T0301065

What's in a Name?

WHAT'S IN A NAME?

*Friendship, Identity and History
in Modern Multicultural Britain*

Sheela Banerjee

sceptre

First published in Great Britain in 2023 by Sceptre
An imprint of Hodder & Stoughton
An Hachette UK company

1

Copyright © Sheela Banerjee 2023

The right of Sheela Banerjee to be identified as the Author of the Work has been
asserted by her in accordance with the Copyright, Designs and Patents Act 1988.

All rights reserved. No part of this publication may be reproduced, stored
in a retrieval system, or transmitted, in any form or by any means without
the prior written permission of the publisher, nor be otherwise circulated
in any form of binding or cover other than that in which it is published and
without a similar condition being imposed on the subsequent purchaser.

A CIP catalogue record for this title is available from the British Library

Hardback ISBN 9781529367591
ebook ISBN 9781529367621

Typeset in Sabon MT by Hewer Text UK Ltd, Edinburgh
Printed and bound in Great Britain by Clays Ltd, Elcograf S.p.A.

Hodder & Stoughton policy is to use papers that are natural, renewable
and recyclable products and made from wood grown in sustainable
forests. The logging and manufacturing processes are expected to
conform to the environmental regulations of the country of origin.

Hodder & Stoughton Ltd
Carmelite House
50 Victoria Embankment
London EC4Y 0DZ

www.sceptrebooks.co.uk

To my beautiful friend Sharon, I'll miss you beyond words.

'Tis but thy name that is my enemy,
Thou art thyself, though not a Montague.
What's Montague? It is nor hand nor foot
Nor arm nor face nor any other part
Belonging to a man. O be some other name.
What's in a name? That which we call a rose
By any other name would smell as sweet,
So Romeo would, were he not Romeo called,
Retain that dear perfection which he owes
Without that title. Romeo, doff thy name,
And for that name, which is no part of thee,
Take all myself.

William Shakespeare, *Romeo and Juliet*

A man's name is not like a mantle, which merely hangs
around him, and which, perchance, may be safely
twitched and pulled; but is a perfectly fitting garment,
which has grown over and over him like his very skin,
at which one cannot scratch and scrape without
wounding the man himself.

Johann Wolfgang von Goethe, *The Autobiography of Goethe, Truth and Poetry: From My Own Life*

There is no social agent who does not aspire, as far as
his circumstances permit, to have the power to name
and to create the world through naming.

Pierre Bourdieu, *Language and Symbolic Power*

Contents

Author's Note

I've thought long and hard about whether or not I should self-censor when it comes to the racial slurs that my friends and I experienced, that were part of the society we were growing up in. I know that in many circumstances – such as on the news – it's now felt they are too offensive to be used in their original form – phrases such as the 'N word' or the 'P word' are often substituted to indicate these terms. I understand and mostly agree with this.

However, I have decided not to take this path, and I want to explain why. I wanted readers to feel and understand the hurt, the shame and the trauma that these words caused us. I wanted to show how they were part of everyday life when we were children. And I didn't feel I could do that unless I could actually write out the words; I didn't want to mask their offensive qualities through the use of asterisks or alternative phrases. I was frequently called these names, so were my parents, I heard them on the streets, at school, and they were sometimes used by my so-called 'friends'.

I also wanted to add that at the time I was growing up – the seventies and eighties – although I'm Asian, the name calling seemed to be interchangeable. I was called everything: wog, golliwog, paki, nignog and n****r. I saw these terms carved out on my desks at school, scrawled on toilet doors, graffitied on the walls where I lived. Maybe that's because there weren't many Black people in my area – our abusers seemed to regard us as one homogenous undesirable mass. We were all on the receiving end of these degrading insults.

I've tried to use the words carefully and to contextualise them properly. I've made an exception in the case of the word 'n****r'. The hurt and offence I might cause by using this term feels too great. It's a complicated issue, but in this era, it is definitively a slur that is aimed only at Black people, and I don't, as a British Asian, feel I have a right to use it.

All these words make me shudder when I type them out, or if I ever say them out loud. If they sound offensive, it's because they are. They are horrific. I understand that. I've agonised over the decision to use them, but I hope, in the end, readers will understand why I chose to do so.

Introduction

Our names: they're so mundane, we barely notice them. We walk around with them all day, every day. They are an invisible layer of our being that surrounds us, like a lexical second skin. Most of the time, we probably don't think anything of them, typing them out in texts, in emails, in forms; introducing ourselves, maybe in a meeting, 'Hi I'm Sheela'; in our voice-mail recordings, 'This is Sheela, please leave me a message'; 'First name: Sheela, Surname: Banerjee'.

But they're a strange entity. A name is intimately you, an inescapable part of your identity. It's the bridge we use from the outside world to our inner selves: to our thoughts, experiences, decisions, memories, our hopes, fears and disappointments. It's the sign by which others know us. 'What's your name?' is the first question we ask of someone who will go on to become a friend, in the playground, in the staff room. In Shakespeare's *Romeo and Juliet*, names are the catalyst for the tragedy about to happen. Romeo's Montague surname is an emblem of dense family ties, a vicious blood feud and centuries of psychic energy, all contained in its three syllables. Unless we take the radical step of changing our names, we cannot escape them – any more than Juliet can transform Romeo into someone who's not a Montague.

•

Once prised open, our names reveal a multitude of stories, reveal feelings, states of consciousness and lost histories that embody who we really are and where we come from. Names are words that contain emotional charge, are filled with associations. If we contemplate them for just an instant, we are thrown down the rabbit hole of memory. I think of my own name and I'm suddenly seven years old. I'm at Wood End Park Junior School in Hayes, on the edge of west London, not far from Heathrow Airport. I'm sitting at my wooden desk, which is covered with scratches and old pen markings, has a lid that flips open, and an old-fashioned well for the ink. This is 1975. Sean Cook rocks back and forth on his chair next to me; I'll play with Wendy and Tracey Howard on the climbing frame at playtime. My name is Sheela Banerjee. It immediately points to difference, to dissonance. It tells the world that I'm the child of immigrants. No one can pronounce my surname. It marks me out as Indian, and the presence of this strange name in this English working-class school points to the story of post-war mass migration to this country, and to the global empire that brought my parents over here.

For our names are not just our own, they belong also to the world around us, to society and to language itself. Names place us within a social arrangement and a set of invisible forces. Names are power. To truly grasp the register of any name, one must gauge its position relative to other names. At the age of seven, my surname, Banerjee, exists alongside others such as Cook, Howard and Allen – it's unpronounceable, inferior – and exists within a society that often feels like it doesn't want us here. Names acquire their full meaning in relation to one another, and there is a political dimension to names and naming.

My parents arrived in this country from West Bengal in the

sixties, along with thousands of others like them. Besides my funny-sounding surname, they've given me a first name that's out of time. They don't know that the name doesn't fit: it's their Indianised version of 'Sheila'. I will grow up with an unfashionable name that belonged to middle-aged English women; I will feel uncomfortable with it for many years, because my parents don't belong to the English society they are living in. My compromise name is the story of my parents struggling, adapting, trying to avoid the humiliations of immigrant life. The politics of race and empire infuses their lives, and my name is the emblem of the cultural no man's land that I, as the child of Indians, will always exist in. I love my name now. My awakening to my heritage, as a second-generation Bengali, had a lot to do with this, as well as an acceptance of my history as an immigrant. My liminal status in this country is inextricably part of me and my hybrid name reflects this.

Indians of my generation have often felt obliged by the constant mispronunciations, misspellings and casual mockery to change their names. Fluctuating layers of emotion, shifting consciousnesses, influence the way we feel about our names in the subtlest of ways. My cousin's original name is Mousumi (pronounced Mo-*sh*umi, a beautiful-sounding name, of a Bengali film star from the seventies). But fed up with correcting everyone, she now goes by the name Mo. It just makes life easier, but at the same time she also regrets the decision. She feels that Mo isn't quite right either, it's become a name torn from its linguistic roots and its intrinsic meaning. I wonder, as Indians, if the act of abbreviating our names is a shorthand for the compromises we make. Is it no big deal, or a reflection of our status as post-colonial subjects in the 'mother country'? We are, after all, only one generation on from the end of empire.

When I was growing up, the person who brought the politics of naming into the public arena was Muhammad Ali. He understood that names are crucial to our sense of who we are, to our identities as human beings, and how they can be a powerful tool of resistance. I remember my parents and my uncles and aunts often talking about him, as they'd settle themselves in front of the TV in the seventies. Like a lot of people, they would repeat his sayings ('float like a butterfly, sting like a bee'), marvelling not just at his physical prowess but also at his mental and verbal agility. And his decision to change his name from Cassius Clay to Muhammad Ali was frequently mentioned – it seemed for them like a powerful symbol of his fight against centuries of white oppression. Ali of course knew this, and announced it to a global audience that was enthralled by him: 'Cassius Clay is a slave name. I didn't choose it and I don't want it. I am Muhammad Ali, a free name – it means beloved of God, and I insist people use it when people speak to me and of me.' Names in that era of American civil rights were about the fundamentals of being.

But it's not just famous names that are intrinsically fused with power and politics. *Every* name, even the most ordinary, tells its own story, acting as a miniature poem, ready to be unravelled, drawing us into its historical and cultural labyrinth as soon as it is uttered. Take John Smith, for example, on the face of it a name so conventional that it seems there's little to say about it. It's almost comically boring, so devoid of interest that it seems like a blank piece of paper, with no markings to guide us towards meaning.

But once unpacked, those two words begin to reveal a wealth of information. If I come across a John Smith, here in London, where I live, it means (most probably) that he is a man, probably British, and of a certain age – most likely in his seventies or eighties. (The name John was, in recent times, at its most popular between 1914 and 1944, but by 2020 had dropped down to 150th in the list of names for baby boys.) It is of Hebrew origin, from the Jewish name Yochanan, but in Britain it is most commonly given as a Christian name, the name of two great saints: St John the Baptist (who anticipated the coming of Jesus) and St John (one of Jesus's apostles and traditionally thought to be the author of the Gospel of St John). The ubiquity of this name across the globe reflects the power and influence of the Christian church during the last two millennia. The fact that so many British boys were given this name by their parents during the first half of the twentieth century (along with the similarly Christian Paul, Matthew and Andrew), and the fact that its popularity dropped away so dramatically in the post-war period, tells the story of how Christianity, once so dominant, rapidly lost its hold on British society during this era; how society changed in more diffuse ways, dropping its previously stifling sense of conformity, shifted its moral stances and its values (more individualistic, more secular, more progressive). All very different from when John Smith was the commonest name in the country, when the name acted as a cipher for a kind of Everyman.

The equally common surname Smith is a quintessentially British name, harking back hundreds of years. It is a history lesson in one word, speaking of a pre-industrial British society, dominated by farmers and artisans. It derives from the Anglo-Saxon occupational term 'smith', used to describe someone who worked with wood or metal. Its etymology can be traced to the Old English word *smitan*, a form of the English verb *to smite*, which also meant *to strike*. Anyone called Smith is likely to be able to trace at least part of their ancestry back hundreds of years to this period in England. A name passed down through the male line, its sense of continuity through the generations is another story in itself, a story of the power of the patriarchy.

And it is these, the ordinary names, that are of interest to me, the names that are right under our noses. In this book, I'll dig deep into my own name, those of my friends and those of our forebears. Behind each of our names are myriad personal stories. I'm now in my fifties, and these are the names that have surrounded me as I have gone through life. I have shared many experiences with the people in this book. They reveal to me their deepest feelings about growing up with their names, the buried family histories, the love stories, the psychological forces at play when their names were chosen. This is a personal journey to reveal the worlds which gave rise to what we are called. This is also a book about friendship, about some of the most important people in my life, about moments of connection.

My friends and I are all outsiders in one way or another. I'm a second-generation immigrant, a British Bengali. Having grown up in a very white, English suburb, in the seventies and eighties, I was probably subconsciously drawn to people who'd also grown up in families that weren't typically English, who had felt different from the people around them and didn't quite fit anywhere. Woven through our names, as a group of people, is a very particular story of race, class and identity in modern Britain. Delving into my name, and those of my friends, reveals how our names exist in a daily dialogue with the British society we live in and the pasts that we come from.

Our feelings towards our names also mutate, as the world around us changes. My own name, Sheela Banerjee, doesn't feel like a stable entity, my feelings towards it have altered and been shaped by the social and political forces of this country over the last fifty years. An exploration of my name opens up the different eras and different places I have inhabited: my world as a child growing up in white working-class Hayes in west London, a place full of skinheads, full of casual but vicious racism; university in Sussex in the eighties where the radical teaching of colonialism changed my view of myself and my culture; at work in television at the BBC, and in academia, where I spent my adult life negotiating the world of privileged middle-class whiteness. These are all particular British microcosms, and our names move through them with us, acting as a kind of barometer of the social energies at work on us, without us even realising it is happening at the time.

For this has been a time of extreme changes in this country, especially in terms of race and attitudes towards Britain's colonial past. Our names, those of our parents and grandparents, tell a personal story of the immigrant experience in modern Britain over the last century. From empire to the huge wave of post-war migration from the Caribbean and the Indian subcontinent, the overt racism of Enoch Powell's 'Rivers of Blood' speech in 1968 to the rise of the National Front in the seventies, and Margaret Thatcher's fears of being 'swamped' by immigrants – these events played out in different ways in our lives, their influence subtly manifesting themselves through the vehicle of our names.

By the time my daughter was born in 2007 and it came to naming her, my life as a second-generation Indian was infinitely easier than it had been for my parents when they named me, in the sixties. Behind this was a series of major cultural shifts and huge political upheavals: the introduction of the Race Relations Act in 1968; countless acts of heroic resistance and protest by people of colour; the birth of the Anti-Nazi League; the uprisings in Brixton, Toxteth and Southall (next door to where I lived) in 1981; a landslide Labour government;

7

the Lawrence Inquiry, to investigate the murder of the Black teenager Stephen Lawrence, and the acknowledgement of something called 'institutional racism' in the police force. Where I live, in London, open racist abuse is not common in the way that it used to be, our food – curry – is famously part of the national cuisine, and at my daughter's school, non-English names are the norm. I move through this society more easily, understand its ways, and am accepted far more than my parents ever were.

But racism, of course, still exists and continues its poisonous work in many other ways. It reveals itself through the way we are treated at work, how and when we die, how the police treat young Black men, and in the intense hostility to migrants that seems in this country to be pathological. In many parts of the country, Muslim women who wear the hijab are often subject to the same kind of terrifying abuse that my mother was when she walked around the streets wearing a sari in the sixties. Huge areas of our lives are dominated by the same homogenous group of white, middle-class, Oxbridge elites – in the media, publishing and academia. And the aftermath of the Brexit vote to leave the European Union saw a re-emergence of the kind of racism on our streets that I haven't seen since I was a child. My friends and I, now in our fifties, are the first ones to live through this era of Britain's race history – good and bad. This is our story as second- and third-generation immigrants.

•

When I worked in television, names like Charlotte, Lucy and Sophie were the norm. I wondered where all the Sheilas were. Or, for that matter, the Lisas, Wendys and Traceys I grew up with in Hayes. Was it just that the name Sheila was an anachronism, or was my first name also a marker of lower social status? In this country, racism is often conjoined with its favourite partner: class discrimination. Most parents presumably choose a name without any explicit consciousness of where it will place their child. But like it or not, they are sending a signal, a suggestion, about the intended place in society their offspring might occupy, and about what sort of person they may become. They are stitching them into Britain's social fabric. The names they choose convey certain values and confer class privilege, often in the subtlest of ways.

Names in Britain are social code that we all understand. We may not think of it explicitly much of the time, but in Britain where I've (mainly) grown up, we all have a highly sophisticated and infinitely attuned sense of what a name means. Camila, Anastasia, Rosalind, Casey, Charlene, Carl, Carly, Levi, Wayne, Shaun, Toby, Keeley, Damian, Sebastian, Peter, Tom, Richard, James, Rupert, Robert, John, Elizabeth, Finn, Lola, Anne, Skye, Kylie, Sharon, Tracey. Any British reader of this book could quickly place those names into crude categories, upper class, middle and working class, and the results would be almost identical. Each name has a set of shared associations. At the BBC or in my university department, not only did I never come across another Sheila or Sheela, but similar names such as Shirley, Sharon, or Sandra were also extremely rare. In these environments, my name – along with my accent, education and cultural tastes – seemed to cement my place in a particular hierarchy of class in this country.

•

Our names are not, however, simply one of the markers of our contemporary class-based tribes. They also carry ghosts of meaning that have travelled across centuries and continents.

My own surname, Banerjee, signals that my family are Brahmins, the elite priestly class within the Hindu caste system. They sat at the very top of a rigid and oppressive social hierarchy that originated in northern India thousands of years ago. Even now, in the twenty-first century, when I meet someone in India and they find out my surname, I feel that a centuries-old conversation has already begun between us before a word has ever been uttered. Although I was born in Britain and so were most of my friends, our immigrant pasts mean that our names carry the imprints of the lives that our parents, grandparents and great grandparents once led in countries thousands of miles away. My surname, though of little value in Britain, is a one-word record of my forebears' unearned privilege and power.

Our names act as a portal to other worlds. As I've listened to my friends' accounts about their names, dug deep into where they came from, searched through records, I've encountered seismic moments in history. From the ancestral story of my friend Marcella's Jewish family, escaping brutal persecution in Tsarist Russia, to the role of names in the post-colonial politics of language and race, to the horrors of partition in India. In hearing my friends' stories I've travelled, in my imagination, across India, Pakistan, to Tsarist Russia, rural Cyprus in the fifties, ancient Greece and across Sri Lanka, Egypt and Jamaica.

Excavating the meanings, the etymologies, behind their names allowed me to journey through time, through the personal and the epic, through the mundane detail of everyday life and through the global movements of history. Our names are fused with tales of caste, religion, revolution, slavery, empire, war and partition. These epic events percolate through to individual lives, and to the detail of our names: a history-laden calling card to the world.

•

When I asked my friends about their names, a host of feelings, anecdotes and histories came pouring out. I felt the same when I came to write about my own name. Each story contains revelations, aspects of their lives that I barely understood, despite knowing most of them for decades: about the circumstances in which they were named, intense likes and dislikes, discomfort, especially about the way in which other people react to their names. This intensity of feeling is almost universal and is the sign of something fundamental to our sense of self. The words we use, through their histories and associations, shape our realities, they give meaning to our experience of the world. And a name – something so intimate to us, so connected to us – is one of the most powerful expressions of this process.

Growing up as Sheela Banerjee

The story of my name begins on a cool autumnal day in London. I imagine my parents in the hospital ward where I was born in October 1967. As he's trying to think of a name for his new-born daughter, my father, Balaji, looks outside through the windows and the leaves are a vibrant mix of orange and yellow – he is still getting used to the colours of autumn in Britain. My parents are young and in love. Although they had an arranged marriage, they knew each other from living on the same small street, surrounded by ponds and jungle, in a small town in West Bengal. In a black-and-white photo my father is smooth-skinned and handsome. It was taken in one of those old-fashioned photography studios in India, and he's looking into the camera, smiling, a bit like a fifties Indian film star. But now, here they are in Hammersmith Hospital, at the start of a new life together in London. It is 1967, winter is approaching and it is a few months before Enoch Powell will make his infamous 'Rivers of Blood' speech, warning about the dangers of immigrants pouring into Britain.

And so, these two young Indians have a baby daughter, born on British soil. They bring to this moment, in that hospital, the world they grew up with in India and the huge psychological upheavals of adjusting to life in Britain in the 1960s. Their decision about what to call me will be influenced by their own experience of living here with their own Indian names.

My Father, Balaji Prasad Banerjee
Wolverhampton, 1959

My father arrived in this country bearing the name Balaji Prasad Banerjee. He was just twenty-two years old when he set off by ship to England in August 1959, desperate to get away from his strict Hindu family. He lived mainly in Wolverhampton for the first few years before I was born. I find the photos of him from that time quite poignant. In one of them he's wearing a smart winter coat, standing on the cobbled streets of the city with rows of Victorian terraces behind him. These were pictures taken to send back home, to his sisters and my grandparents, to show how well his new life was working out. He loved the fact that he had made it to Britain and still talks fondly about those early years. But I don't think this was a comfortable place or time to be a newly arrived Indian immigrant. In 1964, just a few miles down the road, the Tories won the Smethwick election with the most racist election campaign ever seen in this country and the infamous slogan: 'If you want a n****r for a neighbour, vote Labour'.[1] Wolverhampton itself, along with other areas such as Walsall, Smethwick and Leamington, had become the epicentre for some of the most virulent racism in the country. Enoch Powell was in fact my father's local MP, and his inflammatory speech, given in nearby Birmingham, was greeted enthusiastically by local residents. Powell would go on to make several similar speeches in Wolverhampton itself, and his poisonous views would cascade outwards, with a profound effect on British politics during the years and decades that followed. It was a speech whose racist reverberations my friends and I would experience through the decades to come.

In Wolverhampton itself, day-to-day life for my father was also pretty lonely. He had a few Indian friends but often the English were hostile: there was racism on the streets, in the pubs, and he knew that in his office, many of his colleagues didn't want an Indian working alongside them. But he was young, incredibly sociable, always cracking jokes and just wanted to fit in to a country that he had been dreaming of coming to since he was a little boy. He got a place at Birmingham College of Commerce to study 'Office Systems'. For years I never really understood what this was, but I think my dad was quite proud of it. Pre-computers, it was the latest in office organisation, and he later worked as a 'Systems Analyst' visiting companies all over the country, showing them how to organise their payrolls, their filing systems and their HR departments. He was determined to make it work over here: he lived in freezing cold lodgings, assiduously learning English, able even to make jokes in this foreign tongue.

·

Balaji Prasad Banerjee. In India this is a name rooted in the world of the gods, part of the origin story of Hinduism. It is revered and respected. Balaji is another name for the god Vishnu, who along with Brahma is one of the foundational deities in Hindu mythology, responsible for the creation of the earth. Prasad – pronounced *Pror-shaadh* – means 'offering to the gods' and is an intrinsic part of his name, paired carefully by his devout parents with Balaji. Together, the two names enact a mini epic, and it's a common form of name. It is from the 'prasad', or offering, to Vishnu that the child, a miraculous gift, arrives on Earth. But when my father arrived over here, in 1959, Prasad was, wrongly, assumed to be his middle name, which among the British is usually another personal name, a slightly embarrassing entity, quickly forgotten about after a christening. Accordingly, Prasad was barely ever mentioned again, and a vital part of my father's name went missing. More importantly, the name Balaji itself suddenly lost all its 3000-year-old associations, it became a meaningless name, a nonsensical collection of sounds – and a name that no-one could pronounce.

It should be *Baa-la-jee* – with an equal stress on all three syllables, simple enough.

But with the English tendency to put in stresses everywhere, it often became

B'*laar*-ji.

Or even

Blah-ji.

It's horrible to Bengali ears, an aural mockery of the name.

Whenever I ask him, my father says he didn't mind. He was an optimistic twenty-two-year-old, excited to be in Britain, starting a new life, away from the constricting religiosity of his Brahmin parents. He laughed at the English inability to pronounce his name and quickly decided to shorten it to Bala (he'd heard there was a place in Wales called Lake Bala, so he guessed that might work) and that's how he would introduce himself to anyone English for the next sixty-two years.

Bala – a name that meant nothing. It's just a Bengali word for bangle.

My Mother, Tripti Banerjee
Southall, West London, 1967

My mother, Tripti, meanwhile had only just arrived from India in 1966 as a new bride, just a year before I was born. Her enclosed traditional Indian life had been completely different from the world she now found herself in. She was from a devout Hindu family where they prayed every morning, and she grew up having classical singing and dance lessons. She had barely ever left her small semi-rural neighbourhood until she got married. Arriving over here was a shock: she had been to college in India but couldn't really speak English. She found that the English regarded her as inferior or stupid, she couldn't communicate and was stared at, or even abused, as she walked around the local streets, wearing a sari. It was, she says, like being a baby, she was helpless, an outsider, in a completely unfamiliar and often hostile world.

As my mother's name, Tripti, moved from its home country, it experienced an even greater misfortune than my father's. Most British people are unable (or can't be bothered) to articulate its consonants. Correctly pronounced, Tripti sounds something like

Thripthi

The 'th' is pronounced with the tongue rolled tightly behind the teeth, creating a sound that doesn't really occur in English. So as soon as my mother arrived over here, she was condemned to never have her actual name spoken, except by another Indian.

It's a bit like someone called David being called Tavid – forever.

Not the greatest misfortune, but it's not her real name.

So, fast forward to October 1967, to that moment in Hammersmith Hospital. My parents think about how their new-born daughter can have a better life than them, fit in, and not be singled out or ridiculed because of her Indian name. And they call her Sheela – a safe, Janus-faced name, that's conveniently English, but also Indian, one that straddles both cultures. In that era, unsure immigrant parents who were trying to grapple with questions of identity often opted for similar fusion names: like Anita, Rita, Nina and Ruby. And so, having opted for Sheela, I had a name that looked two ways, that meant very different things in London, where I lived for most of my childhood, and in India where I spent three years, on and off, during my parents' attempts to return to their homeland.

An Indian Girl in England, with a Hybrid Name
Hayes, Middlesex, 1975

I'm seven years old. My name is Sheela Banerjee. No other child at school is called Sheela. And everyone has problems with my surname, Banerjee. They're always stumbling over it, it's regularly turned into *Banner-Tree*, *Ban-Jar-ee* or *Bain-tree*. With my brown skin and my funny name, I'm obviously the child of foreigners, and I'm the only person in my class who isn't British.

•

As a child I hated my first name. When I've asked them about their naming choice, my mum and dad say they partly chose

Sheela because the English version, Sheila, was common in Britain in the late sixties. My dad, who's always been a big fan of British sit-coms, had seen the actor Sheila Hancock on television – it was a name that was around. It's also a Bengali name, written as শীলা, spelt with the Bengali equivalent of Sh-ee-l-a, so my parents changed the spelling from 'Sheila' to 'Sheela', to make it phonetically accurate. The trouble was that among the English, the name Sheila reached its peak of popularity in the 1930s and went into decline after that. By the time I was born it was out of fashion as a baby's name, and most people called Sheila were by then in their thirties or forties.

Looking back now, I very much associated the name with these older English women: dinner ladies in my primary school, patrolling the playground in their checked nylon overalls; school friends' mothers, with seventies-style hair, set and curled, faded lipstick, wearing skirts and high heels (my own mother never wore a skirt). These were English women who seemed a world apart from me. I never went inside their houses; their white skin evoked feelings of inferiority in me, as well as a sense of unfamiliarity. They were nothing like me, a seven-year-old Bengali girl, just back from India. I somehow felt ashamed of this name. It felt like an ill-fitting dress. I certainly wasn't one of these women, and Sheela didn't feel like a truly Indian name – I didn't belong and my name seemed to confirm my discomfort.

While I didn't like the English-sounding nature of my name, I was embarrassed by what that double 'e' in Sheela symbolised – my own Indian-ness. I was embarrassed by my parents, our food, our language, cringing at the sound of them speaking Bengali to me in public. But this was not just about being ashamed of difference. As a young child I was trying to adjust to cultural extremes. We had gone back to

India when I was four years old and my parents planned to stay there forever. I'd lived in Mumbai (or Bombay, as it was known then) and with my grandparents in West Bengal for two years. I went to school in India, spoke fluent Bengali and became a typical little Indian girl.

But it didn't work out, and we returned to England in 1974 when I was six. My parents bought themselves a semi-detached house in Hayes, a new yellow Fiat car, and they both found themselves jobs. My dad became an insurance salesman for the Manufacturers Life Insurance Company. My mum worked as a chemist in Slough for a company called Aspro-Nicholas, which made beauty products and Matey bubble bath. They had managed to start their lives again, but growing up as a Bengali child in Hayes wasn't easy. This was a white working-class suburb in outer west London, just off the A40, next door to Punjabi-dominated Southall. My father chose it because he liked its transport connections – the M4 and the M40 were nearby, and it was close to Heathrow Airport. Someone we knew was always going to or coming back from India, and frequently needed picking up and a place to stay. But what I remember is the endless drab grey roads of small semi-detached houses, the scrappy patches of scrubland and ubiquitous parades of shops. And beneath this rather dull exterior was a pervasive sense of racist threat.

Hayes is on the edge of London, part of a grim urban sprawl, a nowhere kind of place next to the Grand Union Canal. It was once full of light industry, and EMI and Nestlé were still there in the seventies, but most of the old factories were empty and falling into ruin. The canal, once a major industrial artery, was full of floating rubbish and was a dangerous place to be. And as Southall became home to thousands of Punjabi immigrants, Hayes became a fertile recruiting ground for the National Front.

I was just a young child who'd recently arrived back from India. On my first day of primary school, I saw a word scrawled on the back of a toilet door: 'WOG'. I had no idea what it meant. But in the coming months and years I soon found out. We'd often be abused on the street, my mum and aunts had been spat at when they first came to this country, and now I heard people call us 'Wogs' or 'Pakis' and youths would sometimes aggressively mimic Indian accents as they walked past us. Heading off to the local park with one of my cousins, I would be wary once I reached the concrete playground, in case anyone called us names.

There was a darkness I could sense when we were out and about. I remember one time, standing with my mother at a bus stop in Hayes, holding her hand, as she tightened her grip. A teenage boy was circling us on his bike, coming at us, threatening us. The sun was dropping out of sight, the bus nowhere to be seen, leaving us standing in the grey shadows of the pavements. I remember sensing my mother's fear. We seemed to be trapped in a taunting circle that the boy created as he slowly rode around us, standing up on his bike, lunging at us, mocking us. I didn't know what was going on, whether or not he was about to attack us. I was a frightened seven-year-old girl just arrived back from India.

•

Life at home with my family, however, was completely different. It was hermetically sealed, a cocoon of pure Bengali-ness. Every Friday and Saturday, my extended family of aunts, uncles and cousins would congregate at one of our homes. When it was our turn, my mum would cook for hours, with the smells of mustard fish curry, lamb and ginger suffusing our suburban semi. All the grown-ups would be laughing and talking loudly to each other and to us in Bengali, with my dad making pithy comments, joking about some relative in India. Meanwhile upstairs in my room, my cousins and I would be obsessing over the film *Grease*, endlessly discussing John Travolta and Olivia Newton John's outfits and recording ourselves singing songs from the soundtrack on my radio cassette player. Despite our parents, as children we were becoming more and more English, being formed by the world around us – we spoke only English to one another, loved Christmas just like everyone else, wore our paper hats, opened our presents and played games of Monopoly that went on for hours on end.

So it was in this environment that I was growing up, partly taking on the English culture that surrounded me, wanting naturally to belong to it, and partly shrinking myself when out in the streets, at the local pool, in school, hoping no-one would abuse me. My feelings about my identity and the Indian aspect of my name increasingly took on the hue of the outside world. I internalised its hostility. I absorbed everything I saw on TV, including the condescension and racism of programmes like *Mind Your Language*, *It Ain't Half Hot Mum* and *Love Thy Neighbour*. I instinctively felt I had to be as English as possible, fool everyone through my accent and my demeanour that I was almost the same as them. It was deeply uncomfortable having friends round to my house – it was suddenly apparent that I was completely different from them. I was self-conscious about my Bengali parents and the pungent smells of Indian food that seemed to stick to our house.

At school, I took great care to avoid any sign of Indian-ness amongst my white friends – no pigtails for me like a traditional Asian girl and I made sure my accent was pure cockney with no trace of an Indian accent. I was quite pleased with myself and took pride in how English I was.

To my complete shame now, I despised other Indian children who retained even a vestige of their parents' immigrant accents, like the children in Southall, whose English was more Punjabi inflected. In an atmosphere like this, standing out was deeply uncomfortable. By now, at the morning register, as the teacher called out 'Lisa', 'Tracey', 'Wendy', I had become grateful that my name, Sheela, blended in. Other Indian children weren't so lucky. They had a horrific time at the hands of their classmates, who mocked them and punned on their names with derogatory English words. So anyone called Pooja (the Hindu word for prayer) faced insulting comments about poo, while the Punjabi name Kamaljit was constantly changed to 'Camel-shit'.

Meanwhile, as the seventies wore on, Southall, just half a mile up the road and with a big Asian population, was seething with racial tension. There were violent attacks on shopkeepers and residents by local youths, mainly from places like Hayes and neighbouring Feltham, with the police generally refusing to do anything about it. In 1976 an eighteen-year-old student, Gurdip Singh Chaggar, was murdered by a racist gang. I wasn't aware of these wider attacks – it was just the place where we went every Saturday, so my parents could do all their Indian food shopping. I used to love going to Southall Broadway, always busy with Punjabi women in their salwar kameez, full of sari shops and the smells of freshly fried samosas wafting in the air. But by 1979 the violence had reached a peak, and in April, thousands of people took to the streets, to prevent the National Front from holding a meeting at the town hall. Hundreds were arrested, many injured, and the anti-racist protestor Blair Peach was beaten to death by the police.

It was just after this that my parents decided once more to try to return to India. I was grateful – I didn't like living in

Hayes – and in February 1979, my parents packed up all our belongings, we said goodbye to all my cousins and aunts and uncles, to all our Bengali friends, and moved to Kolkata.

Kolkata, West Bengal, 1979

We have moved back to India, my parents don't intend to come back. This is it. We have left Hayes. During the twelve-hour flight from Heathrow Airport, as we flew above the clouds, my name became a different creature. As we passed over Europe, Russia and the snow-capped Himalayas, eating our trays of airline food, it completely transformed in meaning. I live in Kolkata now, still known, however, as Calcutta in 1979. I no longer possess the name of an immigrant child, a name that doesn't fit and which sticks out. Although the spelling remains exactly the same, the actual sound of my name is also different. Sheela no longer sounds like *She-eey*-la, with its nasal inflection and elongated stress on the first syllable and a weak one on the second. Here in Kolkata, my name is metrically equal, the syllables flow, the 'sh' is more rounded, it sounds more elegant.

I was *Sheela Banerjee*. A Bengali girl in an English world.

I'm now *Sheela Banerjee*: শীলা ব্যানার্জী.

I will become, for the second time, a Bengali girl in a Bengali world.

Banerjee used to be that strange foreign part of my name, frequently mangled by English speakers, and marking me out as definitively different. It has now become the most normal name in the world, one that doesn't create even the tiniest ripple when I say it.

I am living among tens of millions of other Bengalis – brown skinned, with surnames just like mine. There are more Bengalis here than there are British in Britain. As I travel from Dum Dum Airport (pronounced *Dthom Dthom*), I see hand-painted signs all over the place, many of these are for the rival political parties. Long Communist slogans are painted on every available wall. Alongside these are often names of shops, painted letters in Bengali, with my name. 'Banerjee and Co', 'Banerjee and Sons'. I see and hear my name absolutely everywhere.

In Kolkata it's as common as Smith or Jones.

Each day we drink *Banerjee Tea*, sold in the dark covered market, scooped out from a large tin box and measured out by a cross-legged shopkeeper, sitting on the ground, with hand-held iron weighing scales. Banerjee is not foreign. Banerjee is not strange.

•

As a family, this is our second attempt at returning to India for good, but it's my father's fourth time. I am uprooted from everything I know. Uprooted from my sense of who I am. The three of us will live here forever now. The world I existed in before has gone; it is six thousand miles away. I don't know when I'll go back, if ever. This is the 1970s and flights are hugely expensive. England's orderly grey streets, the fast, straight motorways, the cars, all the television programmes I loved, the pop songs, the damp green grass, its soft cover of grey cloud – all of it has gone.

As a child I'd always lived a liminal, culturally in-between life. I'd been in Britain for five years, but I wasn't particularly surprised my father had brought us back to India; my parents were always talking about returning. My father was the only son in an orthodox Brahmin family from small-town West Bengal. Crossing the water was forbidden by my grandfather's Hindu belief system and my father defied him by going to England. And having done so, it was my father's duty, as a Brahmin son, to eventually return to his family home, in Chandannagar, to look after his parents. That was what they expected, as a conservative Banerjee family. They were rigid in this idea, as was the rest of the family. This was what he always knew he should do. He would struggle, his entire adult life, to fulfil this duty. He would keep moving to India, fail to settle, come back to England. Try again. So here we were.

Frank Anthony Public School
Kolkata, West Bengal, 1979

The sun is the hottest, brightest sun I have ever known. I feel like I can't breathe. Hundreds of students in rows stand in the unforgiving heat of a Kolkata summer. The blinding white sun ricochets off the mildewed white concrete walls of the school and hits the dusty yellow playground. I'm not used to this heat, I feel it pressing in on me, my throat is so dry.

The head teacher bellows:

Attention!

We salute and bring our legs together.

Stand at ease!

A wall encloses us from the teeming narrow road outside the school, a world of hand-pulled rickshaws, piles of rubbish, and the stench of open drains. Here, at my elite public school, I live the life of privilege with similar Bengali children. It is a fee-paying school, modelled on a public school from England in the 1930s. It was established by Frank Anthony, a well-known social activist. He was an Anglo-Indian, his British-sounding name signalling the community he was from – the descendants of mixed Indian and British relationships. Many of the teachers are also Anglo-Indian – they look the same as me: brown skin, Indian accents – but they have Western names like Mr Clarence, or Mr Flynn. It's the only school of its kind my mother could get me into at short notice. She was desperate to get me admitted here, as I can't read and write Bengali, and these public schools are the only ones in West Bengal that teach in English.

.

Those outdoor morning assemblies always felt like they would never end. I remember staring at the endless line after line of brown children. Girls with oiled black hair, thick plaits running down the back of ironed white cotton dresses. Boys with white shorts, brown legs, that would often feel the lash of a stick. Corporal punishment was brutal and rife. I was always in a state of terror. This was nothing like my British state primary school – working class, not strict at all. A place where some of my classmates – with names like Sean, Lee and

Gary – had difficulty reading and writing, and no one seemed to care greatly.

I now go to school with the children of the rich. We are all called by our surnames, as was traditional in English public schools at one time:

Chakraborty (Madhabi)

Alum (Parveen)

Smith (Linda, she is also Anglo-Indian)

Dasgupta (Subra)

Chatterjee (Indra)

My own name is ordinary, but I'm not, as I've just arrived from England. In seventies Kolkata I'm treated with awe by my fellow pupils for a few weeks. I'm from a land that is mythical – in its modernity, its glamour, its riches. However, they soon get bored. And I too start to become more and more Bengali.

I go to school on the school bus. I sit at my desk, arranged in a row, and study like an Indian child. Rote learning, memorising everything. I win a prize for reciting poetry. I learn to read and write Bengali and slowly my Englishness is being eroded. I feel my English accent slipping away.

•

I get up in the morning and my mother prepares a plate of rice, vegetable curry, fresh fish curry and dal. This is breakfast, before I go to school. I grow to love eating fish in India – I eat with my hands, picking the bones out, mixing it with the rice. The deliquescent *rui mach* (a type of carp) has come straight from the ponds that surround us. My mum has got up in the morning and cooked it in a freshly made mustard sauce, and it's the freshest fish I'll ever eat.

I live in Lake Town – the low sea level means that there are 'lakes' or ponds everywhere. Dark green pools of water, covered with huge green lotus leaves. At that time, in 1979, Lake Town was lush and green, a newly built suburb of Kolkata, with beautiful pastel-coloured houses, the Indian approximations of modernist architecture. It was slightly apart from the centre of the city, a long bus ride away, and was wealthy and tranquil. I was always relieved to get back there after the dirty heat of the city, its dark narrow streets crowded with people, and its intense noise-filled roads.

We are part of a group of comfortable well-to-do families, living in an upmarket area. My parents are relaxed here, there is no sense of threat towards them on the streets. Instead, they seem to have an air of glamour about them – everyone knows that they've just arrived from England. People are awestruck when all our belongings arrive from England in a huge wooden crate that is the size of a small room – the TV, the hi-fi, the Scalextric racing set, all my toys are unpacked, and for weeks visitors marvel at all these *things*. This is seventies India and even the middle classes don't own such mod cons. The Indian government doesn't allow many imports so there aren't any shops that sell them.

My parents move in different social circles to those they had in Britain – one of my father's oldest friends is a senior figure in the Indian oil industry. His name is Mr Bose. Sometimes just referred to as Bose. Another close friend, another Mr Bose, lives nearby in Lake Town and has just left his prestigious job as a senior accountant at a large factory nearby to become my father's business partner. For some reason they are both referred to as Mr Bose, rather than by their first names, which are Sunil and Pranab respectively. To differentiate them, my parents affectionately call the first friend Thel Bose – 'Thel' means oil – and the second, Khajanchi Bose – 'Khajanchi' means bookkeeper. I become close friends with the latter's children, Tutul, Tukun and Bubul. Another friend is the wealthy manager of a big Kolkata company. A former film star, Monisha Sen, who lives on our street, often invites us round to her house. Our own surname, Banerjee, fits entirely in the Bengali upper-middle-class world we now live in.

•

Within weeks the very atmosphere of the country seeps into my consciousness. I'm getting used to the crowds, the potholed Kolkata streets, the intense smells of flowers used by everyone to do their puja (prayers) mixed with the ever-present stench of the open drains, swirling with dark brown and green algae. Everything has changed. The language I now speak everywhere apart from during lessons at school, on the streets, at home, see on the hoardings around me, is Bengali. The culture that is around me, the films, the songs, the clothes, the life I'm leading, is different. I start to change too. My name now just feels like a normal Bengali name. I inhabit it more and more easily. It fits immaculately, as my inner self starts to change. I go to school, become immersed in the world of my Indian family, and move around the streets and houses of West Bengal in 1979, with my parents. The world of associations of the English Sheila is fading away.

My Cousin Tuktuki
Girish Park, North Kolkata, 1979

It's a Sunday morning. We've come to see my cousin Tuktuki. Although it's only mid-morning the ferocious May sun is at full blast. I come out of the sweating black taxi, my parents going out first, my dad paying the taxi driver, and I step onto the broken paving stones of Girish Park in north Kolkata. Paving stones laid 200 years ago, by the British. I look up and see magnificent decaying buildings, with intricate wooden balconies that are teeming with residents. Shadowy figures are crammed into dark, bare rooms as I walk past them. These buildings were built during the British Raj, in the days when grand Kolkata mansions were built with the proceeds of doing business with the East India Company. The journey of my surname and how it found its way over to England was part of this story.

I feel the heat all over me and the sun burns through the thick green corduroy trousers I'm wearing, made for an English climate. On the street there is a tiny shack, where a man sits on a raised platform making *paan* – betel leaves filled with lime paste – and selling cigarettes and matches. There are impoverished families living on the streets, their homes a tattered straw mat, the children with tangled, dusty hair and wearing clothes that look like torn rags. Rickshaw walas run along the streets, pulling their impossibly heavy carriages, sweating, as they tug rich, heavy passengers, loaded with shopping. Along with the heat, the street is filled with people, the noise of car horns, bus conductors from packed buses shouting out their stops.

•

I remember Tuktuki's house as a dark labyrinth. It seemed to have no definition – I can't remember where it began and where it ended. My parents and I turn into a narrow dark alleyway, its brown damp walls so close together that they nearly touch me. Looking up, I see a narrow slit of sky far above me, and a black lizard, flat against the wall, perfectly still, gives itself away when it moves its scaly head. It was cool there, the seething life of the crowded Kolkata street squeezed out by the mildewed dank wall. I will remember those walls for the rest of my life.

We enter a dark courtyard inside the enormous house. Patches of light hit the old concrete floor. A woman stoops over a bucket of water, washing the floor, slopping water everywhere. The tin bucket rattles as she dips her old grey rag in it, she wears no blouse, the skin on her arms loose. Her shoulders shockingly bare.

We make our way every week to the top floor, where my cousin Tuktuki lives with my aunt and uncle. Tuktuki's family are also Brahmins, with a similar surname – Mukherjee. But they lost their money in successive family feuds and live in a state of genteel poverty – this dilapidated mansion-block a sign of the Mukherjees' former glory. I climb up endless stairs and look up to see other storeys, with grand marble floors and green wooden doors, closed forever with huge iron locks. The gloom of the courtyard is like a smell, it has entered all the rooms. No one lives in these middle floors, and the black-and-white Italianate marble tiles – a sign of long-lost riches – are never stepped on.

My cousin lives right at the top of this huge building in two rooms, and climbing up endless stairs, it felt like she was a glamorous Rapunzel, living at the top of a crumbling Kolkata tower. A sixteen-year-old, who I adored, who was a huge influence on me and wove into my being the threads of Bengali identity that changed me into an Indian Sheela. A Sheela with two 'ee's.

•

We're standing next to each other, leaning over the balcony of the flat roof. Tuktuki's plait is shiny, a burnished brown, that hangs down her back, thick and smooth. Her face is creamy light brown, she is regarded by everyone as a *shunduri*, a beauty. To me, an eleven-year-old, her prettiness is unreal. Like the clay statues of Durga I see everywhere, drying on the ground – painted goddesses, calmly compact and smooth; solid, beautiful perfection. I always remember her as laughing and joking. Even though we hadn't lived in the same country for many years, we were family. And in India that seemed to be something slightly different, much more familiar, more intensely close and – when they weren't feuding or fighting – more affectionate. Extended families often lived in the same house. These powerful bonds were, of course, why we were back again in India – so that my father could do his familial duty and look after his parents.

•

And within those families, there was an intricate set of naming rules, a tightly constructed lexical net, holding us all together, with each of our names explaining our relationships to one another, and our different degrees of closeness. To start with, everyone in West Bengal had at least two very different personal names. The first was the *dak naam*, a formalised version of a nickname. *Dak* comes from the verb *daka* meaning 'to call', and as a noun, *dak* means 'a call' or

33

'a shout'. So, a *dak naam* literally means 'the name you are called by'. Tuktuki was my cousin's *dak naam*, a name of affection and love that only a close hierarchy of people were allowed to use.

Tuktuki

Pronounced *TOOK-TOOK-EE*

If you say it out loud – the *dak* – the sounds are repetitious and rhythmic.

Tuk

Tuk

As you speak it out loud, the quick clicking of the tongue is an act of aural fun. The combination of sounds is like a tiny rhyming poem, the light stress on the first syllable giving the name a sense of musicality. The *dak naam* is the first name to be used after a child is born. Its sounds emanate out of the primal scene of the family. It's the name that is always used at home and contains all of the emotions and feelings associated with being a child. The *dak naam* therefore is usually babyish in its sounds, a pre-verbal demonstration of love, the sounds of adoration for a little child; enjoyable to say and hear, designed to entice and amuse the young child. And in Tuktuki's case, those of us most closely related to her would often shorten it further, to Tuku, adding another layer of closeness and affection.

The second name given to the child is the *bhalo naam* ('good' name), a much more formal entity, a name that is full of significance and meaning. Although the *bhalo naam* is also given at birth, for the first few years of a child's life, in the realm of home and the neighbourhood, it will only be the *dak naam* that is used. The *bhalo naam*, often carrying great religious significance, like my father's name Balaji, is a polite name meant for the official world, the serious world – for legal documents, when enrolling at school, in the workplace.

Tuktuki's official name – her *bhalo naam* – was Rupa. I often forgot she was called this, as I never heard anyone in my family using it. My other close cousin's *dak naam* was Ranu. Her *bhalo naam* was Pragyaparomita – a name that was so formal, so beyond the realm of family, that I didn't even know she was called that until I was an adult. In Tuktuki's case, her *bhalo naam* seemed alien to me. On the very rare occasions I heard it being used, when we met some of her schoolfriends, she seemed different. Her name, along with her persona, seemed more held together, more polite. There seemed to be an acknowledgement in India, through naming, that we become very different people in different social settings.

When we returned to India, I realised that my parents also had these childlike names. My father Balaji was Khokon ('little boy') to his parents and his childhood friends in India. His parents, uncles and aunts and cousins all called him this. It made me laugh when I heard him addressed with this baby-ish name: I could suddenly imagine him as the child he once was. The relationship to his parents suddenly became clear as the child-like name was uttered by his mother. I'd never heard this name used in England before. My mother Tripti was called Boo by all her sisters and her parents. My parents only had these names when they returned to India, a sign of the life they'd left behind, the closeness of family that they would only have over in India. No one in England ever called them by these names.

In England, I wasn't given a *dak naam* and neither were

35

most of my cousins. I was simply Sheela. Maybe it was because we didn't have extended family around us in the same way, we didn't exist in a Bengali neighbourhood where our friends would all call us by our *dak naam*. Maybe my parents thought it best to assimilate with the British system and not cause confusion with two separate names.

•

There was another layer of naming in India that didn't involve personal names at all, in fact it was characterised as an *absence* of names. I was in a world where respect for age and the familial relationship were paramount – symbolised often by the use of familial titles in place of the individual-ised first name.

So, my father was never called his own name by his (younger) sisters. To them he was *Dada* ('older brother'). In India, younger cousins (who are treated as semi-siblings) kept trying to call me *Didi* ('older sister') but I instinctively didn't like this erasure of my own name. Perhaps the desire to hold on to Sheela was the legacy of my time in Britain. Equally, I didn't like the feeling that I was primarily now an older sister, that I had responsibilities towards these younger children.

Aunts and uncles were also carefully delineated by their position in the family, by their relationship to their own broth-ers and sisters. So, one person was often referred to by multi-ple different titles by different people. My father called his sister, Tuktuki's mother, Lachmi (a shortening of the name Laxmi and her *dak naam*). Her *bhalo naam* was Manjushree. I called her *Boro Pishi* ('boro' means oldest, 'pishi' means aunt, the father's sister) and she was called *Boro Mashi* by her sister's children. She would have been called *Mamima* by her husband's sisters' children, *Jethima* by his younger brothers' children, *Kakima* by his older brother's children and *Boudi* by his brothers and sisters and their partners.

My aunt's husband meanwhile – my uncle – wouldn't have called her anything. In my experience, Bengali couples tended to avoid referring to each other by name, just making a sound like 'oi' or 'eey' when they wanted to call each other. I believe this arose out of the practice of wives not being allowed to address their husbands by name, as they were regarded as deities. One's husband was a *pothi debotha*, translated as 'husband god'.

Thinking about it now, this absence of personal names in day-to-day life, the primacy of the family in the Bengali naming system, seemed connected to the way everyone behaved and lived their lives. My father, in the family, wasn't Balaji. He lived his life as *Dada* in terms of his three sisters, and as such he grew up with enormous respect accorded to him. I saw that in the way my aunts in England behaved towards him: they adored him and looked up to him during my childhood. He encouraged them to come to England, offered them somewhere to live and so they came. Often, he led the way and they followed. So, if he decided it was a good idea to buy a Hitachi television – they would buy the same. Or one year they all, on my dad's advice, bought the same make of car – a Renault 12, with consecutive number plates and a group discount. Later on, again at my father's instigation, they all bought holiday flats in Spain, again with a group discount, in the same complex on the Costa Blanca. But as *Dada*, he also had a set of immutable responsibilities in the family, the most important of which was to look after his parents, to live with them and care for them in old age. The absence of a personal name seemed symbolic of the way personal desires and wishes also came second, after duty to family. And this of course was why we were in India. Despite my dad wanting to stay in England – he always loved it there – he always knew he'd have to go back to India to do his familial duty.

•

And so we lived our lives in West Bengal mainly seeing family: both sets of grandparents, my mother's siblings, and of course Tuktuki. The longer I spent in this world, the more it penetrated my sense of who I was. And even now, decades later, the sound of my cousin's *dak naam* summons for me intense associations, layers of memory. Tuktuki seemed to inhabit the aural playfulness of her own name, its essential jollity. She was always laughing, joking and teasing as we stood on her flat roof, the top floor of a teetering, crumbling building, looking out onto the hundreds of lives on all the other flat roofs in Kolkata. As the sun went down, everyone else was out on the roofs too, enjoying the coolness of the early evening. Saris hung out to dry on washing lines would make curves as the breeze blew them about, and Tuktuki would always be singing a Hindi song, teaching me the latest hit songs from Bollywood musicals.

> *O sathi rey, theray beena bhi kyaa jeena*
> (Oh my love, what is life without you)

Intricate melodies that she'd copied perfectly by listening to the radio stations playing musical songs all day, on the tinny radio she listened to lounging on her bed. It's what everyone loved doing, as television was still very rudimentary and only on for a few hours in the evening. Everyone knew the songs. The sweetness of her doll-like voice, a perfect imitation of Asha Bhosle, the singer of the song, still echoes in my mind.

The sights and sounds of India went deep into my consciousness, so that whenever I hear those songs, I'm still taken immediately back to standing on that roof, with Tuktuki, feeling
the rough floor, the little pebbles sticking to the skin of my
bare feet. Dusk falling suddenly, obliterating all the roofs
around me, everyone disappearing into the blackness of
Kolkata.

We would sometimes flick through the latest film magazine
together, *Stardust*, with pictures of the goddess-like film stars,
Rekha, Zeenat. Two Bengali actresses, Moushumi Chatterjee
and Sharmila Tagore, were huge stars when we were in India,
and my cousins Mousumi and Shormila were named after
them when they were born in the seventies. But in Britain,
where they grew up, no-one knew who they were, no-one
understood the moment and the popular culture that their
names were a part of.

As the months wore on, I stopped thumbing through my
cherished copy of the *Grease* photo-novella, complete with all
the words to the musical. I learnt other songs, the ones that
Tuktuki taught me, and got my dad to buy me a Bengali folk
song that became a hit, *Boli O Nonodi*, full of colloquial
language and innuendo, about a young village wife out shopping and cooking for a big lunch for her in-laws:

Boli o nonodi
(Oh sister-in-law)

Aar do mutho chaal pheley dey hari thay
(Put two more handfuls of rice in the pot)

Thakur jamaiee elo bari-they
(The in-laws are coming to visit today)

Tuktuki and her mother, my *Boro Pishi*, would take me shopping or to the tailors to get new clothes. We'd go to New Market, a huge covered market full of hundreds of little stalls selling jewellery, saris and beautiful salwar kameez, that I now wanted to wear because Tuktuki wore them. Or they'd take me to an upmarket little tailor shop, called *Madame*, where a young woman in a sari would get me to put my arms out and measure me up and make me a perfectly fitted, cotton maxi dress. I admired all of Tuktuki's clothes – the maroon salwar kameez she wore with her clacking platform sandals, and her painted toenails, or the perfectly pleated pink silk sari and the enormous *teep* (bindi) on her forehead. I no longer had any urge to wear my prized corduroy drainpipes – the height of fashion when I left England, in April 1979. They belonged to the world of Wood End Park Junior School and my friends Samantha, Elizabeth and Ceri. I occasionally received a blue airmail letter from one of them, but they soon tailed off. They seemed like they were from another life. Now I wanted to follow Indian fashions, I listened to Indian music, I learnt to read and write Bengali script, and I started, against my wishes, to think in Bengali. I was seeing the world with Indian eyes, inhabiting the consciousness of an Indian girl called Sheela Banerjee.

My Banerjee Surname in India
Chandannagar, West Bengal, 1979

It's a spring day in 1979. We've just got off the train and the three of us are squashed onto a cycle rickshaw. We are in my parents' hometown of Chandannagar, a bustling suburb on the banks of the River Hooghly, twenty miles upstream of Kolkata. We are precariously balanced as the rickshaw wala slowly weaves his way through a dirty, messy road, with vegetable sellers crouched on the ground, piles of onions, potatoes, bananas, melons laid out either side of us. He blasts his bulbous rubber horn and shouts at them to get out of the way.

I'm sitting on the high cushioned seat, enjoying the breeze blowing my hair back on a hot, humid day. I used to love that rickshaw ride, past the huge grey river, the old colonial French buildings. The rickshaw wala weaves through the narrow lanes; we go past one of the larger ponds, the curved trunks of coconut trees looming over its edges. He swerves, just avoiding the rows of clay goddesses laid out to dry on the ground by artisans preparing for the festival of *Saraswati Puja*. I remember their almond-shaped eyes staring up at me, their garish red and gold paintwork. Chandannagar in 1979 was a very different place to Kolkata, and looking back, it felt like the town was in a state of timeless suspension, as did vast swathes of India. Most people didn't have phones, TVs or cars and for the few who did have a TV, the only channel was the state-run *Doordarshan*. There was a waiting list of several years to buy the only Indian-made car, the Ambassador, a lugubrious old-fashioned vehicle that looks like it has come straight out of a forties film – you can still see them today.

Society also seemed like it was from another age. Chandannagar was a highly conservative town, with religion suffusing everyone's life, and caste was absolutely central to this. This is where I can sense the real change in the status of my name, its striking reversal of fortune. It is here, in small-town West Bengal, that I can trace the centuries of power and privilege that lie behind my name. Banerjee, as a Bengali Brahmin surname, clearly identifies my family's position within the Hindu caste system – a form of brutal social segregation, originating around 3300 BCE, with Brahmins at the top and layers of lower castes and Dalits beneath them.

From the moment I got off the train in Chandannagar it was apparent that my surname carried enormous weight. Both my grandfathers, Karthik Chandra Pathak and Ram Chandra Banerjee – a barrister and a former priest – had huge standing in the town, their status resting on the edifice of caste. As we arrived, even the ticket collector knew who they were – to me, it felt like being in another era. Even as an eleven-year-old, I knew that Banerjee was a highly privileged name. Everyone who was introduced to me knew from my name exactly where I was within the structure of this society.

And it's here I can trace the ambivalence I've always felt about carrying the surname Banerjee – I've always loved the connection it gives me to my Bengali heritage, to my grand-parents and my wider family, but I've always been deeply uncomfortable about its inseparable link to caste. I didn't fully understand its implications as a child, and I loved going to see my grandparents. But as an adult I can't escape from the fact that my surname connects me to a rigid social hierarchy, one that was often brutal and degrading, especially for the millions of Dalits consigned to the bottom rung of the ladder.

The Banerjees, Narua Para
Chandannagar, West Bengal, 1979

As Banerjees, my grandparents were part of a long line of ancestors born into the Brahmin caste. Their name and their whole way of life were embodiments of this and everyone in the small neighbourhood where they lived in Chandannagar was firmly embedded within this highly stratified social ecology. Although Chandannagar is a suburb of Kolkata it is divided into small village-like areas (*paras*), which, when my parents were growing up, were dominated by particular castes. My parents lived in Narua Para, a centuries-old, high-caste neighbourhood, extremely conservative, with a strict maintenance of social segregation.

I remember the place as essentially one narrow road, with a few large houses set within acres of lush green jungle. It seemed idyllic in many ways – there were no cars, everyone knew one another and would stop for a chat with my parents. A decaying temple complex, Baro Mandir ('the twelve temples'), was at one end, with intricately carved cone-shaped structures housing a Shiva temple in the middle.

In 1979, when I returned as a child to India, Narua was still very much socially stratified by caste. I asked my father about it recently, and he started by reeling off a list of the families that lived there, by their high-caste surnames: 'Next to us were the Chatterjees, then another Banerjee house. Then there was your mother's family, the Pathaks (also Brahmins) and the Pandits.' The Pandits, historically, were renowned Brahmin scholars and experts in Hindu scripture, and this is the origin of the English word 'pundit'. My father finished off with the opposite house, 'they were Nandis'. They were the odd ones out it seems – as they were from a lower caste, the business and moneylending caste, known as Benes or Bannias. (The same caste as the Mittals – the billionaire Indian steel magnates.)

Unknown to me at the time, at the other end of town, living in squalid slums amongst the mud and slime of the river, were the Dalits (formerly known as Untouchables), condemned to a life of 'manual scavenging', a phrase used in India for cleaning out toilets and sewers by hand and preparing corpses for cremation at the *ghat* (riverbank). The area where they lived was known as *Mathor Para*. Their segregation was absolute: the Dalits were nominally, spatially, psychologically and economically set apart from the rest of society. All other castes would shun them and my grandparents would be horrified if they were touched by a Dalit, even if their shadow was accidentally trodden on by one of them. In the seventies, although untouchability was outlawed, in practice it still existed. When my parents were growing up in the 1940s and 1950s, it was much more formalised – Dalits weren't allowed in the local cinema, they were only permitted to shop for food in their own section of the bazaar. Marriage or socialising with a member of a higher caste was forbidden. In many ways, it was similar to the apartheid regime in South Africa, but to my mind it was even worse. It was entrenched in divine law. Therefore, to go against it would be to go against the gods and the whole religiously ordained structure of the universe. This was the case whether you were the victim or the beneficiary of the system. And the main method of classification was by name.

When I was visiting, I remember occasionally a young woman coming into my grandparents' house to clean the toilet and take out the excrement. I remember her as a shadowy figure, who didn't say much. She seemed to be different from my grandparents' daily servant – somehow even lower down on the social rung – no one would really talk to her. She was never referred to by name, just as the 'Jommadarni' – the term for a female who cleans and sweeps out excrement from household toilets. I now realise she would have been a Dalit and was at the bottom of this inhuman social structure, of which my family were a part. My father loathed the inhumanity and rigidity of caste, and it was one of the main reasons why, as soon as he could, at the age of twenty-two, he escaped by emigrating to Britain.

.

The power dynamics operating within my name tell a story that reaches back through thousands of years of history, to the Indo-Gangetic Plain where my Hindu ancestors lived, from around 3300 BCE, in an area covering northern India, including present-day Punjab, Delhi, West Bengal, as well as half of Pakistan, Bangladesh and southern Nepal. When I studied history at school in India as an eleven-year-old, we were taught a fairly simplified version of how this system came about. We were told that the fair-skinned Aryan warrior tribes invaded from Central Asia in the north and subjugated the darker-skinned Dravidians who had lived in India for centuries. The Aryans set up the caste system and placed themselves at the very top of a four-tier pyramid of priests (Brahmins), warriors (Kshatriyas), merchants, tradesmen and farmers (Vaishyas) and labourers and craftsmen (Shudras). I later found out, of course, that it's all much more complex and that there are, in fact, hundreds of further divisions, with their own intricate set of religious codes of behaviour.

Although reinforced and solidified during the colonial era, it's clear from the history books that this abhorrent tradition of hereditary discrimination existed before the British came to power.[2] For centuries, the Brahmins lived a life of privilege. They weren't usually particularly rich, or politically powerful, but they upheld an oppressive structure of cruel, all-encompassing social and religious control. Some Dalit surnames – including Pariah – again clearly marked out their position within the social hierarchy. (The British word 'pariah', meaning outcaste, was inherited from this inhuman system of Hindu classification.) Others sought to free themselves from this nominative prison, changing to more neutral surnames – that were used across different castes and religious boundaries – such as Das and Mandal.

My grandparents lived their lives according to the Brahmin

scriptures – as they were taught them. Their name was like a box, encasing them, symbolising their Hindu belief system and their Brahmin heritage. And it would have been unthinkable for them, or for anyone around them, to step outside of it. Narua had been a high-caste area for centuries: religiously orthodox, with women barely leaving the home, and caste purity maintained through strict rules around marriage. Religion was woven into the fabric of everyone's lives here: it dictated where they lived, how they acted in their daily lives, and what happened to them when they died. It was in the very air everyone breathed. One's surname was integral to this strict social system – it both gave you your current identity and summed up your actions in the previous life. The name Banerjee was one of the highest karmic prizes you could achieve, signifying to everyone that you must have behaved and acted virtuously in past lives. My grandparents' enormous social standing, therefore, arose out of the idea of cyclical reincarnation across the millennia.

My Grandfather, Ram Chandra Banerjee
Narua Para, Chandannagar, 1979

A hand-painted name plaque on the wall, written in Bengali script:

Mahamayashram

And below it, my grandfather's name:

R.C. Banerjee.

This is the person I most associate with my surname, a stern authoritarian figure, my grandfather, Ram Chandra Banerjee. Named after Lord Ram, the hero of the Hindu epic, *The Ramayana*. The family home was a large old house with numerous rooms arranged around a dark central courtyard. I remember as a child stepping from the sunshine of the street and entering through two huge carved wooden doors. I would be transported into a timeless world of praying, washing, ritual and arcane Brahminical rules around eating and the preparation of food.

Despite his forbidding appearance, my grandfather was a rather lost figure, trapped in a rigid world of religion and ritual, locked in a lifelong battle with his only son – my father – who had run off to England, who worshipped everything British, loved socialising, drinking, smoking and rejected his father and mother's intense religiosity and everything about their devout upper-caste way of life. My grandfather, dhoti clad and grey haired, barely spoke but dominated the household from a separate wing of the house where he spent most of his time. Wandering about those dusty rooms in the old Chandannagar house I'd hear fragments of stories. Behind my grandfather's rather ossified persona were hints of a more idealistic and dramatic past. Now when I think of what my surname carries, it's complicated. Reaching further back in time, I can't help but feel for the young boy my grandfather once was and the hardship he went through, that tied in with his surname and with his Banerjee destiny as a Hindu priest.

•

Ram Chandra Banerjee was born in 1907, when India was still under British rule, in a village outside Tarakeshwar, a rural backwater in colonial Bengal. Like all Banerjee males, he would have been initiated into the Brahmin priesthood around puberty, with a sacred thread ceremony. His surname was inherently connected to the life he was about to lead.

Banerjee is an anglicised version of the name Bandyopadhyay, a term that signifies that you are a priest, a teacher, a transmitter of religious knowledge. It is thousands of years old, derived from the Sanskrit *Vandyodpadhyaya* which means 'venerable teacher', and is constructed from the word *vandyo* ('venerable') and *upahdyaya* ('teacher'). Although they were high-caste Brahmins, my grandfather's family were very poor (as was often the case) and lived in primitive conditions: a mud hut consisting of one room for the whole family. His family couldn't afford to send him to school, so they decided to send him off to the Balaji Mandir in south India – one of the largest and richest temples in India – to train to become a priest and receive an education. So, around the age of fourteen – just a teenager – he left his village and travelled thousands of miles across India on his own, to live at this sprawling ancient complex, full of thousands of devotees and hundreds of priests.

He was clever and quickly rose up the religious ranks to become one of the head priests, but as he did so he discovered that he was living within one of the most corrupt priestly hierarchies in India. This was a long time ago, the 1920s, and I have heard only fragments of his story from my father. But from what I have gathered, among the crowds, the incense, the rotting flowers and the gods and goddesses, my grandfather stumbled across a dark network of fraud and corruption. According to my father, he got to know things he shouldn't know, threatened to expose them and had to escape in fear for his life in the middle of the night. I imagine that part of his own Brahmin code was about leading a pure life and having high moral standards, and from what I gather, he believed in this. It may have manifested itself in his household as a rigid set of religious rules, but my grandfather, I think, tried to be 'good' in a way that seemed right to him.

He eventually married and settled in Chandannagar and, together with my grandmother, created in their huge old house a life of almost monastic religiosity. Despite his traumatic departure from the temple, he never forgot the Vedic rituals and teachings he had learnt and my father's first name Balaji – meaning Vishnu – comes from there.

My Grandmother, Mamata Banerjee (née Ganguli) Chandannagar, 1979

My grandmother was only fourteen when her marriage was arranged. Her family were Kulin Brahmins, an elite Brahmin subcaste, as denoted by her family's surname, Ganguli. Her groom had to be from a similar family, with a corresponding surname. According to legend, Kulin Brahmins were descendants of the four Brahmin priests brought to Bengal by an eighth-century Hindu king in order to revive traditional orthodox Hinduism. The descendants of these four Brahmin priests formed four clans, with the surnames Banerjee, Mukherjee, Chatterjee and Ganguli. For centuries, their high status meant that Kulin Brahmin priests often had multiple wives – up to forty or fifty, some of them just ten or eleven years old – as lower-rank families would see an improvement in their social standing if they managed to marry one of their daughters to one of these men.

Within this insular subcaste was an intense snobbery. For my grandmother's family, marriage had to be strictly to another Kulin Brahmin, and the surnames acted as a filtering device. My grandfather was viewed as a particularly desirable groom: not only was he a Banerjee, but he had also been a senior priest at a renowned Hindu temple.

Once she was married, my grandmother – just a teenage girl – soon became as devout as her new groom. It was hardly surprising, this was a society where women were taught to regard their husbands as demi-gods, obeying their every instruction. I remember her praying for hours at a time. Each day, in her faded white sari, she would create a shrine on her marble floor, carefully arranging pictures of gods and goddesses, placing flower petals in front of each one, filling the room with incense smoke and the sounds of her Sanskrit prayers. As a child I wasn't allowed to disturb her, but I loved the heady otherworldly atmosphere that she created. And afterwards she would let me eat the offerings to the gods, the *prasad,* of freshly made Indian sweets and fruit. These memories too, of spending time with my grandmother, are wrapped up in the complicated feelings I have towards my surname.

•

As a Brahmin Banerjee wife, my grandmother lived what I now feel was an extreme cloistered existence. She seemed to spend all her time in her bedroom. She slept there, prayed there, washed for hours in a primitive bathroom on the side, cooked on the threshold just outside and ate her food on the floor by her bed. It's not that she was forced to do this or was unhappy, but she barely left the house, never went downstairs, never went out onto the street outside, to the shops or to other people's houses. And when I went back to India as a child, this archaic world also became my reality. We had lived with my grandparents when I was younger, during our previous stay in India. This wasn't just an exotic, rather strange version of

Indian spirituality. This was now my normality. I went from living in Hayes, watching *Grange Hill* on TV, living in a modern world, with carpets, central heating, driving over to my cousins' houses, to being thrown into this pre-industrial world of Brahminical orthodoxy.

When my father talks about his childhood spent within the restricted enclosure of a high-caste household there is a feeling of suffocation, a darkness to the religiosity suffusing his world. He describes his mother as someone whose life was filled with obsessions about food, with numerous constraints and daily performances of ritual cleanliness. Cooking had to be preceded by full bathing, and it was strictly no meat, fish, eggs, garlic and onions. There was a fanaticism around the cooking of rice and anyone who touched the pot of cooked rice was viewed as contaminated, unless they touched a drop of water immediately afterwards. Similarly, it was forbidden to partly eat or touch food and pass it on to someone else – it had become what is known as *etto* and was therefore polluted, in an undefined but vaguely religious sense. As a child my father also wasn't allowed to eat at anyone's house unless they were Brahmins – he remembers being severely beaten by his father for eating at the home of a friend who was from a lower caste.

In this Brahmin quest for caste purity, washing was a permanent feature of day-to-day life, overseen by the women of the house. In my grandparents' house there was no running water and I remember my grandmother standing at the threshold of her room, ordering around a man who delivered fresh water every day, weighed down by the heavy buckets that he'd just carried upstairs. In the huge dank bathroom, there was a primitive squatting toilet, and endless tin pails filled with water, used to flush the toilet and clean ourselves. There was always water on the floor of the bathroom and translucent brown lizards lurked on the walls, disrupted by the sloshing from the buckets and the incessant washing after going to the toilet.

This was a patriarchal world: high-caste women like my grandmother were married off when they were children, had to leave their family homes and were teenagers when they started having children themselves. Running the household, obsessing about cleanliness and religious ritual became the entirety of their lives. I remember the derogatory term, *chuchibai*, for a woman who had become fanatical about touch and cleanliness. Perhaps long ago these were practical measures to keep food fresh and to prevent disease, but over centuries they became fused with religious dogma.

It wasn't right of course, this snobbery and focus on caste purity, but it makes me sad now, thinking of the mentally and physically restricted lives of such women. The connections between cleanliness and holiness were extreme in certain Brahmin households, and had my grandmother been born into a different caste, had a different name, perhaps her life could have been more expansive, less obsessive. In some ways, she defied aspects of this life: she was a strong and opinionated woman; she loved reading, talking politics and most importantly, she made sure her daughters were educated. But I think her life could have been so much more, and it was blighted by being born into an enclosed life of washing, cleaning and praying.

•

When my parents were growing up in Chandannagar, if anyone tried to step outside of the reality of caste they faced the prospect of total ostracisation. In the late sixties, my grandmother's daughter, my youngest aunt, broke all social taboos and fell in love with someone from the caste below, a Dutta, a Kayastha surname. My aunt was terrified of what would happen if my grandparents found out. She feared that she would be coerced into leaving my uncle, that she might even be locked up in the house. The fear of bringing social shame on my grandparents was also huge. She eventually got married in secret, telling no-one, not even her sisters. She eloped with her husband to Britain and didn't return to India or see my grandparents for many years.

•

My grandparents were proud of their Banerjee name, but I will always remain conflicted about it. I love many aspects of their Hindu belief system, but their interpretation of it, their unquestioning belief in the caste system, will for me always be wrong. I understand it would have been hard for my grandparents to see beyond or challenge its moral and philosophical universe, given the narrow society they were born into. However, in nineteenth-century India, reformist Hindu movements swept across the country, with inspirational Bengali spiritual leaders, such as Ramakrishna and Swami Vivekananda, who challenged the whole proposition of caste. These were revered household names when I was growing up, and I now wonder why my family didn't turn more towards this egalitarian version of Hindu spirituality. For me, however, in the seventies, the contrast between my 'Indian' and 'British' social statuses was odd, to say the least. I was moving as a child between two starkly different identities. Looking back, in Britain, as Asian immigrants, we were part of a reviled minority, looked down on by much of society, ridiculed, shamed and sometimes abused. But in India, my Brahmin family were part of an oppressive ruling class

– entitled and comfortable in their innate superiority – and my name was intrinsically connected to that.

Sheela Cosmetics
Kolkata, 1979

In India, there was an undoubted sense of opportunity for my parents, free of the shackles of discrimination they lived with in Britain. The names Tripti and Balaji were no longer felt to be slightly contemptible. Tripti was pronounced properly every time it was spoken and sounded beautiful in Bengali. I could feel my parents' ease and familiarity in this world. My mother was reunited with her parents, three sisters and her brother once more, and I could see the strength it gave her to be with them. I loved the fact that my parents could walk the streets without any fear, my mother wearing her sari, an air of confidence about her as she held my hand and we walked together through the streets of Kolkata, to visit a school or go shopping. She was in her element in India.

She was a trained chemist, and soon she spotted a potential opening here in India. There were very few basic cosmetics and toiletries available in Kolkata in the late seventies, especially as there were no foreign imports. She used what she'd learnt in England, her knowledge of chemistry and her experience working for Almay Cosmetics to set up a business, deciding to name it after me.

Sheela Cosmetics

I didn't mind at all – in fact I quite liked it. My name was no longer a source of discomfort, the name of a frumpy-sounding older woman. To my eleven-year-old mind, *Sheela Cosmetics* sounded pretty and as if it could well be the name of an aspirational beauty brand.

I liked using my mum's creams, her shampoos, and was proud of the fact that she knew how to make these things. My name was registered as a business, and it didn't feel embarrassing or odd. Indian businesses often used first names as a title. The leading makeup brand then was Lakme – a version of the name Laxmi – and I used to eat Amul Butter, and often saw signs like Madhabhi Sarees or Leela Tailoring when I was out and about.

In our very basic stone kitchen in Lake Town, my mother unpacked the laboratory scales she'd brought from England, weighed out chemicals from Hatti Bagan market in Kolkata, and started to make batches of mosquito repellent, shampoo and moisturisers – products that weren't very high quality then in Kolkata – and started selling them. She had great instincts. This was a part of the world plagued by mosquitos and yet the only repellent on the market had a nasty smell and no-one liked using it.

•

But despite my mum's promising new business, day-to-day life was hard for all of us, and especially so for me as a child used to living in Britain. This was seventies India, full of political turmoil, which meant there were power cuts every day. Sitting in our flat in Lake Town in the heat of the summer, I would be filled with dread as the fans would suddenly stop whirring, not knowing how many hours until the electricity would come back on. The heat was like a blanket wrapped round my face, claustrophobic and suffocating. This was a country where nature seemed to be encroaching all the time: snakes appeared in our house, huge rats, and when we came back to the house after a few hours away, the kitchen would be filled with gigantic brown cockroaches, with their dark shiny shells, that would suddenly split as they took flight. The darkness at night was enveloping, the seasons harsh, the sun unforgiving. When the monsoon came things got worse, our roads became flooded and when I returned home from school, our white walls had turned black, teeming with thousands of grasshoppers that had crawled out from the ground to escape the water.

Kolkata, in 1979, was incredibly poor. The main train station, Howrah, seemed to me, as we came back from Chandannagar each week, like a modern-day hell on earth. There were thousands of people living on the platforms, or on the cracked pavements around the station, in makeshift shacks, or just on a scrap of dirty material. Children younger than me, their hair matted, would come up to us, arms outstretched asking for money. I often saw limbless beggars, probably victims of child trafficking, shifting themselves around on pieces of wood with wheels attached. I felt uncomfortable about the servants that came to clean in our homes – some just a couple of years older than me. Subconsciously I knew that it was deeply unfair that so many people lived like this – no money, not enough to eat, with no education, no healthcare, and often nowhere to live. It seemed like a gross vision of humanity, but one that was just accepted by those around me. Viewing my relatively privileged life as an outsider, society seemed cruel and inhuman. Just four years later, as a sixteen-year-old, I would remember this, the things I'd seen, and the stark differences in wealth that I saw as a child between Britain and India. It would fuel my engagement with politics, and this too was a part of the identity I had as an Indian child.

•

I make it sound awful – there was another side too. The incredible life force of Kolkata. Being immersed among people speaking the same language as me with a centuries-old, shared cultural heritage. Being close to Tuktuki, I saw my mother's parents all the time too – they too lived in Narua, and I was reunited with all my cousins on that side of the family.

But after a year of living in India, my parents were running out of money and my father's business hadn't worked out. Although *Sheela Cosmetics* was looking promising, they were also fed up with all the struggles of living in India – the rigidity of my grandparents' lives, the constant power cuts, the lack of healthcare, the corruption, the appalling roads, the constant presence of life-threatening diseases like malaria, dysentery and encephalitis. And so they decided – once again – to return to Britain.

An Indian Girl Comes Back to England
Hayes, West London, 1980

We returned on a cold grey day in February, got off the plane and walked through the ordered corridors of Heathrow Airport. As we went through immigration, my name was back to being as foreign and liminal as it had been a year ago. I was once more an immigrant child.

But in just one year the country I had returned to seemed to be a much nastier place.

•

I'm twelve years old and it's 1980. Margaret Thatcher has just been elected while we were away, stoking racist tensions, talking of fears of being 'rather swamped' by people of a 'different culture'. We are the immigrants 'swamping' the country. I start secondary school in the middle of the year, an Indian girl with an Indian name, paranoid that I have picked up traces of an Indian accent while I've been away. Suddenly, around me, it seems that being a skinhead, being a racist, has become just an ordinary part of teenage fashion. The politics of the time, the clothes, the music – two-tone bands like Bad Manners and Madness – have come together to form a powerful identity of casual suburban racism. It's everywhere, it's no longer just a far-right pose.

And in Hayes things had got much, much worse. The streets were suddenly crawling with skinheads with their shaved heads, Harrington bomber jackets and huge Doc Martens. These were the same skinheads going next door to Southall, beating up shopkeepers and attacking Indian families. The trouble was, in Hayes, we were now living among these racists, one of the few Asian families in the area. National Front signs started appearing everywhere, school desks sometimes had 'Wogs Out' etched in biro. We would sometimes be served by shop assistants who had tattooed swastikas on their necks or on their wrists, peeking out from under their overalls. It was clear we were definitely unwelcome here. The National Front may have been trounced in the election, but their influence was powerful on the streets. And in the next general election the residents of Hayes would go on to elect the most openly racist MP in the country, the Conservative politician Terry Dicks.

Even as a child I sensed a threat every time I walked down the street. I would sometimes walk to the town centre with my mum, scared if I saw a group of teenagers walking towards us. I would be anxiously watching to see if they were skinheads, praying inwardly we could get past them without being attacked. I knew they wanted to hurt us. As they got closer and closer, I would imagine them beating me and my mother – and it seemed to me at the time that I was surrounded by stories of Asians being attacked. I've since found out that my mother and my aunt were assaulted by racists around this time, but I wasn't told about it then. I think they were trying to protect us as children, but these attacks filtered through to me as a kind of unnameable fear. The groups of youths we passed would sometimes taunt me by lunging at me aggressively for fun, to make me afraid, or spit at me. Young men with narrow eyes and shorn heads would snarl at us: 'Fucking Wog, go back home'; 'Fuck off back to where you came from'. Every outside space I went to – my road, the shops, the local pool – I would be on the alert, fearful of a pervasive threat from gangs of teenage skinheads.

•

One Saturday, in July 1981, my parents heard rumours that the National Front were threatening to attack. I was told I couldn't go out. That eerie, frightening day is etched in my memory: I stood at my living room window, looking out through the net curtains, by our teak sideboard with the cream-coloured telephone sitting on top of it, my father's work notepad by the side. I remember looking out at the grey road, the blank rows of houses opposite, feeling vulnerable even inside the house. Later that day, rioting broke out in Southall. Hordes of skinheads had arrived there and started throwing bricks through Indian shops and beating up elderly Asians. When the police refused to do anything, the Indians fought back. The local Punjabi youth burned down a nearby pub, The Hambrough Tavern, after it refused to call off a National Front gig full of hundreds of swastika-tattooed men, intent on hate.

When I went into school on Monday everyone was talking about it. I found out that the pub, notorious for its popularity with local skinheads, was owned by an uncle of one of the girls in my class. I didn't say anything to her when she talked about it. It was hard to compute that someone I saw every day at school, someone who was friendly and nice, could in any way be connected to this violent, frightening presence. I don't blame her in any way – it also must have been a shocking event within her own family. We didn't really have the consciousness or the words for the kind of racially charged atmosphere we were living in. We were all just thirteen-year-olds, living our lives, listening to Madness and The Jam, obsessed by the Top 40, but it was a disturbing thing to find out that Monday morning.

I spent the first couple of years after getting back from India nervously watching for signs of racism in my class. Nothing overt was ever directed at me. But I sensed a quiet coldness – a kind of unspoken revulsion – from some of the girls, and the only Indian teacher in the school, a gentle and rather mild man, called Mr Sharma, was derided for his accent and treated with contempt. Indian accents, our languages, all were generally made fun of, as was the smell of curry, Indian clothes, and I felt I had to be on my guard the whole time. But racism didn't by any means blight everything. At school, after a couple of years, I had a tight-knit group of (utterly lovely, white) friends: Siobhan, Erica and Denise. We were a gang of four, and we mainly spent our time talking about bands we liked, laughing at our maths teacher Mr Arnold and giggling a lot in class.

•

And, as I grew up, the atmosphere in Hayes gradually changed. The '81 riots in Brixton, Toxteth and Southall were part of this – Black and Asian communities had fought back for the first time, the children of immigrants were growing up and refused to be cowed. The Southall Youth Movement was formed to resist attacks, with violence if necessary, and together with the presence of local Punjabi gangs in the area they ensured that Southall became a no-go area for the skinheads. The music and fashions of the outer London suburbs had changed – in my school this was the era of The Human League, Duran Duran and Madonna. Poppy androgynous music.

My parents had decided to stay in Britain. I felt a sense of growing permanence. I no longer had a sensation that we might at any minute go back to India and that I would become an Indian Sheela Banerjee again. That life was over. London was home.

I no longer walked the streets perpetually watching out for abuse, no longer shrinking into myself – I became a punk, outwardly visible to the world. My name, Sheela Banerjee, was a British Indian name, part of a new generation of Indians growing up here, who were starting to claim our place.

Marcella Gatsky: The Journey of a Name from Tsarist Russia to Suburban Stanmore

Marcella Gatsky
Harrow Weald Sixth Form College
North West London, 1985

I loved hanging out with Marcella – she was always at the centre of everything. At sixth form college, she brought us all together, organised nights out and would turn up with a little wicker basket of drinks for everyone, and, once she'd got her driving licence, we'd go from party to party in Harrow and Pinner in her second-hand Triumph Herald. She was one of my closest friends at college, and I was always round her house in the afternoons, in Honeypot Lane, Stanmore. We had bonded over our shared dislike of our A-Level maths teacher. We were always whispering; we couldn't keep up with the rest of the geeky male physics students in our class and became mind numbingly bored. Marcella gave it up after a few months to study art instead, and I ploughed on, in the subconscious hope of pleasing my mum, who had desperately wanted me to study sciences and become a doctor, neither of which I was going to do.

I remember Marcella's house as large and bustling – she has three sisters – in a nice middle-class area, just down the road from college. We would walk into her kitchen, with its large wooden table; it was unlike mine, which was pokey and quite dilapidated. My mum had recently started a part-time business making samosas, and it constantly smelt of oil and frying. I always remember Marcella opening up the fridge and getting out a huge array of food: olives, chicken drumsticks, salad and taramasalata. I had never seen such a well-stocked fridge before, with deli food that you could just take out and eat. My favourite was always the taramasalata – it was the first time I'd ever tasted such a thing – an unctuous pale pink dip in a large tub (it was much nicer than the version sold in the supermarkets now). Marcella would spread some on a piece of hot fluffy white pitta and as I bit into the creamy sour fish roe, I would be in heaven. It was so different from all curries, or the typically English school dinners I was used to – shepherd's pie, toad in the hole and apple crumble. This was my first taste of Mediterranean food, and my first experience of spending a lot of time in a family home that wasn't Bengali.

•

Gatsky, I was to find out, is a Jewish surname. And I loved getting to know someone Jewish. Her family were open and welcoming, and there always seemed to be someone staying at her house. Her Uncle Leon would often be in the front room with his large shaggy dog. And then there was her Aunty Ann, her Aunty Faye. The Gatskys were a typically big Jewish family, and it reminded me of my own family, and how we also often had relatives and friends staying at our house, sometimes for months at a time. They seemed uncannily similar to us in other ways too. Lots of doctors and lawyers, the same overbearing parents, quite middle class, conservative, and with their own religious traditions and their own identity. Like us, they too were different from the English, and just like me, Marcella was always railing against having to stay in on a Friday night for a family meal with all her relatives.

·

But Marcella seemed very different from some of the other Jewish girls I was at sixth form college with. Before I'd become friends with her, I'd noticed a group of them, always hanging out together in a large crowd, languishing, laughing with one another, completely at ease. I'd wondered where they were from. These girls had sun-kissed tanned olive skin, stone-washed jeans and long glossy brown hair, cascading in waves down their bare shoulders. They looked like they'd spent endless summer holidays in idyllic Mediterranean villas. I'd vaguely thought that they might be Italian or Spanish but wondered what they were doing here in suburban Harrow. I was still trying to work out who everyone was at my new sixth form college, a Bengali girl who'd never really been outside of Hayes. They were beautiful and seemed incredibly glamorous. I had no desire to look like them – I was a punk – but I found them intriguing. No one at my old school, Swakeleys Comprehensive, which was overwhelmingly English and working class, looked like this. Later, I overheard other Jewish people referring to them in a derogatory way as 'Becks'. I think they may also have appropriated the term for themselves – they didn't seem to care and always appeared to be supremely confident throughout my time at Harrow Weald.

Marcella knew most of these girls from her childhood; she rejected their aesthetic and what she felt was the homogenous world of eighties Jewish femininity in places like Stanmore, Harrow and Edgware. She feels it was a 'girly' environment, dominated by money and looks. Marcella also had long dark hair, but it wasn't glamorous, she wore it rockabilly style, rolled and pinned at the front, and had shaved the underside – it was bald, harsh and unfeminine. She tells me most of the girls – including her – were sent to small girls' private secondary schools nearby, but barely anyone she knew went to university. They weren't encouraged to have careers, it was, she says, 'all very one track'.

She herself had felt pigeonholed and pressurised by the world she'd grown up in to be a 'North London Jewish Girl'. It was the part of being a Gatsky that she didn't like. Outside of school, everyone went to one of the networks of Jewish youth clubs from a young age. Hers, she says, was called Maccabi, she refers jokingly to it as the 'princess-y one', and there were others like BBYO, the one our friend Sarah Leigh, the daughter of a rabbi, went to – 'the hippie one'. The clubs were the hub of most north London Jewish children's social lives, says Marcella. At sixteen, many would go on a 'tour' of Israel together, a formative experience, before they entered the world of adulthood.

These were all-encompassing groups, and most Jewish children Marcella knew stayed within the same social circles, formed in childhood. Marcella says that 'they grew up together, ended up with each other and got married.' This was the life of suburban Friday night dinners with the family, and Saturday nights at Edgware Station – a place where hundreds of teenagers used to congregate to flirt and often meet their future husbands and wives.

I remember Marcella taking me to Edgware once and it was an amazing sight: masses of teenagers outside this drab station at the end of the Northern line, just milling around, lining the grey pavement. I came across a podcast recently, based on a Facebook group called 'I Grew Up in Edgware Station', and immediately recognised the 1980s social scene it described. A middle-aged Jewish woman interviewed on the programme laughs about the strict social hierarchy and the 'cool kids'. She talks about 'the premier Becks' and how they used to stand there 'chewing gum and flicking their hair at the same time'. The host of the podcast, a man in his fifties called Steve Belasco, has really fond memories of that time, and recalls how he and his friends used to meet and get ready at his house in Borehamwood, before making their way to Edgware Station. They would get there by 8 or 8.30pm, by which time there would be anywhere up to 200 Jewish teenagers already there, ready for their Saturday night, which sometimes just involved riding the tube for a while, carriages packed with other Jewish teens, chatting, laughing and getting to know one another. He ends the documentary saying 'it was an amazing thing, I'll never forget Edgware.'[1]

As an outsider, I feel a pang of regret at this lost innocent world. But I can also understand how it felt claustrophobic and restrictive to Marcella, as a young girl trying to carve out her own identity. Marcella had grown up immersed in a tapestry of Jewish traditions and celebrations: the bar mitzvahs, the shabbats, the family get-togethers, which, despite her outward rebelliousness, she had always enjoyed. The Gatskys always went to synagogue, and her family, like everyone else, celebrated a succession of religious festivals throughout the year. Marcella used to love Hanukkah (or *Chanukah*), commemorating the recovery of Jerusalem after the Jewish people rose up against their Greek oppressors. She always remembers the lighting of the Menorah – a sacred candelabra – for eight days and the gifts that went with it, one for each day. They also celebrated Yom Kippur, as well as Passover (or *Pesach*). Marcella remembers how everyone in the family would come round to their house on the first two nights of the seven-day festival and they would all share a huge meal – eating unleavened bread (matzo), matzo ball soup, beef and gefilte fish (poached, minced fish). As Gatskys, her family was part of a much larger history – they all knew the stories – that knitted together Jewish people all over northwest London, in a huge collective that reached way back into the past.

●

But being a Gatsky, for Marcella, also has another meaning. It came from her father, David, who passed away eleven years ago. Through his name, she carries a spirit of rebellion that was always there in the Gatskys, a family of East End Jews. Her grandfather, Myer Gatsky, had gone against religious tradition and married a non-Jewish woman, causing a scandal among the closed Jewish community of the East End. The Gatskys always had an 'open house', which meant that Gentiles would often join them, and mealtimes were raucous and full of politics and debate. In the seventies the name Gatsky became synonymous with her uncle, Jack Gatsky, a left-wing rebel and strike organiser, who was instrumental in bringing Heathrow Airport to a standstill in the summer of 1977.

And then there is a story within the Gatsky name that goes much further back in time. It is a tale of persecution, violence, fear and flight. It's the story of trying to escape a momentous and monstrous history of pre-revolutionary Russia, of waves of deadly anti-Semitism that swept across the country. Within the surname Gatsky is the experience of deep and lasting trauma, which carried on through generations.

●

The Gatskys weren't always Gatskys. Names, like people, often go on a journey, metamorphosing as they pass through the centuries, through places, cultures and religions.

Gerginski. Gatskei. Gates. Gad. Gerswhin. Gatski. Gerskyn. Gershovitz.

I see so many variations of their name as I'm researching Marcella's story. It's unclear what the Hebrew version was but I try to fill in the gaps along the way. The Gatskys were originally a Russian Jewish family, who along with two million others fled in terror from persecution in Tsarist Russia at the turn of the century. Their original surname has disappeared – it's a symbol of how the Gatskys lost their entire existence, and were forced to leave behind everything they knew in Russia. Their oldest living relative, a cousin called Rita, thinks their name may have been Gerskyn, but there appears to be no record of it anywhere. In the *Dictionary of Jewish Surnames from the Russian Empire,* the closest I find is Gats, also listed as 'Gots, Gotts and Gostev'. Gats means 'righteous, proselyte, true convert to Judaism, and was also the name for the official in charge of alms and charities'.[2] This is the name I have to assume the Gatsky family went by at this point in time. As the Russian Revolution was about to unfold, the Gats made their way across Europe in a horse and cart, escaping with nothing: no money, no belongings, in fear of their lives. Eventually they got on a boat and made their way over to Britain.

It's story upon story, and like Chinese whispers it's different every time. One story goes that every time they crossed the border their name was changed: people couldn't pronounce it, or they spelt it wrong. Or perhaps the Gats changed it themselves to hide their Jewishness? Their mutating name became an outward manifestation of the horrors and deprivations they endured and all the countries they passed through, a marker of how nineteenth-century Europe treated its Jewish population. After travelling thousands of miles, they eventually settled in the East End of London. By then they had changed their first names and become the Gatskis. Other members of the family were thought to have become Gads. Their identities and their story underwent radical transformations. They went from Yiddish-speaking, Orthodox Jews, scraping a living in Whitechapel, living in grinding poverty, working in the rag trade, to a family that lived through two world wars, sometimes with barely enough to eat, who eventually became the Gatskys that I met in 1984, an affluent family, part of a diaspora of middle-class British Jews, living in British suburbia, to finally my friend, Marcella, who still carries these stories, which can be glimpsed faintly in the outline of her name.

Marcella's father, David, was the youngest of five siblings, and once he passed away, all the family stories, the anecdotes, the memories, the history of the Gatskys started to fade. As with all families, there are just scraps of information passed down, repetitions of images, fragments of events: the Russian great grandmother who wore her hair in a bun and spoke Yiddish, who gave birth on a boat; hiding under the table during the war; nights out in underground jazz clubs in Soho. I know that Marcella adored her father David, and she still carries his surname. He was the one who gave her that spark of energy as a teenager, the refusal to conform, who encouraged all the Gatsky girls to go to university, to be independent, broaden their horizons and go out into the world. He was, as Marcella remembers, always laughing, joking, creating the open, hospitable home that I remember visiting as a teenager. With Marcella's father now gone, the only living family members who can shed light on the Gatsky history are

Marcella's mother, Maureen, and Cousin Rita, who is in her eighties. I talk to both of them, to see if I can start to understand the dark forces of history and the tales of individual survival that lie behind the Gatsky name.

Chaia and Myer Gats
A *Shtetl* outside Odessa, Eastern Ukraine, around 1884

If we spool backwards through time, to unfurl the long history of the name Gatsky, we arrive on the edges of Tsarist Russia, at a deeply conservative Jewish *shtetl* (village), and meet Chaia and Myer. These two young people will begin the train of events that will eventually lead to Marcella's name as it exists today.

•

It is Chaia's wedding day. She is fifteen years old.

Chaia. The Hebrew word for 'life', it means 'our gift from God'. A name of deep spiritual significance. Chaia. Chaya. Khaya. Khaja. Haiyyah. Pronounced Hi-yah, it starts at the back of the throat, with strength, with a rasp, and an expulsion of air in the second syllable 'aah', the sound lifting itself up into the heavens.

Fifteen-year-old Chaia is my friend Marcella's great-grandmother and on this day she will take on the Gats name, when she marries Myer. He is twenty-two years old, and Chaia has barely spoken to him, as her marriage has been arranged by the old matchmaker, the *shadchan*. Chaia looks in the mirror and shakes out her long dark hair, that she usually wears tied up in a bun. It comes tumbling down, shiny and brown, and will only ever be seen like this by her husband, as is the custom for all the women in her *shtetl*. We will never know if she was nervous, excited or worried about marrying a man she barely knew, seven years older than her. But she might have thought it was a good match – Myer from an educated family and according to Cousin Rita, at the time was studying to be a doctor.

As a Jewish wife, living in Russia in the late nineteenth century, Chaia's duty would have been to bear children, a vital part of her faith. Her life in the *shtetl* would have been imbued with a strong sense of community, deeply rooted in religious culture. The men and boys would have spent several hours a day studying religious texts, the Torah and the Talmud, at religious schools known as *yeshivas*.[3] And like most societies at this point in history, this was a patriarchal world, where women weren't allowed to study or work and were confined to household tasks and raising children.

This is the life that fifteen-year-old Chaia Gats was expecting to lead.

•

Chaia and Myer Gats: their shared surname symbolised their marriage, but more than that it defined them clearly as Jews. And being Jewish in this period of history in pre-revolutionary Russia meant living under a vicious, anti-Semitic autocracy. The Gats, along with the rest of Russia's Jewish population, were stripped of basic human rights, denied the right to vote or work across most of imperial Russia. From 1791 to 1917 they were confined by Tsarist rule to an area known as the Pale of Settlement, covering mainly the Ukraine and parts of Poland and Lithuania. Within the Pale, the community existed in a condition of virtual apartheid, allowed to live and work in Jewish-only enclaves (*shtetls*), with race laws barring most Jews from owning businesses, or from becoming doctors, teachers, or even from becoming educated. The resulting poverty meant that huge swathes of the population found themselves unable to feed or clothe themselves and survived only through the Jewish spiritual tradition of charity (known as *tzedakah*). Myriad welfare organisations provided food, medicine, education and housing for orphans in the *shtetls* to help as many people as they could. Historian Martin Gilbert writes in *Atlas of Jewish History* that in Ukraine, where Chaia and Myer lived, over a fifth of the Jewish population was being supported through charity at this time.[4] This was also a period of terrifying violence. Brutal attacks against the community swept through the country, especially in the Pale. Gangs of Russian Cossacks on horseback would rampage through *shtetls*, burning buildings, beating, killing and raping villagers, with the tacit approval of successive Tsarist governments.

Leaving the *Shtetl*
Odessa, Eastern Ukraine, around 1900

It's now six years since Chaia and Myer got married. They have three young children and Chaia is pregnant with a fourth. The Gats don't know this, but within a few months they will lose their name forever. Behind the eventual disappearance of their name lie historical forces beyond their control, as well as countless individual decisions, emotions. Among them fear and terror.

Tsar Alexander II has been assassinated. Revolution is in the air, and rumours spread that he was murdered by communist Jews. Violence against the community has become increasingly deadly as the years have gone by. Pogroms are about to sweep through the city of Odessa, by the Black Sea coast, just a few miles from where the Gats are living. Murderous mobs will go round beating and mutilating Jewish men, women and children; they will hurl people out of windows, rape and cut open pregnant women, slaughter children in front of their parents. All that is to come.[5]

For now, here they are, the Gats, a young family. Myer can no longer train as a doctor – under the Tsar's decree most Jews are barred from entering the medical profession. But beyond this is a growing sense of dread and physical threat that surrounds their life in the *shtetl*. Fear crawls in Chaia's stomach. She is scared every day. She has three children and another one is on the way. Russian gangs are burning down neighbouring villages. At the market all they talk about is how the Cossacks roam the countryside hunting down Jews; she hears about women being raped and mutilated in Odessa. She dreams every night about the hoofbeats of Cossacks, she sees smoke rising in the sky, imagines the crackle of burning wooden houses. Like everyone around her, she wonders if their *shtetl* will be next.

If you look hard enough, behind its anglicised appearance, terror lurks somewhere in the Russian history of the name Gatsky.

It was in this atmosphere of fear that Chaia and Myer decided to pack up their belongings and flee Russia. The transformation of their surname begins from this moment.

The Gats took just a few belongings – including their Menorah candelabra – loaded their suitcases onto a horse and cart, and set off across Europe, to try to get to Britain. As they travelled they may have wondered if they would even survive

74

the journey. The Russian countryside was a dangerous place; they knew that their lives were in danger if they were caught outside the Pale of Settlement, or even beyond the boundaries of their own *shtetl*.

•

Among the two million Jewish migrants who fled Tsarist Russia between 1881 and 1920 were Chaia and Myer, their three young children and their unborn baby. I look on the map and I'm guessing that the Gats travelled across Europe, maybe, as Marcella has heard, on their horse and cart, until they reached a port, from where they could get to Britain. This would have been a terrifying and precarious journey for this deeply religious family, unused to going anywhere outside the boundaries of their *shtetl*. As Robert Winder, author of *Bloody Foreigners*, writes: 'Documents had to be bought or forged, policemen had to be bribed, borders had to be sneaked across at night.'[6] Sometimes these were illegal border crossings, fraught with the possibility of imprisonment or deportation, full of shadowy, unscrupulous characters. Was this when the name Gats started to mutate, as it was written down in haste, by criminal forgers, corrupt officials, the middlemen who didn't care? Or did the Gats change it to protect themselves?

I have hardly any information about their journey, what they must have felt and the hardships they would have endured. There are just their original names that tie them to Russia, and a few memories that have been handed down, floating down through the generations, fading with time, about to disappear into the future. What did they eat? Where did they sleep and how did they keep warm? Where did they find the will to survive? The scant information, the shadowy form of their name, was a reflection of their precarious sense of being, shorn of shelter, and of a way of life that had now vanished forever.

•

Finally, the Gats and their three children boarded a ship bound for London – along with thousands of other Jewish migrants. Most likely they would have made their way to places like Rotterdam, Libau in Latvia, Hamburg and Bremen – where weekly crossings transported around 150,000 people by steam ship to ports in Hull, Grimsby and London. Conditions on these boats were appalling: there was virtually no sanitation, and the migrants were often jammed below decks alongside livestock cargo, including horses, bound for Britain's coal-fields. A reporter from the *Evening News and Post*, writing in 1891, who made a similar journey, described a state of complete misery, where men and women were 'so enfeebled that one might have fixed their age at nearer seventy than thirty'.[7] Below decks, the Jewish migrants were 'packed together like cattle' and vomit, filth and the fetid poisonous air combined to create a scene from hell.

It was in these desperate conditions, possibly having been seasick for weeks on end, weak and frightened, in the cargo hold of a steam ship covered in vomit, that Chaia gave birth to her fourth child.

Chaia and Myer Gats and Their Four Children
Tilbury Docks, around 1900

At every border their names were changed. So the story goes. The last border the Gats family cross is the one here in

Britain, as they get off the boat at Tilbury Docks, with hundreds of other penniless and bewildered immigrants. It's a confusing cacophony of harsh sounds, 'cries and counter cries', and the 'hoarse laughter of the dock loungers', mocking their strange outfits and broken accents. And if they don't have the money for the landing fee, they face the wrath of the angry boatmen.[8]

This is the moment when the exhausted Gats arrive at the immigration desk. They have travelled for months, Chaia has just given birth on a stinking ship, and they are fleeing terror and death, at one of the most vulnerable points in their lives.

An immigration desk, with an official behind it. An exhausted, traumatised family arrives in this country. The desk is a site of demarcation. A border, from one country to another but also from one identity to another.

And it is also a site of power.

This is 1900. I imagine the official can't understand what these funny-looking foreign people are saying when he asks them for their names. He doesn't care. The Gats don't speak English, they're refugees. They are probably filthy from their months of travelling, in primitive conditions. Maybe they all look the same to him. There may have been other relatives with them. Maybe there were, we don't know for sure, but anyhow, if there were, they're long gone. I hear this story from Maureen, who in turn has heard it from her husband David Gatsky. More whispers, stories that disappear, about lives long gone, with memories fading.

The immigration official just writes down what he thinks they've said. He can't be bothered. He writes down Gatsky for one, Gadd for another. So this story goes. Marcella's mother thinks they were originally Gershwins. Cousin Rita thinks they were Gerskyns. Marcella thought they may originally have been called Gatskei, or even Gerjinski, but can't remember where she heard that. Names change, people die, stories mutate.

.

As soon as they were done with immigration, the Gats would have been in an existential struggle once more. Within minutes the hundreds of arrivals would have been dispersed to the slums and backstreets of Whitechapel, left to fend for themselves in a cutthroat atmosphere. Beatrice Webb, the social historian, writing in 1899 (exactly the point in time the Gats arrived in Whitechapel), described how within days, most of the immigrants were 'robbed of the little they possess'. The Gats may have ended up in the Jewish Temporary Shelter for a few days but soon they would have been turned out and left on the streets 'destitute and friendless'.[9]

The thousands of Jews who came to Britain at the turn of the century arrived with no money, desperate and unsure if they would even survive. The systematic transformation of their names, symbolic of the carelessness with which they were treated, tells a much bigger story: not only of brutal Russian anti-Semitism, but of the powerlessness of Jews through the centuries. It speaks also of ways in which immigrants are almost always forced to accept whatever situation they are faced with, just to survive.

Annie Gatski, Census, 1901
Louis Gatski, Census 1901

A name is like a guiding light, a faint glow that can lead you back into the pathways of the past. Without a name I have nothing. I type the names that I have been given by Marcella's family into my computer: Marcella Gatsky, Maureen Gatsky, David Gatsky. I type in their dates of birth and I'm led through the centuries back into the mazes of past lives. I'm searching for Chaia and Myer, looking for them in recorded history, through the names of their descendants.

Other names that I've had pop up on my screen: the Gadds, the Gates, the Gatskeis.

And then finally, I can't believe it, there they are, in black and white on a laptop in front of me. I find the Gats living in Whitechapel, in the census of 1901. But the names are different:

Name: Louis Gatski
Name: Annie Gatski
Address: 5D, 197 Fieldgate Street

These new names take me into a whole world, the world of the Jewish East End in Whitechapel in London. Chaia and Myer are gone. They are now Annie and Louis. One of their first acts of survival is to change their first names. They are a Russian-Jewish couple who now live in London. They are no longer who they were, and their name change is the beginning of a journey that takes place over the course of a century, their new identities intrinsic to a long and arduous process of assimilation that will take them from the poverty-stricken East End to northwest London suburbia.

But the change of name can't completely disguise who they are. They are still listed in the census as 'Russ. Foreign subjects' (Russian Foreign Subjects). That 'i' at the end of Gatski would also have clearly identified them to any English person as a foreigner. They were part of a highly visible community, thousands of immigrants crammed into a tiny space, their insularity viewed with a mixture of hostility and fear by their British hosts. And so, in the Gatskis' case, that tell-tale 'i' would disappear too as decades went by, as the process of assimilation went on.

Cousin Rita tells me that the family were poor. When I talk to her, she doesn't know the exact details, but she stresses it, *they were very very poor* she says over and over again. This is the history contained in the name Gatsky, the history of desperation.

•

Names are tools of classification, and as such they put the Gatsky family in a place, in a very precise place at a precise time. In 1901 the Gatskis, as they were then, were living in Fieldgate Street, off the Commercial Road, the heart of the Jewish community in Whitechapel. This was an overcrowded, poor and disease-ridden place that was ninety-five per cent Jewish. Charles Booth, in his famous *Descriptive Map of London Poverty*, had painted the wealthy areas of the city in shades of red, and the poorer ones in blue. The darker the colour, the more squalid the conditions. Whitechapel's most impoverished streets were tinted with a shocking deep blue, its dingy houses crowded with the new arrivals, tens of thousands of them packed into one square mile, escaping the horror of the pogroms, eking out a life – just about.

•

I talk to Marcella's mother to try to understand the journey that the Gatskys made – the seismic geographical and cultural transformations that lie behind the change to their original name. We speak from the comfort of our carpeted homes, pictures and photos on the walls behind us, our modern laptops on. But I feel during our conversation that I've stepped back in time, been transported into a world of life and death, of astonishing feats of survival. The Gatskys' flight from Russia to the East End is hard to imagine, the scale of their hardship, the dangers they faced. The change in their name emblematic of the story of an entire people and their plight, as the wheels of history turned around them. Of the two million Jews that left the Russian Empire at the turn of the century – mainly from Ukraine and Poland – 120,000 ended up in the Whitechapel area of the East End. As we talk, what I'm struck by is the astonishing will to survive of the family. Penniless and persecuted, Chaia and Myer Gats made their home, like successive waves of desperate immigrants before them, in the most poverty-stricken area of London, the East End, with the thousands of other desperate Jewish refugees who had recently arrived in this country from Imperial Russia. They spoke only Yiddish, and could barely make any money, but somehow managed to cling on to life.

•

Myer Gats had been a young Jewish boy, growing up in Tsarist Russia with dreams of becoming a doctor. He'd been steeped in religion, spent hours in his *shtetl*, studying the Talmud and the Torah, the sacred books of Judaism. But now all that was gone. His home, his nationality, his identity vanished. He was a different person: Louis Gatski, a man who by 1916 had nine children, and was living in Britain, desperately trying to feed his family.

Aged twenty-eight, Louis was now a tailor, one of the few ways of earning a living in early twentieth-century Whitechapel for a Jew who spoke little English. He's listed in the 1901 census as a 'capmaker', which meant he would have been working in one of the hundreds of sweatshops that had sprung up within the square mile of Whitechapel.[10]

This was a brutal immigrant world, with poverty wages and no job security. As tens of thousands of Jewish immigrants arrived, they became part of a highly exploitative 'sweating' system. In Whitechapel, there were over a thousand small workshops by the late 1800s, each employing a handful of desperate immigrants. Workers such as Louis, known as 'sweaters', often hung around street corners, looking for jobs, waiting for employers to pick them out from the huddled masses.[11] When he was lucky enough to have a job, Louis would have been working in dirty, cramped conditions: dank, dark buildings, disused rickety sheds, people's backrooms, garrets. They were overcrowded and stank, littered with rubbish. Floors were sometimes smeared with faeces, toilets leaked into the rooms where tailors sat working, and urinals were open, emitting foul odours. Hours were long. One historian writes of how workers toiled in sweatshops for 14–18-hour days, with their health suffering irreparable damage. Respiratory diseases were rife among these exploited garment workers, spending their days in 'damp, steamy, overheated workrooms and inhaling toxic fibre particles'.[12]

·

When Marcella talks about what her name means to her, where it comes from, she talks about how the Gatskys, like so many Jewish families from the East End, worked in the 'rag trade', a catch-all term including capmakers, tailors and an assortment of piece workers in the garment industry. To our ears, the phrase 'rag trade' evokes something archaic, even nostalgic. But life in these sweatshops was short and brutal, with employers taking advantage of the powerlessness of the Jewish immigrants. And it was no different for Marcella's great-grandfather; these were the hellish conditions in which Louis Gatski worked day after day and year after year.

I keep looking through the records, and eventually find Louis Gatski's name on a death certificate. He's changed his name once more, to Lewis Gatsky. It's now 1926 and Lewis is only thirty-five years old when he dies. He has tried to provide for his family – his wife Annie and their nine young children – but lung disease probably killed him, like thousands of other garment workers around that time.

The name on the gravestone in 1926 signals the end of the journey for Louis, his young life cut short by the brutality of life for Jewish migrants in the early twentieth century.

Annie Gatsky and the Nine Gatsky Children
Whitechapel, London, 1926

This was a time when the Gatsky name could have completely disappeared. Annie Gatski, still using the old version of the surname, was left penniless, with nine children to feed. She had no way of earning money, spoke little English, and Jews, as foreigners, were generally treated with intense hostility and xenophobia. But families like the Gatskis were part of a tight-knit, religiously devout community. They partly stuck close together for survival, but these networks were also a continuation of the religious structures that had been central to their previous lives in Russia. Annie and Louis may have changed their names, but they were still, according to Cousin Rita, an extremely devout family and together with their neighbouring Jewish families would have been immersed in a very particular version of Jewish immigrant life in the East End. Everywhere were Jewish shops, with signs in Yiddish, that sold kosher food, salt beef bagels or *gefilte* fish. Men in tall black hats, with long hair and beards, would be seen hurrying every day to prayers. It was an isolated community – religiously, linguistically and culturally. Annie Gatsky, despite her British-sounding name, even by the time she was in her eighties, could barely speak English.

A name ties you, through numerous threads, to a wider community; the name is a marker that you belong, and this was the world to which the Gatskis belonged. It was, as Charles Booth notes, a community held together by a dense network of religious and charitable associations. It included the Shabbat Meals Society, the Soup Kitchen for the Jewish Poor at Spitalfields, the Jews' Hospital (which started off at Mile End but later moved to Norwood and became the Jews' Hospital and Orphanage) and the Jewish Board of Guardians, which provided loans for the poor. However, at the heart of the newly arrived Jewish community were the *chevras*, the multitude of informal religious institutions which sprang up in each neighbourhood. These were often named after the district in Russia or Poland from which the members had emigrated and continued the charitable and religious traditions that had existed in the poverty-stricken *shtetls* of Tsarist Russia.[13] And it is this dense network of spiritual and charitable collectives, together with the close community around her, that saved Annie and her children from starvation after her husband died.

When he was alive, Annie would have walked with Louis and their children, across the rubbish-strewn streets of their area, and entered their own *chevra*, which may well have been housed in the same building as the sweatshop that Louis worked in by day. The Gatskis would have mingled with people from the same region as them in Russia, sometimes with others who had come from the same *shtetl*. They formed

84

close bonds with families who went through the same terrifying ordeals to get to this country. These small religious societies, in decrepit, dust-filled rooms, were at the heart of Russian Jewish life in Whitechapel in the early twentieth century. Once inside their local *chevra* with other families, such as the Harrovitzs, the Endelmans, the Solomons, London – the inhospitable city of the faithless – no longer felt quite so unfamiliar. Within its atmosphere of devotion, with the intonation of prayers, the smell of the candles burning, there was a respite from the harshness of daily life. The community came there to worship but the *chevras* also looked after people when they were sick, providing benefits for their families, carried out the religious rites of mourning and burial when people died and also helped look after the families that were left behind. In effect, these were spiritual collectives, groups of families who supported one another, who organised themselves, so that if one fell down, others could hold them up, in a spirit of mutual aid and co-operation.

Marcella's Grandfather, Myer Gatski
The Jewish Orphanage, Norwood, 1926

He was named after his father and given his Russian Jewish name: Myer. He will always carry that heritage through his strange-sounding foreign name. But his family call him Mick, a decidedly English nickname; a sign of how with the second generation, the family's Russian ancestry is starting to recede. The other children are given names that work in both cultures, names that are familiar to the English, that won't cause any problems. Like Becky (Rebecca), Rosy, Fanny, Harry, Davey (David) and Sadie (Sarah). A lot of diminutives, comfortable, acceptable names. Except one of Mick's brothers, who is called Lazarus. A biblical character, famously raised by Jesus from the dead, but more importantly in the Gatskis' case, a name of Hebrew origin, from 'Eleazar', which translated means 'God will help'. Perhaps it is a name given as a wish, a prayer, by a family in desperate need of salvation?

Meanwhile, on official records – on census forms, school enrolment applications – their status as outsiders is in flux: the family sometimes still go by the surname Gatski and sometimes they become Gatsky. When the 'i' is removed, Gatsky remains a name that is slightly unusual, with origins that are opaque, but overall the effect is to remove any lingering traces of Otherness.

Mick (Myer) Gatski is just twelve years old when his father dies. Annie is desperate, she has gone to the Jewish Board of Guardians, and they have given her some money. But it is nowhere near enough, she has nine children to feed and no income. They will get kicked out of their home soon, the rent is due. There is no social security, no family to help them. During this time of catastrophe, Marcella has heard how her grandfather was sent across London, miles away from every-thing he knew, with three of his siblings to the Jewish Orphanage in south London. (It's not completely clear which of the Gatski children were sent to the orphanage – but this is the story Marcella grew up hearing.) But as Gatskis, they are part of a close-knit community, and despite the horror of having to send away her children, Annie knows that they will at least survive. The *chevras,* the neighbours, the friends, the Board of Guardians, the charitable orphanage, part of a Jewish collective that stood together. Without this, the family would have starved. They saved the Gatskis from possible death, and their name from possible extinction.

•

And so, another part of the Gatsky story begins here, one that is also common to the Jewish diaspora in this country. Somewhere along the line they definitively lose the 'i' at the end of their name, the last traces of their Russian heritage disappearing for good. Alongside that story of becoming British is the Gatskys' astonishing trajectory through the British class system. Within just a couple of generations they will move from a world of squalid housing, destitution, men dying young, widows trying to keep their children alive, to the life that my friend has now – one that is comfortable, educated and secure.

In order to tell that story, we have to fast forward through the years. There are emotions that we have no record of, conditions that would have been almost unbearable. The Gatsky children are afraid, there is no food. Becky, Annie, Rosy, Fanny, Lazarus, Mark, Davey, Harry and Sadie experience gnawing hunger. They are going to be torn apart as a family; some of them will spend their childhood in an orphanage, they won't see their other siblings for months at a time. Marcella's grandfather Mick (Myer) is one of those children, starving and exhausted. He has to go out to work as soon as he is able, he is still a child, barely educated, forced into the hell of the sweatshops. Mick Gatsky is just a teenager, he has watched his father die and now experiences yet more of the same degrading poverty.

It was around this time that Jewish immigrants were starting to fight back against their brutal working conditions, getting angry about their poverty-stricken lives, the damp, mould-filled houses that they lived in. After returning from the war, workers across the country began to join forces.

This was 1918 and a new generation of Jews in the East End had started to become radicalised. The sweatshops became a symbol of the most exploitative aspects of capitalism. A multitude of tailors' unions were formed, as well as the Capmakers'

Union, and the Cigarette Workers and Tobacco Cutters Union. Workers' groups – such as the Hebrew Socialist Union, the Jubilee Street Club, several anarchist collectives – sprung up in East London. Radical thinkers, political activists, unionists met in dingy rooms, on street corners and in places of worship. According to one writer, 'they saw no conflict between praying in a synagogue and then sitting in the same room to discuss socialist principles and organise industrial stoppages.'[14] 40 Berner Street, in Whitechapel, became a renowned meeting place for left-wing Jews and like-minded Gentiles. The 'Berner Streeters', as they were known, also put on Russian plays and folk concerts in the evenings for entertainment. These radical groups were, says Robert Winder, 'ambitious not just to improve the lot of London's Jews but to alter the social injustice that plagued all working-class Londoners'.[15] They realised there was strength in numbers, across the cultural and religious divide. This was a younger generation, who were starting to become more assimilated, were angrier and less timid than their parents. In 1902, there were over thirty Jewish trade unions in Whitechapel. This increased rapidly, as revolutionary activity swept across Europe in the 1920s after the Bolshevik overthrow of Tsarist rule in Russia. Left-wing Jews in Britain saw themselves now as part of both a national and global collective force. They would go on to play a huge role in the British trade union movement – including during the General Strike in 1926 – and large numbers of them joined the Communist Party and other left-wing organisations. And when, in the 1930s, the fascist Blackshirts marched through London, it was the Jewish left that was at the forefront of mobilising against them and seeing them off, during the famous Battle of Cable Street, just a short walk from where the Gatskys had first settled.

•

Mick Gatsky grows up. As with his mother and father, there are no photos of him. And once more, I just have a name, a few stories. I find him on an electoral register, where he is still listed as Myer Gatsky, his father's Jewish heritage still visible in his name, on paper at least. The Gatskys still live in east London, but they have moved to Ridley Road in Hackney. The Jews are leaving Whitechapel, spreading northwards towards areas like Stoke Newington, Dalston and Stamford Hill. There is a thriving market on Ridley Road itself, full of Jewish and kosher stalls; there are several synagogues nearby including the grand Poets Road Synagogue in Dalston, with its gothic Victorian architecture and magnificent stained-glass windows.

The Gatskys, like the other Jews they know, have put down roots in this country. They no longer congregate in temporary fashion in the dingy rooms of the *chevras*, like they did in the olden days. But Mick, unlike the rest of his family, feels his faith weakening. He is not as strict as the others. That rebellious streak associated with the Gatskys begins here, as he breaks the strict Jewish social taboos and falls in love with an Englishwoman, a Christian. More shockingly, she already has a child – a daughter called Anne. He will bring her up as his own. Many in their orthodox community in Hackney disapprove of this relationship, the family don't like it. Some of them will never accept her. But the couple are determined to make it work, and Mick wants his family to accept the woman he loves. So before they get married she converts to Judaism and she takes on a new name: Charlotte. It's not strictly Jewish in origin, but is common among the more anglicised members of the community. Charlotte starts going to synagogue, all her children will be Jewish and Marcella's grandmother will always be known as Lotty, her Gentile past no longer visible in her name.

As well as Anne, Mick and Lotty Gatsky go on to have four more children. There will be no more unusual Russian Jewish names, that part of their history is over. They call their children Jack, Sylvia, Leon and David. The Gatskys are becoming more and more assimilated into British society, but life for Jewish families is still desperate. For Mick, it's again the story of a brutal working existence – he is a tailor, a 'sweater', like his father, doing painstaking work for eighteen hours a day. The rights that others have been fighting for haven't come in time for him. Like thousands of other sweatshop workers, he suffers due to the appalling conditions he has been working in since he was a child and loses his sight.

Blind at forty, Myer can no longer work as a tailor and the Gatsky family are, once more, facing destitution. There's not enough to eat. Again, it is up to the woman of the family to somehow find money, keep them alive. Mick's wife, Lotty, cooks, keeps house, looks after the children by day and takes in sewing work by night. They live through the Second World War; there is deep and painful poverty. And always a lack of food. None of this is recorded, very little has been passed down, there are just stories about the Gatsky family's will to survive.

One of those Gatsky children, hiding under a table during an air raid over the East End, feeling pangs of hunger after their father can no longer work, was Marcella's uncle, Jack Gatsky.

'Red Jack' Gatsky
Heathrow Airport, 1977

Thirty years have passed. The little boy who didn't have enough to eat during the war has now grown up. It's April

1977. Heathrow Airport has been brought to a standstill by a sixteen-week strike of airplane engineers. Newspaper headlines talk of 'Airport Chaos', with pictures of thousands of passengers sitting on the floors, piles of suitcases around them. The name Gatsky is all over the news, as Marcella's uncle Jack, one of the Gatsky children, has become a powerful national figure in the trade union movement. He is on the front page of the *Times* newspaper, thousands of his members are pictured in the *Evening Standard*, voting for strike action; he's on television, interviewed the whole time.

The role of the unions in the seventies is often vilified, the all-powerful union barons are supposed to have held the country to ransom. But for Jack there was an alternative narrative: an ideal of collective action to help one another, to fight for and stand up for workers' rights. Jack would have seen in his own Gatsky family how lives can be destroyed by dangerous working conditions. His father Mick was a blind old man by now, often angry at what the world had done to him. Jack Gatsky saw all this as he grew up, his seamstress mother sometimes barely able to put food on the table. As soon as he was old enough, he got a job, and eventually worked at Heathrow Airport as an airplane engineer. He joined the union, quickly rose through the ranks to become a shop steward, fighting for better pay, better conditions, for health and safety at work, at the forefront of the British trade union movement.

By 1977, the name Gatsky had become part of the national political conversation. Questions were asked in parliament. Gatsky, says Marcella's mother, was an unusual name, and Jack's politics meant everyone knew who they were. She didn't particularly enjoy all the attention, and it felt sinister when she realised their phones were being tapped. Jack Gatsky, the man who brought Heathrow Airport to its knees, was a person of interest to the British state. The media portrayed him, as they did with a previous generation of left-wing Jews, as a dangerous subversive, and his name, now splashed across the papers, became 'Red Jack'.

This caricatured title, given to him by the right-wing tabloids, reflected how individual leaders were often singled out and demonised. The seventies saw industrial action by coal miners, rail workers, bin men and for the first time, in 1977, firefighters. Perhaps Jack Gatsky felt a glimmer of confidence, of hope. He was part of a powerful moment in the long history of the trade union movement. It may have felt to Jack, as he regularly spoke to crowds of thousands, that by standing together they could bring about real change. His own family would have benefited from a multitude of laws, reforms, acts of parliament, that had been passed to keep workers safe, to make sure they didn't work cruelly long hours, that they weren't underage, that they didn't breathe in toxic fumes that could kill them.

Personally for Jack it may also have been a natural continuation of the kind of collective action that had stepped in at vital moments throughout the Gatsky family history – like the Jewish shelters, the soup kitchens, the *chevras*. However, 'Red Jack' became too threatening for the establishment. His employers, the airport authorities, eventually managed to get him sacked. He paid a heavy price for fighting for what he believed in, for sticking his head above the parapet, for being a rebel. And despite the best efforts of his members to save him, with another mass walk-out, he was, in the years to come, no longer part of the union leadership.

Marcella's Father, David Gatsky
St Margaret's, London, 1950s and 1960s

As Jack Gatsky goes out to work in the 1960s, starts getting involved in politics, his little brother is also determined that life will be better. He works hard, looks up to his brothers. This is David, Marcella's father, the youngest of the Gatsky tribe. They all still look after one another. They have to, the alternative is that there is no food and the children go into an orphanage. Still alive through all these years is Annie Gatsky, a Yiddish-speaking grandmother from Russia, who knows very well what happens to your children if you can't put food on the table. 'They had nothing,' says Marcella. The joke in the family was that whenever the other Gatskys came round, there were no leftovers. 'They would never leave food on the table,' says Marcella, because 'they know what it's like to be facing starvation.'

The experience of intense poverty formed the backdrop to the lively political debates in the Gatsky household; people were often coming and going, Jews and Gentiles; political friends of his older brother Jack. David watched as his brother started taking on his bosses, speaking his mind. That Gatsky streak of rebelliousness was ingrained in David too. The family were known for it in their community, ever since their father Mick had 'married out'. Marcella always associates her own defiant side with this aspect of her father's family. They knew they were part of the wider Jewish community, but were also prepared to stand alone, voice their opinions, if they had to. David sees that some within the community still won't accept his mother Lotty; they make petty remarks at religious gatherings, but the Gatskys don't care. In any case, Lotty's Jewish identity is so complete within her own family that barely anyone can remember her original Gentile name, and when I ask Marcella she has no idea as she's never heard it mentioned.

It's the 1940s and David is growing up. He is part of a post-war generation whose lives are very different from their parents'. He is six years old when the war ends and the Labour Party wins the 1945 general election, transforming the country through the establishment of the modern welfare state. Swathes of social housing are built, and, in 1948, the NHS is born. It was envisaged in that optimistic era that the welfare state would provide a safety net – so that families like the Gatskys no longer faced the prospect of starvation or homelessness. And as Britain recovered from the war, the worst of the inner-city slums were cleared.

Many Jews from the East End, like the Gatskys, moved out to the suburbs. The Gatskys started to better themselves. Marcella's father David Gatsky, the son of a poor Jewish tailor who went blind at the age of forty, the grandson of Russian peasants who escaped the pogroms, was part of this huge social change. In post-war Britain, he – like millions of working-class children – had an education that his family didn't have to pay for. He was clever – he passed his 11-plus and got a place at the local state grammar school.

Marcella says he was determined to do well. She grew up hearing stories of how he would sit and read the English dictionary to better himself. One of Marcella's sisters still has it. Marcella tells me it's a 'lovely red bound book, with gold leaf lettering'. He was trying to make sure his English sounded as educated as possible. He wanted more than his parents had, wanted to study and to expand his world, and escape the insular environment he had grown up in.

David Gatsky and Maureen Solomon
Soho, London, 1960s

David Gatsky and Maureen Solomon. Two young British people, who meet and fall in love. Although both come from Russian-Jewish families, they both have anglicised surnames and personal names that are popular with Jews and non-Jews alike. Maureen, born in 1945, has an English version of the Hebrew name Miriam, a biblical prophetess and one of the seven female prophets of Israel. It was common among many British Jewish girls of her genera-tion, emblematic of the general wave of assimilation, after the traumas of the early twentieth century. Like David's family, her parents had also grown up in conditions of extreme poverty, and she too was the granddaughter of Russian Jewish immigrants. After the war the Solomons moved out of the East End and settled in Chingford, in Essex. Here in British suburbia, they were one of the few Jewish families. Maureen remembers it being a difficult time: there was, she says, some 'nastiness', name calling in the playground, anti-Semitic comments; a feeling some-times that they were unwanted. But she and her brother learnt to keep their heads down, and by the time she was a teenager in the sixties, life felt easier, freer.

She left school at sixteen and got a job as a pattern cutter for a fashion house in Great Portland Street, earning three pounds a week. She was creative; she too had come from a long line of tailors and capmakers. She'd take home scraps of material from the fashion house during the week. And during the day on Saturday, she'd sit at her sewing machine at home, make a dress and wear it out the same evening. She'd meet her friend at the tube station in Chingford and they'd travel into central London to go out dancing. They became friends with the Gatsky brothers David and Leon, and they'd go to all the little clubs around Soho and Tottenham Court Road.

Maureen is now seventy-nine and still remembers exactly what these clubs were like, the ones she went to every week, as a teenager. There was a little club in Shaftesbury Avenue, she recalls, in the pit of a disused church called St Anne's: 'We'd pay our money on the door and go down some tiny winding stairs into the crypt, or we'd go to Whiskey-a-go-go in Soho, or for a treat to Ronnie Scott's.' She remembers how she'd take two trains and a tube to get there, and they'd 'have a blast' every Saturday night. It sounds like it was a real scene. 'We were all good dancers,' she says, 'and David and I used to sometimes "take the floor" where we'd be in the middle and people used to stand back and watch. It was such good fun.'

•

It all reminds me of Marcella herself, when I first met her, when we were both young, also making our own clothes, styling ourselves, going off to clubs, gigs. Her father, David, later went to university – the first of the Gatskys to do so – supported by his brothers. After his degree he did an MA in metallurgy and he became an engineer. Maureen and David got married, at Twickenham Registry Office. And it was in that open and optimistic time that they named their second daughter Marcella. It's an Italian name – they just liked the sound of it, so they went with it. They didn't feel pressure to choose a Hebrew name, or one that was, in some way, connected with their families. The spirit of lightness associated with Marcella's name reflects the times that her parents were living in, their relaxed attitudes, her father's distance from some of the more insular ways of his community. And it's all a long way from the pressures they once faced as the

Gats, fleeing the terror of the pogroms, trying to stay alive. In its own way, it's telling of the huge transformations that have taken place within the Gatsky family, their lives so different from the traditional *shtetl* life that their forebears had over a hundred years ago.

•

In the end, when Marcella, her mother Maureen and her Cousin Rita tell me about the story behind the Gatsky name, one of the most powerful things that remains with me is the story of Chaia. Who took on a new name, became Annie, a British citizen, a Yiddish-speaking immigrant. Whose original surname, like most women of her time, was lost. Who somehow, with her family, made her way over to Britain – giving birth on a ship, surviving with nine children and no money in a hostile foreign country, thousands of miles from where she grew up. The stories of a generation of these women are not recorded, their voices are absent, there are just a few scraps of information about them. Often their names too have disappeared but the Gatsky one has survived. Only just, however, as none of the grandchildren in Marcella's family bears the Gatsky surname and it too will soon disappear. But for now, it's still here. A faint light leading us: from Gats in the village, to maybe Gatskei at a port along the way, to Gatski, to Gatsky in London – the differing versions of the name are an act of remembrance and a portal to stories which might otherwise be forgotten.

Liz Husain:
From Hyderabad to Harrow

Liz Husain
Harrow Weald, September, 1984

It was our first day at Harrow Weald Sixth Form College, in September 1984. We were both Asian punks. I had my back-combed hair and my skull and crossbones dungarees on. I remember Liz leaning against a radiator: spiky hair, dressed all in black. I couldn't place her: she was brown skinned, but her name was *Liz*? I hoped subconsciously that she was Indian like me, but no Indian I'd ever met was called Liz – such an English name, so *comfortably* English. Liz – short for Elizabeth. The Queen. A diamond-encrusted crown fused with stories of a little princess who grew up to sit on a golden throne. Christmas dinner, the Queen's speech. The Silver Jubilee, a rainy party at the end of our road. Weeks sitting awkwardly at an English neighbour's house, making decorations with people that never spoke to us again as soon as the celebrations were over. Bunting. British flags. Elizabeth, still one of the most popular British girls' names in 1968, the year that Liz was born.

And then I was confused by her surname – Husain. Was she Muslim, an Indian Muslim? She *looked* Indian to me – black hair, brown eyes, brown skin – despite that English first name.

But as we did our A-Levels, watched bad punk bands, got drunk at the Royal Oak pub in Harrow on Friday nights, we never talked about it, and I didn't see any trace of an Asian background. Liz's mum was English and I later found out her dad was half Indian Muslim and half English. But I never met him – her parents were separated, the Husain side of her was perplexing, missing. A mystery.

Liz's name embodies her mixed heritage, but on a much deeper level it's about a profound sense of absence. Her father, who bequeathed her the Husain name, left the family home when Liz was thirteen. And despite his Indian surname, there was nothing Indian about him. His first name, John – so very English – seemed to epitomise this. Liz barely ever heard him speak of his childhood in India and any history that lay behind her name was missing. A name usually gives immediate clues as to who someone is, anchors them to a nation, maybe to a religion, to a culture. But my friend's surname seemed free floating; disassociated. Liz always felt her name had no meaning behind it – it represented a void at the core of her identity.

•

Harrow in the eighties was, in fact, a multicultural area, far more so than Hayes, and there were lots of Indians at college, mainly Gujaratis. There were even a couple of Bengali teenagers I'd known from my parents' social circle: a boy whose parents were good friends with mine, who went by the nickname 'Biz', a shortening of his surname, Biswas, and another girl I vaguely recognised, called Shami (short for Sharmishta).

Liz and I also hung round in a culturally mixed group of friends. There was our friend Vimal (Shah) – I understood his background lot better than Liz's. I'd often heard the name Shah mentioned by my dad. Just as Banerjee is Bengali, I knew immediately that Shah was Gujarati. Like Patel, it was a common surname across the Harrow and Wembley area. When I used to phone Vimal's house his mum spoke with a familiar Indian accent and it all seemed completely understandable to me. As a child I'd often overheard my own parents doing a quick assessment of where another Indian was from or what their religion was based on their surname: 'Oh he's a Singh, he's a Sardarji,' (meaning a Sikh from the Punjab); 'Patel, they're a Gujarati'. My dad's friend was known only by his surname, Jain, which meant literally that he was a Jain, as in the religion, and probably from Mumbai. Our friend Sarah Leigh, whose father was a local rabbi, was Jewish, as was our friend Vanessa Taub. Liz's friend Trish was Ghanaian and our friend Gerard Barry, who lived near me in Greenford, was from an Irish Catholic family. There were also plenty of typically middle-class English people at college, from suburban families, with names like Helen, Alex and Chris. These were all friends with names that I had no trouble placing, but after several months at sixth form college I still hadn't asked Liz where her Husain surname had come from.

We were interested in other things then. I was often round Liz's house with our friends, upstairs in her room, chatting, smoking out of the window. I remember the David Bowie posters in her room and she had lots of vinyl records that we used to listen to whenever we went round. She seemed to possess a knowledge that I didn't have – and was funny in a quiet, dry, sharp way. She knew about music and had proper likes and dislikes. Her mother was welcoming and relaxed, and their house emanated a feeling of calm, with its pale green walls and shelves full of books. I used to like going round there, it was far less fraught than inviting anyone back to my house, where I'd be worried about the smell of Indian cooking and what my friends would think hearing my parents speaking to me in Bengali.

The thread that connected us through our names, that led back to India, to our histories, never came up during those afternoons spent hanging out in her room. Banerjee and Husain, of course, were names that were connected. Bengal, where my name was from, was the epicentre of Muslim rule before the British arrived, and Husain would have been an extremely common name throughout India. Our ancestors had lived on the same subcontinent and our fathers had both grown up in India in the thirties. But we were teenagers, saturated with the English culture all around us, and none of this was ever present in our conversation or in our shared teenage lives.

•

I didn't know it during those sixth form days in the eighties, but I would be friends with Liz forever. Four decades later we are still close. After our A-Levels, and university, we both came back to London, and she moved in with Paul, her boyfriend. He seemed very glamorous – he had a job at the BBC and owned a flat in Hackney. They had two sons, got married. She worked full-time, took on a demanding managerial job for a while. But she was, I know, always looking for something else. She studied and taught yoga, and then retrained as a counsellor. She listens to people's stories, helping them to work things out, to see the patterns in their lives. She loves it. We laugh a lot when we chat. We went to each other's weddings, and a few years later I went to her mother's funeral. At some point, I realise that this is one of those amazing long friendships, that I'm lucky to have, that it doesn't matter how long we haven't spoken to one another we can always just pick up where we left off, that we can talk for ages on the phone, and that we have known each other since we were teenagers.

•

During all those long years of our friendship, I never did end up meeting Liz's father and we hardly ever spoke about his side of the family. He passed away in 1999, and this added to the sense of elusiveness surrounding her Husain surname. There was a sense of disconnection that was always perplexing, a form of absence that I could never quite pinpoint. But I realised that things had been changing for Liz when we met up for a lunch to celebrate our fiftieth birthdays. I found out that she did in fact attach an importance, in terms of who she was, to the Indian Muslim side of the family. She had been to a rare gathering of her cousins and uncles on her father's side, and this had had a profound effect on her, bringing up a lost connection with India that she wanted to try to understand. They talked about their upbringing as Husain children – being raised as essentially white and English. None of them, it also turned out, had any clear idea about their family's past.

Maybe it's something about turning fifty, it's an age when you really start to think about your parents, where they came from. Your own childhood and the forces that have shaped you assume a greater significance. Liz had also talked with her cousins about the racism that she had experienced despite her lack of connection to India. I realised that there was a complex emotional story behind her name, arising from a deep inner conflict about who she was as a child and a further layer of absence connected to the mystery that existed at the centre of the Husain family.

It all started to reveal itself when I asked her how she felt about her surname. I thought that Liz was comfortable with her identity, that she saw herself as essentially British. Yes, her surname was something of an anomaly, but I assumed, wrongly, that she didn't give it much thought. We'd never had a proper conversation where we'd talked about her Indian past, her feelings about being mixed race. We'd also never really talked about her name specifically, but it led to a quite emotional response when we did. Although I'd known Liz for so long, I wasn't expecting the vehemence of her reaction. I felt from her a real sense of resentment at the way in which her name had always categorised her. I'm slightly ashamed to say that I was surprised. I should have known what she felt about her name after all this time, but I didn't, not really.

Growing up, she explained, Husain was to the world an obviously Muslim name. There were 101 different ways of spelling it – and everyone always spelt it wrong. It's Arabic, it has real connotations, she said, in terms of your identity. But she wasn't a Muslim and neither was her father.

She felt her name didn't signify who *she* was.

She would get called a 'Paki' at primary school. I heard something in her voice that was partly anger, partly sadness. Sadness that as a child she couldn't place herself, categorise herself and feel a sense of belonging, anger at the hostility of the outside world, precisely because it would insist on labelling her because of her name and her brown skin.

There was an uncomfortable dichotomy in how Liz saw herself and how the world viewed her. People assumed she was from India, or maybe Pakistan; there were negative reactions from the society around her. It was hurtful, but also incongruous and unsettling. She had, she says, Indian friends at primary school, and her own name labelled her clearly as belonging to this community. But she felt nothing like them, she felt she was British and they were 'proper' Indians. Their mums wore saris, they spoke another language at home. Thinking about it now, she said to me quietly, 'my Indian friends were the genuine article and I was not. And everyone assumed I was.'

It must have been extremely difficult – to feel neither Indian nor Muslim, yet not feel accepted by the British around her as one of them. She felt she had no rich cultural heritage. This was a time of intense tribalism, it was no melting pot and mixed-race families were uncommon. Mainly, this was due to hostility and racism on the part of the English, but not completely. We all lived entirely separate lives. In my own family, my parents never had any close English friends, and we barely socialised with them inside our home. And Liz is right to feel that she didn't belong within these communities. A few Bengali men married English women, and even as a child I felt that they were never fully accepted or welcomed. As a mixed-race child, Liz felt she was in a no man's land, moving through the world with a name that didn't belong, neither in one camp nor another.

•

There are, as Liz mentioned, many permutations of the name Husain:

Husain
Hussain
Hossain
Husayn
Hussein
Hossein

Husein
Huseyn
Huseyin

It is also, as Liz points out, the epitome of a name that would classify someone as Muslim. Husain, one of the many derivations of 'Hassan', meaning 'handsome' or 'beautiful', is a deeply revered name across the Islamic world, appearing sometimes as a personal name and sometimes as the patronymic.[1] Its origins are said to have come straight from Allah himself: according to legend he instructed the Angel Gabriel to whisper it into the prophet Mohammed's ear when his grandson was born, the youngest son of his favourite daughter Fatima. The baby boy Husayn ibn Ali would grow up to become a martyr, the 'peace-loving prophet', the spiritual leader of the Shia Muslims, and his name would travel through time, through fourteen centuries, embodying a deep association with divinity and justice among the world's 1.5 billion Muslims. Hussains, Husseins, Hossains, Husayns, Husains and all the permutations of this classically Muslim name are found all over the world, in India, Pakistan, Afghanistan, Indonesia, Iran, Iraq and Turkey.

Its linguistic roots are Arabic; it is part of a patronymic system of naming intrinsic to Islamic culture. This means it can appear at the start of someone's name, in the middle or at the end. In Arabic tradition, one has a personal name, followed by the father's name, followed sometimes also by the grandfather's name.[2]

Liz's particular version of the name, Husain, probably came from Iran, as Islam spread to Central Asia and India in the eleventh century, during successive raids by former Turkish slaves turned warriors. During this period, the city of Lahore, where Liz's grandfather would be born 800 years later, became a centre of Islamic culture, as the religion made its first significant incursion into northern India.

It was, however, during the early seventeenth century, when Mughal rule in India reached its pinnacle with the rule of Akbar the Great, that the name Husain would have really made its way across the Indian subcontinent. The Mughals spread their Islamic faith across India, and the name Husain and all its variations became more and more common across the land. Lavish and fantastically wealthy Mughal courts established themselves in cities such as Lahore, Hyderabad, Kolkata and Delhi. Islamic art and learning flourished, alongside the growth of an enormous expansion in the global trade of silks, spices, textiles and jewellery. At one point the Mughal empire controlled nearly a third of the world economy – its extraordinary wealth symbolised by magnificent monuments, like the architectural wonder of the Taj Mahal. Hyderabad, in northern India, where Liz's father was born, became an important trading centre for diamonds and pearls, its wealth symbolised by the beautiful palaces dotted around the city – with their Mughal domes, their intricate stucco pillars, and their exquisite pools and fountains. Now the Indian subcontinent – India, Pakistan and Bangladesh – has, at 500 million people, the largest Muslim population in the world. It is all this – the magnificent, brutal, repressive, inventive and spiritual hinterland of Islam – that the name Husain carries within its lexical borders.

Growing Up with the Surname Husain
Harrow, North West London, 1975

It is true, as Liz says, Husain is a powerful name. There is a charge to it, an energy that surrounds it, that is at odds with who Liz always felt herself to be as a child, at her core. It is a box, a carapace, constructed from associations, symbols, feelings that are hundreds of years old. Its edges and lines mark out the boundaries of religious and cultural belief systems. Within its sounds reside the faithful, followers of a centuries-old creed. But, in Liz's case, this box was empty. I thought later about what Liz had said and it seems to me that a name should match your vision of your self, your inner world, in a meaningful way, otherwise it becomes alienating. It becomes an empty signifier; a lacuna where family, history and culture should be. Husain – an Asian surname, with powerful Muslim associations. Yet for Liz there was nothing Muslim about her life and her world; it was, in 1975, as a seven-year-old, almost completely British.

She lived in a three-bedroom terraced house, on a quiet back street in Harrow, on the edges of London, with her mother, Heather, and her father, John, her older sister, Anna, and their cat. It was a typically middle-class world. Liz recalls that their house was filled with books. Her parents were the last people she knew to get a TV, and once they did, they only watched programmes that were on the BBC. Her mother loved reading but had left school at fifteen and become a secretary, then a housewife. Once Liz was a bit older, her mother studied part time at the Open University and got her degree, going on to teach English at the local college of higher education. She was a single parent by then, working and raising her daughters. Liz's father, John, worked as a lecturer teaching economics at North East London Polytechnic.

There were barely any objects in Liz's childhood home to suggest an Indian connection – a pair of wooden elephants, a carved table lamp. These fragmentary glimpses had no accompanying stories to anchor them to another world, to the fact that her father was born in India and had lived there for the first twelve years of his life. Like her surname, they remained unconnected to any sense of personal history. There was just a single photograph of the Husain brothers, but none of the wider Husain family, nothing of the origins of their name, the ancestry of their family. There was little evidence of the language that must have been spoken; no sense of the culture Liz's father once belonged to. The Indian part of her father's life was absent, and as a person, he seemed unknowable. He was called John – and as far as Liz could tell, he was treated by everyone around them, by their neighbours and friends, as if he were English. He was, as Liz's mother often said, 'more English than the English'. The question of Husain, where it was from, how it had arrived on these shores, never came up. Liz knew her father was Indian, but it was barely discussed. Liz's house, like her life, was almost completely British.

·

Liz remembers walking home from her primary school nearby. She would sit at their Formica table in the kitchen after school, having a biscuit and a glass of orange squash. There were still hints of a bygone era in Britain then – a rag and bone man would still occasionally come up and down the road, on his horse and cart, while Liz and her friends would play nearby. She remembers the coal bunker in the garden and deliveries of coal before they had the central heating put in.

Harrow itself was once the epitome of well-heeled British suburbia, with its endless rows of mock Tudor semi-detached houses, with their curved bay windows, paved parking areas and neat borders. It had lodged itself in the nation's imagination as an aspirational place to live and, in the interwar years, became the unofficial capital of a commuter belt known as Metroland. The area was originally the farmland surrounding the Metropolitan line, developed by its private owners in the early 1900s. Metroland was originally a marketing name that caught on, designed to seduce young couples looking for an affordable home, selling the dream of a modern house in the country with a quick railway service into the city. Metroland brochures were filled with pictures of timber-clad 'country villas' with lush lawns and bathed in a warm golden glow. The language used to describe the area – a band of countryside stretching from Neasden to the Chilterns – evoked a semi-rural English Eden, all winding footpaths, wildflowers and forgotten hamlets. And this arcadian vision was, of course, completely white.[3]

But the world was changing. By 1975, when Liz was growing up, Harrow's status as the capital of Metroland, a dream-like English suburban idyll, had been disrupted by hundreds of Asians who had started moving into the area during the late sixties and early seventies. They were mainly Gujarati Indians, descendants of indentured labourers brought over by the British to build railways in Africa. They were forced out by a wave of anti-Indian sentiment sweeping through Kenya, Malawi and Tanzania. And in 1972 in Uganda, the dictator Idi Amin led a coup and ordered the expulsion of all Asians within ninety days. Suddenly 28,000 refugees – British citizens – arrived in Britain, moving into places like Leicester, Wembley and Harrow.

There are images of the new arrivals, Asian women with windswept saris, men in their dusty suits, looking bewildered as they stepped off the planes. Many had fled with nothing, left their homes and arrived with just a suitcase. But much of the reaction in the media was hostile. Newspapers whipped up racist hysteria – including a bold front page headline from the *Daily Express*, proclaiming: 'Asians . . . No Need to Let Them In!' Others had cartoons depicting refugees luxuriating in taxpayer-funded hotels. Leicester City Council took out a notorious advert in the *Ugandan Argus* warning Asians to stay away. There were, it said, no houses, no jobs and the schools were full. 'In your own interests and those of your family you should not . . . come to Leicester,' the advert read. Protests and attacks were organised against the refugees by the far right, contributing to an increasing hostility against the Asian community in Britain over the next few years – part of the larger context of the race hatred that I too was experiencing as a child growing up in Hayes.

•

In places like Brent, Wembley and Harrow, Asian newsagents and grocery shops, run by the new Gujarati community – with unfamiliar surnames like Patel, Shah and Sharma – were starting to appear. Liz would be out with her mother and see Indian women in their saris out shopping, bending over tilted carboard boxes filled with bitter gourds, ginger, okra, picking up handfuls of small green chillies and carefully putting them in small paper bags. Liz's neighbours were Indian, as well as several of her friends at primary school – all part of this wave of immigration. When we talk about what the name Husain meant to her, Liz frequently recalls the sensation of growing up alongside other Asians, one of them in name only, feeling that she didn't belong to their world.

She remembers going round to her friend Raju's house after school, and it felt very different from her own home. For a child, it would have been like entering a different universe. These would usually be noisy houses, sometimes with two or three generations under one roof – Liz would no doubt have heard snatches of another language. The smells of spices and curries, of roasted cumin, cinnamon, cloves and fried mustard seeds, would have seeped into the thick brown carpets. I imagine her walking past a cluttered front room, with a statue of Ganesh on the mantelpiece, sofas covered in plastic, cabinets filled with cut glass tumblers, saved for formal occasions, and maybe a framed black-and-white photo of Indian grandparents, in their younger days, staring out from a photographer's studio in 1950s Kampala.

Liz remembers Raju's mother standing at her gas cooker frying Indian food in a huge dark pan, full of bubbling hot oil, wearing a sari. The fact that her Indian friends' mothers always wore saris comes up whenever Liz and I talk about her name. Saris were a palpable, visually striking sign of difference between British and Indian cultures. For the children of Indian immigrants like me, these pieces of material marked us out as foreigners – through the bodies of our mothers. I loved them for their beauty but in chilly, racist, seventies Britain they also evoked feelings of shame and inferiority. I didn't like seeing Indian women out and about on the streets wearing those flimsy, floating bits of material, a dowdy cardigan over the top that completely hid whatever splendour the material had originally possessed.

But for Liz the sari was different – an emblem of Indianness that she felt herself to be lacking. Part of a heritage that she didn't possess. It was one more sign that she wasn't, as she'd put it, 'the genuine article', a visual reminder that she didn't belong, despite having a name that seemed to suggest she did.

•

The long, hot summer of '76.

Liz and I didn't know one another, but we were living just a few miles apart, in outer west London. Liz's surname Husain, her feelings about it, swam in the same sea of racial and political currents as mine, despite our very different experiences of being eight-year-old, brown-skinned little girls. She felt she was essentially British; I was a recently arrived immigrant child from India.

That strange summer we would have both looked up and seen endless days of harsh blue skies; played on suburban pavements, the cracks filled with flying ants. Neither of us would have known it, but this was the same summer a pool of blood surrounded the Indian teenager Gurdip Singh Chaggar as he lay dying on Southall High Street, stabbed by racists.

The more I think about what was going on from the vantage point of the present, the more I understand quite how threatening the environment was in that period. It was the same summer Eric Clapton went on a twenty-minute bigoted racist rant in front of a crowd of 20,000 fans at the Birmingham NEC, telling them:

Get the foreigners out.
Get the wogs out.
Get the coons out.
Keep Britain white.

Fascism was no longer something in Britain's black-and-white past. David Bowie casually announced soon after, in *Playboy* magazine, that 'Adolf Hitler was one of the first rock stars' and that he believed 'very strongly in fascism'. Sid Vicious and Siouxsie Sioux were seen sporting swastikas. Four years after the arrival of the Ugandan Asians, the National Front was gaining in political power, winning support. In Blackburn, they won forty per cent of the vote in the 1976 local elections and the following year would go on to get 120,000 votes during the local elections in London, with a toxic message linking high unemployment with the recent growth in the Asian population.[4] Far-right calls for the compulsory deportation of all non-white immigrants infected the mainstream discourse, with politicians openly debating the idea of voluntary repatriation for Black and Asian immigrants.

Racism spread across Britain during that decade, a blanket of poison gas, a dark miasma that hovered across the country, suffusing the population. There was a palpable threat out there that felt dangerous. It reached into Britain's suburban corners, its streets, its schools, in diffuse ways. It was a poison that seeped into the cracks of our psyches and into our consciousnesses, tainting the texture of ordinary life.

Liz Husain. A little girl who lived in Harrow, who felt herself to be British because that's how her parents felt themselves to be. But to them we were all the same. Nig nogs. Wogs, Pakis. It's no surprise that Liz grew up hating her surname.

•

A boy at a school disco came up to Liz in 1978. They had all just been dancing to the Bee Gees' 'Staying Alive', from the film *Saturday Night Fever*. John Travolta in his white suit on the dancefloor. Liz had brought in her favourite 7" single to play Queen's 'Don't Stop Me Now'. She couldn't wait for the DJ to put it on. They were all ten-year-olds, excitable, on the cusp of growing up but still innocent at that age. The boy was her friend, she played with him every day in the playground. He explained in a matter-of-fact voice, nothing malicious, that he would have asked her to dance, but he couldn't. He was really sorry, but his father wouldn't have liked it if he danced with a Paki. So he couldn't. He was sorry about that.

Liz still looks upset when she suddenly remembers the incident and talks about it to me forty-two years later. 'It was horrible,' she says quietly. Recalling the shame of racism, the shame that we were all growing up with.

•

Nazism seemed to be lapping at the edges of society. And so, the Anti-Nazi League was born in 1977 – to fight back. Thousands of people – Black, white and Asian – joined forces against the National Front. There were running street battles across the country between the ANL and the far right. 'Rock Against Racism' was founded – partly in response to the racism of Clapton and Bowie, as well as the rise in racist attacks and the growth of the far right. It mobilised hundreds of musicians, and brought together Black, white and Asian music fans in a common love of music. One spring day in July 1978, eighty thousand people marched seven miles from Trafalgar Square to Victoria Park in Hackney, for an open air concert – headlined by The Clash and Tom Robinson – one of the largest anti-racist events ever seen in the United Kingdom. And over the next few years the Anti-Nazi League, together with Rock Against Racism, organised a huge grassroots political movement, with hundreds of carnivals, concerts, marches and fêtes across Britain, whose anti-racist activism reached deep into the British population.

•

One Saturday afternoon, in 1978, nine-year-old Liz Husain walked along the road holding her father's hand. They arrived at what she thought was a local fête or jumble sale in Harrow – she wasn't sure. She remembers lots of people milling about in a field, lots of homemade stalls selling food. Liz asked her father where they were and he replied that it was an 'Anti-Nazi League rally'.

She asked him what that was.

And he explained it very clearly, so that even as a child she could understand what was happening. And now, over forty years later, she repeats it to me, almost uncannily, word for word. She recites his explanation from the darkened space of her memory, where hurt and fear remain intact.

Her father's answer is like a speech that's been set in stone in her mind:

> There's a group of people and a movement in this country who would like to see anyone who is from elsewhere go back to their own countries, even if they've made a life here and are settled here. If this movement gains power, I would be sent back to India, even though I haven't lived there since I was a boy.

Could that happen, she asked him, feeling for the first time a chilling fear. He replied that he didn't think so, but that they'd have to make sure that it didn't.

Liz remembers being scared.

That day, she suddenly felt for the first time an awareness of her father's race. Although he lived his life for all purposes as an Englishman, his Indian identity – symbolised to the world by his surname and his skin colour – meant that somehow he could be at risk, that there were people who meant him harm. He wasn't born here, his father was Indian and his surname, Husain, despite who he felt himself to be, marked him out as clearly not belonging in this country. It seems to me that Liz's father knew, deep within himself, that hatred can be ignited quickly with deadly consequences. That your life, your home, your citizenship can be taken away in an instant.

John Husain, Liz's Father
Harrow, West London, 1970s

Liz describes her father as quiet, fairly shy and reserved. She remembers him as a loving parent, but as a child she felt like she never solved the mystery of him. He was the kind of person, she told me, who would be the one at a party on the edge of a group, listening. He would also be the one you might want to talk to if you had something serious on your mind. But he didn't really voice his opinion and you never knew quite what he thought.

Then there are some facts and details, clearer to see. He loved books and had a degree in Economics from the LSE. He was clever – he taught economics and he'd even done another degree in Geography – just as a hobby. He loved mountains, rocks, rugged landscapes, and would take the whole family camping in remote parts of Wales and Scotland. Liz remembers how he taught Liz and her sister to put up tents, to repair bikes, all kinds of practical skills. But emotionally she felt that he remained elusive, often working all weekend at the dining table reading, marking student papers. Once her parents split up and he moved into a flat in Mile End, the sense of distance between them increased, as well as the feeling that there was something missing, a feeling that has stayed with Liz all her life.

I sometimes feel that the story of Liz and her father is in many senses the story of their shared name. Words that keep coming up during my research are absence, gap, mystery, unknowability. These are words that might describe how Liz felt about her father, but they reflect something about their shared name too. There's a history within it that Liz's father John never managed to share with Liz. It's something she is still reaching for, like a shadow or a phantom that can't be grasped.

Liz's father died at the age of seventy-two and Liz finds it sad that they never really spoke about his childhood in India. For Liz that part of his life was never there. And her name Husain embodied a silence where there should have been a story. The absence itself hovered around them, in the house in Harrow, as she grew up.

•

Apart from two saris that were tucked away in a cupboard on the landing.

Liz tells me about them, and I notice that the saris have come up again in our conversation – those visible signifiers of Indian identity. And there they are, two long pieces of exquisitely embroidered material, tying her Husain name to a fragment of India.

Liz and her older sister Anna would sometimes go upstairs and take them out, dress up in them. As they would open out the endless folds of material, a musty smell of camphor would emerge, speaking of a different world, of something unreachable. There was one sari for each of them – a pale blue silk one for her sister, and for Liz a red, silk chiffon sari, gossamer thin, with gold embroidery.

Liz always remembers the saris.

She would hold the sheer, delicate material against her cheek. Contained within its folds was a link to their father's childhood homeland, the life he never spoke about, an imagined world of heat, sunshine, relatives they'd never know. Liz remembers trying to drape the sari over herself, wrapping it round her body and tucking it into her trouser waistband. It was a confusion of material, it went everywhere, and was unmanageable. The chiffon was too slippery and wouldn't stay in place. And there was no female member of the family to work a dexterous magic with the material, turning it into an elegant series of pleats, folds and tucks.

But still, when they put on the saris, the two sisters would feel that they had transformed themselves, momentarily, into an approximation of Indian womanhood. But they knew it wasn't how it should be, the overall effect a bit of a mess, and the girls would give up and start playing something else, leaving a heap of material lying on their parents' bed.

Although they never wore the saris out and only used them to dress up, Liz and her sister knew the saris were *theirs*. It's clear they were something the sisters treasured. They were among the few things that meant they belonged, albeit in a fragile sense, to their father's family, to the Husains. Liz didn't know who exactly the saris had come from, but they evoked a fragmentary sense of connection to the women in the Husain family. It was a bridge to another world. And when they put them on, Liz and her sister would look in the mirror, enveloped in another identity that, for an instant, was part of them too.

•

Once Liz's father, John Husain, had passed away, the sense of her family's heritage, one that should have been part of family folklore, passed down through her surname Husain, felt like it had gone. But together we start to put together the pieces of a jigsaw puzzle, about the absences behind the Husain name. She tells me the fragments of her father's history that she has managed to pick up over the years, from having occasionally met up with some of her uncles, her father's brothers, and their children. It's a question of feeling around the details, picking up the scattered pieces, trying to patch together a life, trying to imagine what someone may have felt at a particular time, guessing at a story.

She recently started looking through a suitcase full of letters that had belonged to her father. It had lain in her loft for many years, and contained fading letters and records, belonging originally to his father, to Liz's grandfather Qazi Mohammed Husain.

We talk about what she has managed to find out, and we also get in touch with her father's only surviving sibling, his youngest brother Asif. Liz hadn't seen her uncle for a few years and had never had a long conversation with him about her father. Asif is in his eighties, but it's after talking to him that we really start to understand the mystery and the missing details of the story behind her name.

Arif Husain
Hyderabad, India, 1938

Eleven-year-old Arif Husain stares into the camera for the posed family photograph. It's a beautiful old black-and-white print that Liz has unearthed and was taken around 1938. Arif looks like a typical upper-class Indian schoolboy, dark hair, stiff oversized blazer and shorts. It's a formal portrait, obviously taken by a professional photographer. The family are arranged in front of a grand colonial-style building, looking into the camera in front of white stucco pillars and a patterned black-and-white rug placed in front of them. Liz's grandfather, like many upper-class Indian men in that colonial era, is wearing a suit, a sign of wealth and privilege.

Liz's father John is the schoolboy in the photograph. He is, at this point, known by his Indian name Arif. It is a Muslim name, common across India, and everyone – parents, brothers, friends, schoolteachers – all call him this. Arif: a classical Arabic name, meaning 'knowledgeable, educated'. A prophetic name as it would turn out, for this eleven-year-old boy would go on to become a scholar, a man who would devote his life to books, to learning and teaching others. His first name is actually John, but no-one uses that.

To the world around him, Arif is Indian, his father is Indian, and he looks Indian. Arif was born in India and lives with his mother and father and four brothers, in a large house in the Banjara Hills, an exclusive area on the outskirts of the ancient Mughal city of Hyderabad. There are acres of land surrounding the house – it is lush and green, and once was a hilly, forested area, a place where royalty lived in grand palaces and went big-game hunting. His father is the Pro-Vice Chancellor of the University of Osmania, founded by the Nizam of Hyderabad, and a courtier at his palace. The Husains are an established, privileged family.

Arif Husain lives a comfortable life, and I try to imagine what it was like. He and his four brothers would have slept on high hand-carved teak beds, covered with mosquito nets. Outside would have been the particular darkness of India, the simmering heat of the summer nights, the sounds of crickets, frogs and wild animals emanating from the depths of the trees and the vines surrounding their house.

And in the morning, the bright sunlight would have poured into his room, the servant opening the wooden shutters as he and his brothers sipped their sweet, milky tea. Arif would have got ready for school and heard the slosh of tin pails full of water, as the servants washed down the marble floors of their house. Decades later, some part of him, no doubt, would always be, in his mind, this boy. The same boy who steps out of the house in the morning and sees the twisted bark of the banyan tree in the corner of the garden, the leathery green leaves of the banana trees, and that giant old gecko, blinking sleepily, waiting and watching him from the corner of the wall as he gets in the car to go to school every morning.

•

Arif Husain was born in India in 1926 when it was still under British rule and would have entered into a world of complex, dissonant identities. His mother was a working-class woman from Croydon in south London and his father a devout Muslim, from an educated, well-to-do Indian family. Olive and Qazi Mohammed Husain were a mixed-race couple and here they are, living in India in the 1930s. She is smiling in the photograph, wearing a flowing floral chiffon dress, but the Husains were a highly unusual couple for this time and this place. Their relationship, between a dark-skinned Indian and a white-skinned memsahib, was taboo. As David Gilmour writes in *The British in India*, the children of these relationships were known derogatorily as 'half castes', looked down on by the British for snobbish and racial reasons.[5] Perhaps that's why the Husains made their home in the much more open-minded circles of the Nizam of Hyderabad's court, where the couple mixed freely with the Muslim, Hindu and British elite of the 1930s. Arif speaks fluent Urdu. But he is being educated at an elite English-speaking public school in Hyderabad, St George's Grammar School, alongside the children of British officials, and outside the house is discouraged from speaking in his 'servant's Urdu'.

•

The Husain family photograph, with its elegiac quality, its sepia hue, the men and boys standing stiffly in their suits and ties, was taken in the midst of a turbulent time. It was the 1930s – the height of the Indian nationalist struggle for independence. There were strikes, mass protests, bombings and killings all over the country. Arif was growing up in colonial India with an English mother and an Indian father at a time when millions of Indians wanted the British out of India. Revolutionary groups were active, particularly in Bengal, launching bomb attacks on railway lines and assassination attempts on British officials, especially after the partition of Bengal along religious lines, seen by many Indians as a cynical example of divide and rule. Strikes and mass protests by Indians, followed by reprisals in the form of brutal British crackdowns, fed into the visceral racial tensions that existed across India at this time.

This was the era of mass boycotts of British goods, and there were public burnings of imported cotton cloth. Up and down the country millions joined the movement to buy only Indian-manufactured textiles, known as *Swadeshi*. Foreign garments were despised, and nationalist leaders were only seen in Indian outfits. Questions of Indian identity, pride in being Indian, were being asserted with huge intensity all over the country. In 1930, when Arif was four years old, Mahatma Gandhi began his first mass civil disobedience campaign, *Satyagraha*, or 'Truth Force', against the British. He demanded the right for Indians to produce their own salt, leading thousands of protestors through the neighbouring state of Gujarat to the coast where they would make their own. 60,000 Indians were arrested, Gandhi was imprisoned for a year, and the campaign marked the beginning of mass civil disobedience throughout the thirties and forties that would eventually lead to the end of the British Empire in India.

From the photograph it is obvious that the Husains are well to do. Maybe they are sheltered from the turmoil in the country as they are living in an Indian princely state. Its ruler, the Nizam of Hyderabad, was described by *Time* magazine as the 'Richest Man in the World'. He appeared on the February 1937 cover in a gold turban festooned with enormous jewels and the accompanying article said he reputedly had '$250 million in gold bars and $1.4 billion in cash', as well as owning the 'fabled diamond mines of Golconda'. As well as being fantastically wealthy, the Nizam was a dedicated philanthropist, building railways, road, hospitals and an airport in Hyderabad. He founded the first university in India to teach in a native language – Urdu – and Arif's father, Qazi Mohammed Husain, was a Professor of Mathematics there before becoming Pro-Vice Chancellor, and a courtier in the Nizam's palace.

Liz has never heard her own father discuss this period of his life. But now, over eighty years later, talking to her Uncle Asif – just a baby in that black-and-white photo – it becomes apparent that the Husains had quite an extraordinary lifestyle. Liz's uncle shows us a photograph of the courtier's outfit his father would have worn to meet with the Nizam, an archaic colonial-style suit, knee-high riding boots together with a long silver sabre. There were also the receptions, parties and royal events the Husains attended. Liz has uncovered an invitation to a glittering high-society banquet in 1938, given by the Nizam in honour of the Viceroy of India, Lord Linlithgow, the head of the British Indian government. Another invitation is for 'luncheon' with the Prime Minister of Hyderabad, Sir Akbar Hydari, and his wife, Lady Amina. The Husains would have mixed with Mughal royalty, Hindus and white Europeans, alongside the leading freedom fighters of the day. Rabindranath Tagore, the Bengali poet and nationalist, came to stay in the Banjara Hills, at the invitation of the

Nizam, and the Husains themselves were friends with Sarojini Naidu, the most prominent woman in the independence movement and a close ally of Gandhi's.

•

I peer and peer at the photo that Liz has sent me of her father and his family. Does Arif Husain think of himself as Indian? Is there an instability in who he thinks he is, his sense of self? I don't imagine so. The formally arranged features of the photograph, his mother in a flowing chiffon dress, his father – upstanding in a formal suit and tie – the baby perched on a piece of antique-looking furniture, speak of a confidence in identity, of solidity, of permanence. The framing of the picture, the fact that it was obviously taken by a professional photographer who has signed his name at the bottom, speaks of wealth, of respectability, of a picture that will hang for a long time in a family home, perhaps in the living room alongside other family photos that will be taken as the years go by.

But it is a moment frozen in time, as history swirls around all the subjects in the photograph. Arif Husain, the young boy, will find that war, Indian independence and partition mean that in a few months' time his life will be irrevocably altered – he will go from being a secure Indian schoolboy in an affluent, influential Indian Muslim family, the son of a Pro-Vice Chancellor at a Muslim-run university, to living in semi-poverty in war-ravaged London, his Indian father becoming a distant memory.

Liz's Father, John Husain
London, 1939

It is May 1939. Twelve-year-old Arif Husain has arrived in Britain with his mother and four brothers, to visit his English grandparents. The moment that he stepped off the boat at Tilbury Docks after a three-week voyage from India, his life, his identity and eventually his name would change forever. By the time he reached adulthood his transformation would be complete – he would become John to the rest of the world. And his relationship to his surname Husain, and the history within it, would be irrevocably altered.

On 1 September 1939, just a few months after he arrived, the Nazis invaded Poland, marking the start of the Second World War. Arif, his mother, Olive, and his five mixed-race brothers were now suddenly trapped in Britain, while her husband Qazi Mohammed Husain was six thousand miles away in Hyderabad. The Husains had travelled by ship from India, sailing across the Indian Ocean, through the Suez Canal, but passenger transport was quickly suspended, as it was now too dangerous to travel. Many people initially believed that the war would be over in a matter of months, and his mother had probably assumed they would soon be able to return to India, but the war would last for six more years.

Arif would grow up. He was a young boy, thrust into a new environment, with a new identity; he would never return to India and he would never see his father again. Month after month, Arif Husain would hear planes flying over Croydon, one of the most heavily bombed areas in Britain, as night after night the Nazis carried out their air bombardment of London. The process of change, the psychological shift from a young Indian schoolboy called 'Arif' to a young Englishman called 'John', would begin now, as he lived through the war, going through a time of existential threat and intense patriotic fervour.

Arif Husain Turns into a Young Man Called John
Croydon, South London, 1940s

In September 1939, Arif was enrolled at Whitgift Grammar School. Arif Husain is introduced to his teachers and pupils with his Indian first name. But there is another name, sitting in front of it on his enrolment form, in his reports, on official documents: his first name, John. For now, it is silent, but it belongs to an alternative self, his English one, that will slowly grow in strength as the name Arif, and all that it symbolises, begins to fade away. As much as possible, Arif is now going to become an English schoolboy – despite his surname Husain, his brown skin and his Indian father.

From this point, I imagine, would begin the myriad psychological changes that would take place, that would turn him into the man he would become, a person called John, who was 'more English than the English' – to the father that Liz knew, who bore no trace of his Indian heritage.

In September 1940, the Blitz began as the Luftwaffe rained down its bombs on London. Liz's uncle Asif, now in his eighties, remembers spending night after night sleeping in the cupboard under the stairs with his older brothers. They didn't have an air raid shelter, and this flimsy part of the house was their only protection against the deadly doodlebug bombs that they would hear buzzing through the air as they dropped on nearby houses. The Husains woke one morning to find their neighbour's home destroyed, and later a house across the road was also reduced to rubble. His mother Olive spent the nights wondering if they would be alive in the morning, while Arif and his brothers would play after school inside bombed-out houses in the neighbourhood. Arif, like everyone else, was surrounded by patriotic war-time propaganda: he would have seen the newsreels, the posters calling on the public to 'Dig for Britain', to be 'British and Proud of it', and excitable messages proclaiming 'Greatest Battle of the Century! Blitz on Britain'. Arif was living in a country that was now in a fight to the death against the Germans. He was now part of the British population, held together in a spirit of collective solidarity, where to be British was to be on the side of unquestioning good.

•

John, the ultimate name for someone of English heritage, would no doubt have been a much more comfortable name to go by in this atmosphere. Being called Arif may have meant experiencing daily moments of irritation, humiliation or worse: dealing with sniggering mispronunciations, explaining to people where the name was from, explaining that he was half Indian. Culturally, the might and right of the British Empire was constantly celebrated and it wouldn't have been surprising if Arif, like most people, had absorbed some of this ideology. The boys in the school playground at Whitgift Grammar School would have celebrated the annual 'Empire Day' with a half-day holiday and would have grown up on a diet of *Boy's Own* and the imperial adventure stories of Rudyard Kipling. Books such as *Kim*, set in colonial India, were wildly popular, as were his short stories, tales of derring-do, often set in the colonies, with heroic white protagonists.

At Arif's grammar school, teachers would have called the boys by their surnames. Alongside Husain would have been

English surnames such as Smith, Jones, Williams and Taylor. Perhaps he wouldn't even have been conscious of it, but in order to survive, as a schoolboy, he would quickly have abandoned any trace of the Indian and Muslim heritage contained in his surname and become as English as he possibly could be. Standing among his friends, in the playground, John Arif Husain, a child with an English first name, an Indian surname, an English mother and an Indian father, might have subconsciously experienced a peculiar sensation. He might have possessed what the African American writer W. E. B. Du Bois described as a 'double-consciousness', a sense of looking at his Indian consciousness through the eyes of his own, more powerful, imperial British consciousness, of regarding his Indian heritage through the veil of imperialist values that surrounded his young mind.[6]

•

As the war went on, Arif Husain moved through school. He did well and made good academic progress – his school reports describe him as a boy who loved reading and as 'contemplative' and 'intellectual'. The letters from his father became infrequent – air mail was no longer possible, there was only sea mail, which took months to arrive. One time, there was great excitement when a battered parcel arrived from their father containing a cricket bat and some stumps. (His youngest brother Asif would remember that day for the rest of his life.)

•

Meanwhile, six thousand miles away, India was heading inexorably towards independence, with violence, strikes and brutal repression part of the battle between millions of

Indians and the might of the colonial British state. In 1942 Gandhi launched his Quit India movement, exhorting Indians to 'do or die' and to throw off the 'foreign yoke'.

In Hyderabad, Arif's father, Qazi Mohammed, was getting increasingly worried about his family, whom he hadn't seen for many years. His letters were going unanswered, and he was terrified that he would never see his sons alive again. There were daily headlines in Indian newspapers about deadly bombing raids over London, with terrifying reports on the number of casualties.

Finally, to Qazi's immense relief, the war ended. On 3 June 1946, having still not seen his family for seven years, he wrote to a friend in London, asking him if he could check in on them:

My Dear Nawab Sahib

I enclose herewith my family's address in London. I have numerous children – 5 boys. They all went to England six months before the War and were caught there. They lived in London and went through the Air Raids on London of the last War. The children would be in various schools when death would be dropping each moment all day, from planes above and the mother would be torn with anxiety, not only about raids on the house, but if all the children will come home alive that day. Soul harrowing times that would make the human mind melt. But God saved them.

Qazi ends the letter with his polite request, hoping that his friend will find time to look up his boys, and not 'mind their modest ways of living'. Qazi describes his 'gratitude to God' as being 'boundless' for an end to the war. He was looking forward to his family's eventual return to Hyderabad; he was making plans and, most importantly, he had begun construction of a grand new house in the hills of Banjara.

.

That was the last letter Qazi would ever write from his home in Hyderabad.

Liz's Grandfather, Qazi Mohammed Husain
Cambridge, 1912

Who was Qazi Mohammed Husain, the father that was separated from his sons at this point in history, the grandfather that gave Liz her surname? Who was the man that brought over the name Husain to British soil? The answers lie even further back in the past, before the First World War, in Edwardian Britain.

Qazi Mohammed Husain arrived in England in June 1912, a young man, just eighteen years old, according to Liz, a devout Muslim, a gifted mathematician. He had won a scholarship to study Maths at King's College, Cambridge and was the first member of the Husain family to leave India. He was a product of centuries of British rule in India, one of the sons of the Indian upper classes, whom the British had educated, who helped them govern their empire.

I imagine him a gauche young man, praying in his rooms at Cambridge. Stunned by England; the buildings, that probably seemed so unreal in their beauty, their Englishness, their power. This was a time when many sons of rich Indian families made their way over to this country, to study subjects like law and maths. These were elite young men, often studying over here in order to practise in the judicial system or join the colonial state bureaucracy of the Indian civil service. The presence of these young men on the streets of Britain at the turn of the century was also a sign of the inevitable mixing of the two cultures. The British Empire may have rested on brute military and economic might, but British culture and society couldn't help but be permeated and influenced by India too. Three generations down, fifty-six years later, his granddaughter, Elizabeth Husain, was born, a product of the cultural, societal and political threads that were weaving through both countries, influencing one another and planting the seeds for the multicultural country that Britain would become. And the name, Liz Husain, is a product of that great mixing of those two civilizations.

Qazi Mohammed Husain went on to study law in London and was called to the bar at Lincoln's Inn Fields. He would have wandered the streets and squares of Bloomsbury, which had long been a haunt of the young, besuited Indian men who came over here to further their education. The aim was to create a generation of Indians in the image of their British rulers – British educated, with British tastes and values. However, many of these students turned against their masters. Among them was a generation of Indian nationalists, who eventually took a leading role in overthrowing their colonial rulers.[7] Mahatma Gandhi also came to London to study law and lived in Tavistock Square at the same time that Qazi Mohammed was there. In the next square lived Rabindranath Tagore, who was to have such a huge influence on literature and politics in the West, befriending W.B. Yeats, Aldous Huxley and Virginia Woolf, who was a neighbour. Jawaharlal Nehru, the first prime minister of India, also studied at

Cambridge and was called to the bar around the same time as Liz's grandfather. These were the generation of Indian men who would go on to become the leaders of the Indian National Congress, who would lead India's fight for independence. They would absorb the Western ideals of justice, democracy and freedom and turn them on their British rulers, to get them out of India.

•

When he arrived in Britain, Qazi Mohammed Husain's name would have been an obvious sign of his colonial status and of his Muslim heritage. Qazi means 'Judge' or 'Justice' in Urdu, and Mohammed is, of course, the founder of the Islamic faith, the Prophet Mohammed. A British person, hearing his name, seeing this bespectacled, dark-skinned young man, would have been in no doubt that this was a foreigner, a stranger, a colonial subject, someone of a different faith.

And yet, while in England, a deeply racialised society, Qazi fell in love with an English woman. But like everything connected to her name, it wasn't a story that was ever talked about in her family, says Liz. There were just a few rumours that she'd heard through the years: that Olive was working as a servant when she met Qazi, or perhaps she was a shop assistant and he was one of the customers. As a child, the circumstances of her grandparents' meeting – the origin story of her name – were never mentioned. It was yet another layer of absence contained in her name. In the end, according to Liz's uncle, it turned out that Olive had been working in the accounts department at Harrods. But Liz found this out only many decades later. Perhaps this was because this relationship broke all the rigid taboos of imperial Edwardian Britain – of class, race and religious belief. White working-class Christian women were, after all, not supposed to fall in love with dark-skinned, upper-class Indian men.

Olive Stowers Becomes Olive Husain
London to Hyderabad, 1920s

Qazi's new bride, Olive, signed her name in the registry of marriages after the ceremony. This wouldn't have been the kind of name that was usually found in the large volume – as mixed marriages were so unusual, and there were very few guests at this wedding. She wrote out her maiden name, Stowers, followed by her new signature, Olive Husain.

Stowers. A fairly common English surname, a topographic title, belonging to a group of people who originally lived close to the River Stour in Essex. I look up 'Olive Stowers' and find her on the register of births; and she is indeed from Essex, born somewhere near Colchester, in 1896.

And when we ask him, Liz's uncle also confirms that the Stowers were originally from a village somewhere in Essex, and that they were poor and lived off the land. But he adds that the Stowers were driven from their homes by the famine that struck Essex at the turn of the century. Starving and hungry, they travelled to the city. And once they arrived in London, they did whatever they could to earn money. Eventually the Stowers settled in a small house in south London. Olive, their daughter, came from a class of people who were not afraid of hard work, from a long line of women who were used to labouring on farms, doing their own house-work and cooking their own food. They were used to doing it for themselves – and sometimes for other people.

But Olive was now a Husain and her life was about to be

transformed. There would be no more menial work. Soon after her wedding, she travelled to India with her husband, the first time Olive had ever left Britain. She and Qazi built a life together. They made their home in Hyderabad and had five sons. And as she left her working-class roots, she became part of Hyderabadi high society, in her exclusive home in the Banjara Hills.

.

Hyderabad: an ancient Mughal city, a trading centre for diamonds and pearls, built over centuries around the architectural wonder of the Charminar mosque, with its arches and intricate minarets, a city famed across India for its cooks and its cuisine. Olive Husain, a memsahib, loves the food – the Hyderabadi biryanis especially, a combination of basmati rice, goat meat, yoghurt and cinnamon, cloves, garlic, caraway and saffron. The Nizams have ruled the city since 1724, and the dish is said to have originated from their vast kitchens.

Olive Husain often goes into her cooks' quarters at the side of the main house. (Liz's uncle has told us how she would stand by the cooks, watching them as they made their biryanis.) She asks in broken Urdu what ingredients they are using, finds out the best moment to add the spices, learns just how long they need to release their flavour before they burn. She goes into the dark kitchen, with its rough floor, where her cooks sit on the floor cross-legged, slicing pieces of goat meat on a *boti*, the curved iron blade attached to a piece of wood. Sometimes the smoke from the onions and chillies makes her eyes water. She shouldn't be here, she is the lady of the house, a memsahib. The servants laugh when she asks them exactly which spices they use, and in the years to come she will remember these lessons.

You can of course tell by Olive's surname that she is very different from the other memsahibs in India. They will be married to men with surnames such as Smith and Amherst, maybe a Wilson. Most memsahibs don't particularly like Indian food, they find it too spicy, and they order their servants to make British-Indian concoctions such as kedgeree and mulligatawny. In all things – food, clothes, social activities – they try as much as possible to live the life they might have had in England. They wouldn't dream of going into their servants' quarters and learning how to cook Indian food.

And they certainly wouldn't have dreamt of *marrying* an Indian.

Just the sight of the name Olive followed by Husain would have been shocking in itself in many quarters of British society. This was still a time when it was taboo for an English woman to marry an Indian. The basis of empire was a racial hierarchy, a quasi-system of apartheid, where Indians were not allowed to govern themselves, live in certain areas, sit in certain sections on trains, go to school with or mix with the British in their exclusive 'whites only' private clubs, as they sipped their *burra pegs* (large whiskies). There was also, according to the historian Rosina Vizram, a deep anxiety about the 'whole issue of race, gender and class', a hostility towards relationships between Indian men and white women, based on 'a fear of miscegenation, the loss of authority in India'.[6] This was the psychogeographical reality of colonial India at the point in history when Olive Stowers, a young woman from Croydon, married and made a life with Qazi Mohammed Husain.

Olive Husain
London, Second World War 1939–45

It is 1942, Olive Husain is subsisting – just about. She and her sons have no money, they are getting by day to day, living through the Second World War, which is now in its third year. She is separated from Qazi Mohammed by war, by geography. As the years go by, she is losing hope that she'll ever see her husband again or return to the life she once had. She has her husband's name, but that's all. Sometimes people ask her where her surname Husain is from. They are surprised, perhaps disapproving, when she explains that her husband is Indian; they ask where he is.

She hasn't had a letter from him in months.

Olive was no longer a visiting, rich memsahib, living in high society. As the years wore on, she became once more a working-class woman who was struggling for money. Sometimes, as a treat to cheer everyone up, she would make a biryani. She would send one of the older boys to Tottenham Court Road, to one of the few shops in London that sold ginger. She'd get hold of some garlic, and her youngest son, Asif, still remembers how it was his job to crush it with the mortar and pestle. Using the few spices she could find, Olive would conjure up those biryanis she had watched being made in her servants' kitchen, remembering the cook telling her not to burn the cumin, otherwise the dish would be bitter. Remembering not to add too much water, so the rice would stay fluffy. Remembering the husband she loved and the life they once had.

She clings on to the idea of returning to her old life in India. 'Once the war is over . . .' she says to herself, over and over again as she goes about her day. Qazi's letters, though infrequent, have kept her hopes alive. He is building them all a new home to come back to. It's nearly finished, he describes it as a 'beautiful white house on the hill'. Her sons will grow up hearing about this white house on the hill. They will live in their new house together, reclaim the life they once had.

But the war seems never ending, and the dream of the beautiful house on the hill, of seeing Qazi again, is looking more and more unlikely. Olive is stuck in Britain, can't go back to India. In her small, terraced house in Croydon, she is barely surviving.

India, 1947

In August 1947, the British finally left India. As they departed, the country was split by the British into two new nation states, hastily carved up along religious lines, Hindu-majority India and Muslim-majority Pakistan. The partition of India became one of the greatest horror stories of the twentieth century. Millions of people found themselves a minority in their new country, suddenly terrified for their lives, forced to flee the countries of their birth. The split caused the largest mass migration – apart from war and famine – that the world has ever seen: 10–12 million people were suddenly on the move. Millions of Muslims in India fled to West and East Pakistan (now Bangladesh), and Hindus and Sikhs moved in the opposite direction. There was an outbreak of inconceivable savagery on both sides. In the months before and after Indian independence, over a million people were murdered and millions more were raped, tortured and mutilated in an orgy of communal violence.

Behind these epic movements of history are horrifying personal stories. Then there are the reverberations through time, the painful memories, the horrors of the imagination that are passed down the generations.

Sometimes though, there is nothing, a painful absence, an obliteration.

Qazi Mohammed Husain
The Journey from Hyderabad to Lahore
Eve of Partition, 1947

Qazi Mohammed Husain looked the same as any other Indian, but his name identified him clearly as a Muslim. He was a prominent Muslim professor, a courtier in the Nizam's palace, an Urdu speaker in a Hindu-majority state, in a Hindu-majority country. Hyderabad: ruled for centuries by a Muslim aristocracy, their ostentatious wealth on display in contrast to their subjects, most of them poor, most of them Hindu. But power was ebbing from the Nizam's court, and violence had erupted in the region, with armed uprisings across thousands of villages and peasants seizing land.⁹ Gandhian non-violence was over. The British were leaving and law and order had broken down; across the rest of India, violent Hindu and Muslim militias were getting ready to fight.

In this atmosphere of fear and uncertainty, Qazi decided to leave his job, his home, the beautiful new house he had just finished building for his wife and sons, to head for Lahore, just three months before the partition of India. It's not clear why he left – was he afraid? Had he, as an eminent Muslim professor, been driven out of his job? Was he one of the millions of Indians caught up in the violence surrounding partition? There were barely any facts telling Liz why he left, no stories passed down to her father.

Qazi would, I imagine, have watched with horror the approaching partition of India, witnessed the descent of his country into chaos and violence. He would have been filled with anxiety about his Husain relatives in Lahore, one of the major cities of the Punjab. But there was no mention of this in his letters, and nor was it ever discussed in Liz's family in the years that followed. Thousands of people were already on the move, fearful about becoming a minority in the new nations of India and Pakistan, terrified by reports of brutal killings and violence that had already engulfed the Punjab and Bengal, the two states due to be split down the middle.

Qazi travelled by train to pre-partition Punjab, sometime in 1947. He arrived in Lahore, the city of his birth, which was by now in a state of disintegration. Government across the region had largely collapsed, and the region was being run, in effect, by hostile communal militias. Though partition was a few weeks away, in Lahore the killings and mass violence had already begun.

On 3 June 1947, it was announced by the British that India would be divided into two – with a new border snaking down the Punjab. The violence in Lahore and surrounding areas intensified. Roads, railways and bazaars were bombed and the local population – Hindu, Muslim and Sikh – were now living with a palpable sense of terror. There were riots, bombings and violence, including two huge explosions in the main vegetable market; there were random attacks on streets. Hospitals were overwhelmed. Yasmin Khan writes that Lahore was, at this time, a 'war torn city', with life becoming nightmarish for its residents. No knew where the border dividing India and Pakistan would fall exactly, in which country their city, Lahore, would fall. Fear, she says, was the dominant emotion. Thousands started fleeing, while others grew or shaved off their beards to fake their religious identities; others stockpiled missiles and ammunition, and many sent their daughters away, fearing for their safety.[10]

Qazi hadn't seen his wife for eight years, but wrote to her from Lahore, looking forward to being reunited very soon. The war was over – they would, he believed, all be together as a family once more.

But in June 1947, in the middle of this time of mass violence, of terror and confusion, Olive Husain received a telegram saying her husband had died in the Albert Victor Hospital in Lahore.

• •

It was always unclear what the circumstances of Qazi's death were. Liz's father never spoke of it, and all she herself knew was that her grandfather had died during the Indian partition. Now, over seventy years later, she has been searching in letters and papers for more clues. There are just a few scraps of information. She has found a couple of letters from Olive, saying Qazi had died in the Albert Victor Hospital, that he was 'on holiday' in the Punjab, 'visiting family'. There was mention of health complications: maybe diabetes, possibly typhus. Liz isn't sure. These are polite accounts to acquaintances; there is no mention of the shocking violence taking place at the time. There isn't any detail, and what Liz was left with growing up, and even now, is still that recurring sense of uncertainty, an absence of detail and a silence. And maybe there is a silence because partition was horror.

And that is the silence carried in her name.

•

There are, however, a few things Liz has since found out. Online shipping records show that her grandmother travelled back to India, setting off by boat in July 1947. She was intending to go to Lahore, the place her husband had died, to be near him for one last time. In the midst of her grief and trauma, after a two-week voyage, Olive Husain arrived in India in August 1947, at the precise moment the country was partitioned and descended into indescribable butchery.

Punjab was divided in two, and Lahore, the city where her husband had died, became part of the newly created Pakistan. The violence in this magnificent old city suddenly reached staggering levels. Its streets became a bloodbath: entire Hindu quarters burned down, women and young girls raped, pregnant women attacked, bloody corpses lying everywhere as marauding groups of men from all religious sides unleashed their savagery on a terrified population. It was impossible for Olive to travel there.

She had not seen her husband for eight years, and the violence meant she wouldn't even be able to see where he was buried, or speak to the people that were with him when he died. It was too dangerous, her Husain in-laws warned her. They were still there, in Lahore, in the midst of the slaughter.

The railway lines into the city had become sites of mass murder. Gangs of armed men were deliberately derailing trains full of refugees, massacring and dismembering passengers or setting carriages ablaze with petrol. 'Ghost trains' were arriving at Lahore Junction Railway Station, full of the bodies of slaughtered Muslim refugees, trying to cross the border. In one of the most gruesome attacks of the period, the Amritsar massacre, knife-wielding men boarded a train and killed 3000 people on board and wounded 1000, chopping off limbs and raping women. The train pulled into

Lahore Station, bodies hanging from the carriages, the floors covered in blood.

Olive Husain found herself in India during the grisliest, most barbaric period of its long history. She would never see her Husain in-laws again and Liz would grow up not knowing who they were.

•

Unable to travel to Lahore as it was so dangerous, surrounded by the violence of partition across India, Olive stayed in her old home city of Hyderabad. But this was no longer a place that Olive Husain recognised, its streets seething with a dangerous tension, filled with lawlessness and violence that had escalated in the months since her husband had left. The Nizam of Hyderabad, its Muslim ruler, was refusing to join the newly independent Indian state, and the atmosphere was febrile. Paramilitary groups were arming themselves. Indian troops would soon invade and depose the Nizam. Tens of thousands of Muslims would soon be killed by Hindu gangs, abetted by the Indian army. Like much of the trauma of partition, this too would remain secret, the vast scale of the massacres not entirely known to this day.

She was now alone, she and her sons had no money but there was still the beautiful new house her husband had built for her. She hadn't seen it yet, but she imagined, maybe, one day, they would all return to live there. But in the post-independence chaos, Olive was devastated to find that the house had been illegally seized. India was now a dangerous place, especially for an Englishwoman; she had no power to get the house back, and her old high-society friends couldn't help. The dream of returning to India to her husband vanished: she would never set foot in the 'white house on the hill', and Olive would mourn its loss for the rest of her life. She would make fruitless efforts from England over the decades – writing letters to old friends, filled with anxiety – trying to claim it back. But the world she knew had disappeared, engulfed by terror, and the house was gone forever.

•

Olive Husain didn't ever talk about the extent of the violence that was taking place in India while she was there. Perhaps it was too frightening to comprehend, or maybe she didn't really understand the scale of it. Or perhaps she preferred not to know. She was under immense pressure: the death of her husband, the loss of her home and the life they had shared together. And the loss of the 'white house on the hill' was not just about the seizure of a building but something more profound. It was about the violent erosion of the structures of her previous existence.

I find myself wondering about the void of information that Liz had grown up with, the uncertainty, the absence of discussion. Why did no one in Liz's family ever talk about India, about partition, about their grandfather Qazi Mohammed Husain? Was his death connected to the brutality and violence of partition, or did he just happen to die an ordinary death at an extraordinary time? Is the account Olive gave to friends and to her sons a sanitised version of events, a story told by a mother to protect her sons from the full horror of what was happening when their father died?

•

Liz will never know why her grandfather left Hyderabad, what his thoughts were in his final days. I picture him walking, in earlier days, along the old streets of Lahore, a region once invaded by Turkish slaves from the Middle East who came with violence and their unfamiliar ways; who built buildings with minarets; brought religion, centuries of learning, praying. But this city of architectural splendour, of spirituality, learning and music, was part of a deadly, fractured land. As Qazi Mohammed Husain lay dying, in June 1947, the Punjab was about to be violently split in two. Outside the Albert Victor Hospital, the roads, bazaars, alleyways were already throbbing with bloody hatred.

But there was also another Lahore. The one Qazi carried in his memory, the one of his childhood. His younger aunts, living in the old rooms with the shutters closed. Screened from the sun, screened from male visitors, lying on the bed, laughing, singing sweet tunes. The olden ghazals and one sari-clad aunt taking up the musical thread from another. Looking out across the veranda at the sweet seller shouting out his wares.

John Husain
London, 1938–1999

By the time he was an adult, John had abandoned the name Arif and shut away his memories of his father. That part of his life, the Husain part, was eradicated. Liz thinks it was too painful to go there. I look at my notes of our conversation, and she tells me:

He shut it down. He locked it down. He locked it away.

It's hard to imagine the consciousness of a schoolboy, arriving in Britain, where he'd never lived before, slowly coming to understand that he would never return to his old life. He would never see his father again. He would, in time, come to realise that this was his new life – his mother barely subsisting, the family impoverished. The comfortable, privileged Husain existence was gone forever. A curtain had suddenly dropped across that world, and Liz's father, John Husain, would never return to India again.

He abandoned any outward longing for his old home, for his father, for India. But memories, the imprints left on the mind, were harder to let go of. Maybe they return, through the years, flashes of another life.

Standing on a dusty playground, the bright sun creating shadows of Arif and his friends, as they work out who will bowl first during a lunchtime game of cricket.

The tiny lizard that he watches, moving across a wall, coming out in slow darts from behind a picture frame, as he sits at his school desk in the morning.

The bright pink, paper-thin bougainvillea on the borders around the lawn, watered by the old *mali* (gardener). He comes in every day wearing his *lungi* and a cloth around his head to protect him from the power of that sun, that smothers everything with a golden, harsh light.

•

John Husain closed off that part of his mind, never speaking of his life in India to Liz. She would never know her grandfather, not even through the stories that a family passes down to its next generation. All she had was her surname.

It's not surprising that there is often a collective silence around partition, a trauma that is often not discussed by the people that went through it. Many don't want to burden the next generation with the experiences they have endured.

Although he was six thousand miles away in Britain, John Husain went through his own particular form of suffering, his own grief. When Liz thinks about her name, this helps explain why there was always that void and that absence of connection. This is what has been handed down through history.

Liz has tried to find her own way of redeeming this generational trauma, through talking to her relatives, looking through letters, family records. As her friend, it's not surprising to me that she works as a counsellor. I'm almost certain that her knowledge of psychotherapy, her years of experience with clients, must have helped her understand the pain of separation and bereavement her father went through as a child.

Many years ago, Liz went to India herself – she was in her twenties then, before she'd begun to explore her past, or even thought much about her heritage. It was just a holiday. But she always remembers the conversation she had with her father before she set off. She'd asked him why he'd never returned to India – even as an adult. He'd replied: 'You can never go back. You won't find what you're looking for, it's no longer there.'

Why My Friend Maria Found It So Difficult to Name Her Son

My friend Maria and I met when we were both students in the late eighties in Brighton. She was at the art college and I was studying politics at Sussex University. We were housemates for a while in a huge bohemian house, a converted nunnery full of art students, with their friends coming and going, parties going on all night. We often laugh now about its ridiculously carefree atmosphere. We'd watch TV in the scruffy living room, looked down on by a huge papier mâché sculpture mounted on the wall of a chubby-faced angel wearing a tutu. In the summer everyone would sit around in the overgrown garden, smoking joints, sometimes sketching and creating beautiful scraps of art. I loved Maria's drawings – intricate, gorgeous illustrations the colour of jewels – deep pinks, sea greens, turquoise – and used to beg her to give me ones she was about to throw away to hang up on the walls of my tiny student bedroom.

It all had to end – obviously – we had to enter the real world. Maria and I moved back to London, where we were both originally from, got jobs, flats, had various boyfriends, at various times. It wasn't always easy. Maria tried to find work as an illustrator but she struggled. Eventually she managed to get a job in children's television. She was always really creative – she was really good at it, she won awards. She got married to her Nigerian-French boyfriend, lives in Bounds Green. Miraculously, given how close we are, we had children within weeks of each other. We live just a few miles apart. Our histories and our lives are intertwined.

●

I've never thought too much about Maria's name in the many years I've known her. It's a name that feels familiar, and I know it's also very much a part of her own culture. She comes from a traditional Greek Cypriot family and Maria is a variation of Mary – as in the Virgin Mary. Her father was deeply religious, her mother less so, but both, like all of Maria's relatives, went to church and believed in God. So for them, it was an ideal choice.

There are multiple variations of my friend Maria's name across the Western world, including:

Marie (Czech, French, English, Danish, German, Norwegian, Swedish)

Mary (English)

Marya (Russian)

Mariyka (Ukrainian)

Marja (Dutch)

Mariah (US, and the name of the globally famous American popstar)

Mariam (biblical, Greek)

It's always been one of the most popular female names in Cyprus. (I have another close friend, also Greek Cypriot, who is also called Maria.) It's of course an entirely easily understood name in this country too, it's always seemed well liked. So, growing up in Catford in the seventies and being called Maria was not an issue for my friend. But when it came to naming her own son, who was born in London in 2007, things weren't so simple.

•

'You have to understand,' Maria tells me, 'you can't just name your kid anything. It was ONE BIG pressure,' she tells me slowly and dramatically. If she'd decided to call him Josh or Jeremy, or whatever, she says, the whole family would have had something to say about that. 'Where did that come from? Why did you name him that?' She does an impression of some interfering nosy relatives. But it's not a joke, it's much more than that.

Names, for Greek Cypriots, are not a matter of fashion or individual whim – they follow rules and conventions that have been handed down through the centuries. They are supposed to be a timeless entity – a direct connection to the otherworldly, eternal realm of religion and Greek mythology. As such, the overwhelming majority of Greek Cypriots are named after Christian saints of martyrs, or divine figures from Greek mythology, like Achilles or Athena.

Another sign of the importance of names among Greek Cypriots is the tradition of celebrating name days. Most people on the island have a special day, an annual celebration centred around their name, that's often considered as important as a birthday. This takes place on the feast day of their saint, or on All Saints' Day if they are named after one of the

Greek gods. Maria's name days are on 15 August and 21 November. (She has two, as Maria is such a holy name, and the first one is a public holiday.) Everyone called Maria across Cyprus will celebrate on one of these days with parties, food, cake and gifts.

When it comes to naming, equally important is the idea of following a familial tradition that has been followed forever in villages in Cyprus. And that tradition dictates that the first son must be named after his grandfather, on his father's side. And everyone still follows that tradition – 'even the modern ones', says Maria. She had already upset tradition by marrying a non-Greek. And so, as there was no Greek paternal grandfather, tradition dictates that Maria's son should take her own father's name.

.

'So . . .' she begins when explaining what the problem was. 'My dad's name was Polycarpos.'

Poly – CAR – poss, she says again, in her wide south London accent, with the stress on the CAR, which emphasises how different and odd it sounds in this country. How out of place it is spoken in English.

The name Polycarpos originates in ancient Greece, some time in the first century BC, during the heyday of Greek civilisation – which spanned the Mediterranean and reached all the way into parts of Asia Minor. Like many classical names, Polycarpos is dithematic – comprised of two elements: 'poly', meaning 'many', and 'carpos', meaning 'branches' or 'illustrious fruit'. In Greek mythology, Karpos was the son of Zephyrus, the west wind, and Khloris, the goddess of fruits and spring, and so the name Polycarpos is a powerful name, a metaphor for growth and renewal.

Maria loves the name: it's beautiful, she says.

'Polycarpos.'

She says it again, this time as it should be said: long and full throated, with a magnificent Greek roll of the 'R'. Maria is bilingual and speaks fluent Greek, and as she says it, I feel like I've accessed a different world, away from the mundanity of our London estuary vowels and our thirty-four years of shared (English-speaking) history. It's an *old* classical Greek name, she tells me, drawing out the word *old* as if she's about to begin an epic fable, a story of ancient times, alluding through her tone to centuries of classical myth, summoning images of supernatural heroes, the Greek gods and the whole edifice of Greek civilisation. Polycarpos: a name that sits alongside those other great classical names such as Achilles, Aphrodite or Adonis; names that are still commonplace in Greece and Cyprus, but sound archaic and pompous over here. I like it, she tells me again. But in a matter-of-fact way, she says it's too weird and unusual for this country.

In Greek Cypriot tradition, naming a child after a parent means that they carry, in symbolic form, the essence of that person. Maria's father died over thirty years ago – and her widowed mother always assumed if Maria had a son, he would be called Polycarpos. To *not* choose Polycarpos would not only be to dishonour family tradition, it would also be to dishonour the memory of her late father.

Maria had lived her own life, made her own decisions, all her adult life. But suddenly when it came to naming her son, she didn't know what to do. She wanted to honour her family, but didn't want her son's name to become an object of fun, of ridicule. In north London, where Maria now lives, diverse names are admired. It's all supposed to be a world away from the narrow-minded attitudes of the seventies. But even in liberal circles – full of Alfies, Joes, Freddies and Isaacs – a name like Polycarpos would stand out. She imagined the playground bullies, the sniggers over its unfamiliar vowels, her son having to spell it out the whole time. She worried his Greek grandfather's name would become a lifelong burden.

It all fused into a sense of impending stress, as she walked through the front door of her terraced house in Bounds Green on 1 January 2007 with her new-born baby. She walked past the framed photograph of a christening in 1973 at the Greek Orthodox Church in Camberwell hanging in the hallway, alongside a sketch by a friend from her art college days. As she carefully put down the car seat on the floor with her baby in it, Maria knew she had to navigate her own sense of duty to her father, for whom tradition had been fundamental to the way he lived his life. Suddenly her whole Greek Cypriot family was there inside her head: the voices of her aunts; her glamorous but traditional cousins back in Cyprus ('the Wags' as Maria laughingly calls them), with their designer clothes, their beautiful apartments and gleaming kitchens in Limassol; and most importantly her own Greek Cypriot alter-ego – a powerful fusion of memories, tradition and duty – judging her as she decided what to call her son.

Back in Cyprus her mother and the rest of her family were already calling the baby Polycarpos. It was already decided, that was the tradition, and it didn't matter what Maria thought. These were not just abstract centuries-old rules, they were part of Maria's reality, the whole world that Maria had grown up in; the one that had shaped her consciousness, her sense of self, her sense of Greekness. It was a world that she didn't want to feel that she was rejecting as it formed the deep pool of her childhood memories.

Polycarpos Timotheou
The Tasteful Fish Bar
Commercial Road, East London, 1967

Maria's mother and father came over to the UK in 1961 from a village in southern Cyprus called Maroni, two young people in a great sea of migration from Cyprus in the sixties, just after the country had gained independence from Britain. Most Greek Cypriots from that era came from rural areas that were fairly poor, but they were enterprising and looking for opportunities. They were mainly from small villages, had very little education and, on the whole, didn't speak very much English, so they set up their own businesses – barbers, dress-making factories, restaurants and chip shops. They would rely on one another to help each other out, so when Maria's father first arrived, he worked for his brother-in-law, who was already over here and owned a couple of fish and chip shops. Polycarpos worked every hour he could, saving every penny until, six years later, he had enough money to buy his own chippy.

And so, in the summer of 1967, a new sign was put up above a fish and chip shop on the Commercial Road:

The Tasteful Fish Bar

With Polycarpos Timotheou as its new owner.

•

When Maria remembers her father, in her mind he's getting ready for work every morning in their house in Catford, often when it was still dark. At 6am he would already be in his shirt and tie, preparing to leave the house. She remembers him putting on a V-neck jumper, and once he got to the chippy, he would put on his white overalls and serve customers all day. Maria adds that he wore a tie every day of his life, even on his one day off on a Sunday.

Her parents scrimped and saved to buy the fish and chip shop for £2000 in 1967, and her father worked in it for forty years, six days a week, leaving the house to first go to Billingsgate Fish Market to buy a van load of fresh cod, haddock and plaice, and then heading to the chippy. Maria's mother would join him there at 9.30am and, together, they would work there all day, returning at midnight. Maria remembers spending all her holidays there, while her parents served the long queues of East End customers. She would sit by the window at one of the tables, getting bored, and her father would give her some chip paper and some pencils to keep herself entertained.

She draws a little diagram to show me what it was like. 'So,' she says, 'this is where the chips were fried, the doorway,' and she then draws in some tables with salt and pepper shakers. 'That was my job,' she explains, 'to put out the salt and pepper, and the condiments. And then,' she adds, sketching in a road, some other buildings, 'there's the Commercial Road, with the traffic thundering by, the Methodist Church, the Bangladeshi corner shop and to the left was the Chinese take-away.' Her parents spent nearly all their waking hours in this chip shop, on this shabby, ugly brute of a road, one of the largest arterial routes in London.

The Commercial Road was, I later find out, constructed in the early nineteenth century as a direct route to transport the spoils of empire from the docks straight to its financial heart in the city of London. By the time Maria's father arrived here, in the sixties, it was home to the various immigrant communities that had come to Britain as a result of this process of colonisation, a dingy corner of London where they congregated, one of the few places they could afford to buy a small business to try to make a living in an inhospitable country.

Her parents were on their feet all day, cooking, frying, serving; the mix of heat and grease from the fryers gave her father lifelong eczema. At the back was a kitchen area, where they used to cut the chips. But it had no door, remembers Maria. So, it was freezing cold, and her parents were constantly having to go out and bring in the cut chips from a giant bathtub in the icy kitchen area. I imagine their hands raw from the cold and wet, sacks of potatoes everywhere. Looking back, Maria says, they worked really hard, 'it was dirty, greasy work, a tough life' she tells me. Their only priority was survival.

•

Maria remembers the long school holidays that she spent in the chippy, day in day out, a real mix of people in this dirty, sooty, grim stretch of London. Standing at the steamed glass counter, laughing and cracking jokes, talking about the weather, were working-class cockneys, local prostitutes, the Christians from the Methodist church, a handful of lesbians, some opera singers – part of a small bohemian population – as well as Bangladeshis, Afro-Caribbeans and the other immigrants that had settled in the area. Maria remembers a strong sense of community among the customers; it may have been a tough, ugly area, but it was much more welcoming and friendly than Catford, where the family lived in the suburbs of South London.

When it came to her father's name, Maria remembers how the English couldn't (or wouldn't) pronounce the name Polycarpos and shortened it to Polo. It now had a familiar, cosy ring to it – it was a word that was around in that era, like the mint, or the posh sport that Prince Charles used to play. Even worse, Polycarpos sometimes became Polly, a girl's name. In the openly homophobic seventies, Polly had an aggressively derogatory ring to it. Even as a child, Maria could sense that the beauty of the name, its centuries of history, its classical allusions and its meaning, all disappeared once it was transplanted to seventies London.

The Christening of Maria's Cousin
St Mary's Greek Orthodox Church, Camberwell, 1973

For one day a week, every Sunday, the backbreaking work stopped and an alternative world came into existence. Aunties, uncles and cousins, going to church, weddings, christenings and huge parties afterwards. This was Maria's childhood. As we're talking, Maria takes down that black and white photograph hanging in her hallway, with everyone standing in front of the St Mary's Greek Orthodox Cathedral in Camberwell for her cousin Vasoula's christening. The Timotheous and their extended family were all there. Maria points out her Aunty Vasilou (her mother's sister) and Uncle Andreas, as well as her brothers and cousins, young men in suits, looking solemnly at the camera. Maria is the youngest one in the photo, about six years old, smiling, looking pleased with herself, wearing a velvet party dress with puffed-out netting underneath. It's embroidered with flowers with a lace front and a high neck that Maria describes as 'a bit Little Lord Fauntleroy'. It's both funny and poignant, this world of family gatherings, cousins and aunties.

Inside the church, they would have watched the priest anoint the baby with holy oil and name the child. Each person would have lit a candle and offered up a prayer in front of the gilt-edged icon of the Virgin Mary shipped over from the Kykkos Monastery, one of the holiest spots in Cyprus. Maria says the baptism ceremony was like theatre, especially when the priest, dressed in white-and-gold silk robes, with a huge dome-shaped crown on his head, walked through the arches, intoning the words of the liturgy, carrying long, lighted candles. Once they had stepped outside the incense-filled church, after the christening, someone captured that moment on camera, one day in 1973.

If there was no christening or wedding, Maria's father usually insisted they all went to church on a Sunday anyway. But sometimes he'd take them all for a drive instead, in the family car, a second-hand Wolseley, an old-fashioned contraption that looked like it had come straight out of a black-and-white film. They'd pick up Aunty Froso along the way. Froso was short for Aphrodite – the goddess of love and beauty – a common name among Greek Cypriots who believed their island to be her birthplace. Maria says it was no big deal as a name. No one expected her aunt or anyone called Aphrodite to 'look like a goddess, as if Angelina Jolie had walked into the room or something'. She adds that Greeks don't also, for example, expect anyone called Adonis to be incredibly handsome.

They'd all drive an hour and a half to Green Lanes in Haringey, a huge bustling road, full of Greek kebab shops, sweet shops and green grocers, with their arrays of giant green peppers, cucumbers, courgettes, aubergines, and bunches of fresh thyme, oregano and parsley. They'd wander up and down, stop in a few places, have a coffee and some baklava, with Aunty Froso telling them about her big new house in Sydenham, and boasting about how well her sons were doing.

Green Lanes was the epicentre of the Greek Cypriot community in London in the seventies. The Cypriot immigrants had all settled in an arc across north London suburbia, moving out from places like Camden and Archway, where they'd first lived, into a series of more salubrious areas along the Piccadilly Line – Wood Green, Palmers Green, Arnos Grove, Southgate and Bounds Green, where Maria now lives.

•

Maria had always loved coming on those trips from Catford to north London as a child, sitting in the back, listening to the grown-ups chatting in Greek as they drove across London, and enjoying the bustling atmosphere of London's main Greek Cypriot shopping street, seeing her parents suddenly seem comfortable as they spoke in Greek to the owners, as they picked up bunches of parsley, or decided which was the best shop for baklava. The Greek businesses have disappeared now, replaced by Turkish restaurants, green grocers and jewellers. But the Greeks still tend to live in places like Wood Green and Bounds Green, in those same areas that spill out from this long stretch of road.

It's why, in fact, Maria moved to north London, just before her baby was born – she wanted a connection with the Greek community, one that she felt she was losing. She sent me a text after I went to chat to her, about the move to Bounds Green, which I think says quite a lot about her frame of mind and how questions of identity were playing on her mind when she was trying to decide what to name her son:

Can't remember if I said this yesterday about the move to north London but I think I was looking for a sense of Greekness, hence Saturday Greek school, making friends with my elderly Greek neighbours and Greek orthodox schools. Then for me it's the thrill of going into a shop and hearing the language being spoken or going into Despinas Deli in Arnos Grove with all the ingredients and brands that remind me of Cyprus.

•

Sometimes, on a Sunday, after church, they'd all go for a big family lunch at Aunty Vasilou's flat, above a fish and chip shop in Hackney, which she owned with her husband Uncle Andreas. Maria always remembers the food on those Sunday afternoons. Aunty Vasilou would have cooked huge amounts; it all came out at once and was put on the table: stuffed vine leaves, a roast lamb, a nice pasta dish, potatoes, salad. 'There weren't any fancy starters or anything like that,' Maria tells me. 'There was no performance, no fuss, just get on with it. And it was all delicious.' And what was amazing, Maria now realises, is that Aunty Vasilou would have made all this single-handedly, having worked a seventy-hour week downstairs in her own chip shop, as well as looking after her four grown-up sons, who still lived at home. She was always cheerful, says Maria, and her husband, Uncle Andreas, was a kind of lovely, funny man. He was a little bit short and smoked a lot, she says, and 'they had a great marriage'. Maria remembers that unlike most of the other couples, they were 'romantic and all loved up'. By the end of the afternoon, the carpeted living room would be dense with cigarette smoke, with the men all smoking: 'My Dad smoked, my two brothers smoked, Uncle Andreas and their four sons smoked. It would be loud and noisy, with the television on very loud in in the corner of the room, and I'd leave feeling slightly lightheaded.'

Like Maria's parents, Aunty Vasilou and Uncle Andreas

were a tight-knit couple, working together day and night, running a fish and chip shop in a rough inner-city area. This was Hackney in the seventies, one of the poorest areas in Britain, with high levels of crime. Immigrants who'd set up shops and businesses in the area were constantly vulnerable to attack from local gangs and thugs, who saw them as easy targets because they were foreigners.

But Aunty Vasilou was a tough woman, she knew how to stand up for herself. Maria tells me a family story that she'd picked up when she was a child. Two rough-looking men had come into the chip shop one day and threatened Uncle Andreas, demanding money. They sneered at him, saying 'Your food's off, we found something nasty in it. You better give us some money not to report it.' Maria says her uncle was scared and about to open the cash register when Aunty Vasilou came down and stopped him. 'Stay where you are,' she said to her husband. 'Don't open that till. There's nothing wrong with my shop, and nothing wrong with my food.' She was really feisty, says Maria. 'She saw them off with her dog, an Alsatian called Tarzan, at her side, and they never came back again.'

•

I look at the photo Maria showed me of the christening. The men in their dark suits, women in their old-fashioned A-line dresses, crosses hanging from their necks, carrying handbags from another world: it's as if we are looking at the scene through a window of unreality. We look from this present moment, sitting at Maria's kitchen table, both of us with our in-between Western lives. We talk about the time when we named our children, fusing our own inchoate yearnings for our lost childhood world, our parents' stories, and their tales of struggle and survival as we told it to ourselves. The past becomes a mythic world, particularly for the children of immigrants like Maria and me, because it's vanishing before us: as our parents die or become too old and weak to preserve the olden ways. And so, naming becomes a small act of resurrection. To go against something so important as a naming tradition that's been handed down for centuries in Greek Cypriot families would be yet another loss for Maria, another break from that cocooned world of Greekness that she had grown up in.

Maria and Her Grandmother
Catford, London, 1975

The person who most embodied this vanished Greek world was, for Maria, her beloved grandmother. Maria points out the stiff-looking dress and matching jacket her grandmother is wearing in that photograph of the christening and tells me how she used to get all her clothes handmade by a Cypriot seamstress they knew. Her *yiayia* (grandmother) looked after Maria while her parents were working until midnight at the chippy.

Every afternoon at five o'clock, after she'd got home from primary school, Maria's *yiayia* would set out a china tea set on the folding dining table and they would both sit down and have a proper tea – made in a pot – with a piece of Mr Kipling cake. It was their own ritual and as a little girl, Maria loved it. Maria adored her grandmother, who only spoke Greek and looked after her until she was twelve. Most of the time Maria barely saw her parents – instead she was ensconced in the happy love of her *yiayia*.

Maria says she was much more light-hearted than other Cypriots. Her grandmother – whose name was Christina

– had been abandoned by her husband when she was young; she had raised her children on her own and took little notice of the dour patriarchal rules that everyone else was obsessed by. She loved socialising with the neighbours, even though she only knew a few words of English, and communicated with sign language, bits of Turkish and some heavily accented English: 'Maa-yee thaughthar come Cyprus aeroplane' (my daughter has come over from Cyprus on a plane). She was the one who'd make Maria English food, asking if she wanted 'fish finjas' or 'hum-boor-gas' for dinner as a treat. In this world of Maria's childhood, it was Them and Us. The outside world was Them, the English, with their alien ways, while inside the home was Us, the world of family, that was completely Greek; everyone spoke Greek, they ate Greek food and all their traditions were the ones they'd brought over from their villages in Cyprus.

•

The aunties, uncles, her *yiayia*, the smoke-filled Sundays; a table filled with food, the smell of roast lamb and thyme spreading around the house; the glisten of olive oil on a plate of spinach and black-eyed beans; an echo of laughter from her mother and her aunt, as they stood frying meatballs. It was a one-generation phenomenon, an in-between world that Maria's parents and their extended Greek Cypriot family created with their language, their food and their village traditions. As a child of immigrants, Maria was growing up very differently from her parents; she was living in London, speaking a different language, absorbing different values.

She was being educated in British redbrick schools. And as she sat cross-legged in assembly, on those chilly parquet floors of her seventies school hall, the old traditions were all slipping away, without anyone realising. Everyone's childhood is full of strangeness and nostalgia, and all families have their stories. But for a second-generation immigrant like Maria, the intensity of her closed Greek family, surviving in a hostile country, learning how to *be* from one another, only exists in her mind now as a bubble, a quasi-magical world. Maria would never be able to hang on to this world; she would, like all the other immigrant children, like me, slowly become part of a different culture. She'd always longed to go back in time, to tell her *yiayia* how much she loved her. Could her baby's name act as a tiny dart of light, a star sent out to try to reach that old world again, to connect with it now she'd become a parent?

The Memory of Polycarpos Timotheou
Maroni Village, Cyprus, 1940s

To call her baby boy Polycarpos in 2008 felt impossible to Maria. But of course, in a 1940s village in rural Cyprus, where her father was from, it was a perfectly natural name. In this Greek community, 'Polycarpos' was a name not just rooted in centuries of myth and tradition: Maria's father himself was part of a Greek family that had lived in the same place for hundreds of years, known to everyone for miles around. A place where each person's name was accompanied by family apocrypha, fragments of histories, anecdotes, following them around throughout their lives, like unfurling banners in the air, preceding them wherever they went.

A name in itself was not always enough for this, and villagers often acquired an additional moniker that added another layer of depth and information to their original identities.

And therefore, Maria's father wasn't just called Polycarpos Timotheou, there was a fable-like appendix to his actual name, unverifiable but believed in by everyone around him. Maria tells me it as she's explaining her father's history, and it sounds like the start of a fairy tale: 'Well,' she begins, 'he was known as "The Cleverest Man in the Village".' She goes on to explain how it came about. She tells me that in the village, everyone left school at the age of eleven to go and work in the fields, but her father was allowed to stay on until he was eighteen. Maria reflects that he wasn't particularly well educated – especially by middle-class Western standards. She tells me about his title of 'The Cleverest Man in the Village' partly as a joke, adding that 'he only stayed on until the equivalent of sixth form and everyone talked about him like he had a PhD!' But this was the story accepted and used by everyone around him, this was the Polycarpos Timotheou who was rooted in the collective imagination of his village, his extra title breathing drama, life and character into his actual name when the villagers summoned it to their minds.

But Maria also says her father had a natural intelligence and 'a respect for learning' which was unheard of for a man from his background. She thinks back to Sundays at home, her father's one day off, when he'd watch informative documentaries, or if he managed to get home in time on a Monday night, sit himself down and tell everyone to be quiet because he was watching *Mastermind*. Really, she says, he would have loved to have become a doctor or a teacher, something like that, not work in a chip shop all his life.

Instead, at eighteen years old, Polycarpos Timotheou went to work on the land, like everybody else around him. This was the 1950s, when most families had a plot on which they grew crops – watermelons, cucumbers, tomatoes, courgettes, lemons and carobs. Her father's family also had an ancient olive farm, and Maria describes gnarled, old olive trees stretching across their small patch of hillside, overlooking the deep blue waters of the Mediterranean Sea. The olives would be harvested and placed in a huge cauldron and pressed, using a donkey to turn a grinding stone. Her mother's family meanwhile used to keep silkworms and make their own silk. They would weave their own cotton and her grandmother used to crochet beautiful tablecloths and sell them, as well as making her own honey and cheese.

There's an elegiac quality to what Maria tells me, the stories of the life that her parents had led back in Cyprus in the forties and fifties. She had grown up hearing of a lost culture, through the filter of her parents' longing for their homeland. Maria held in her imagination yet another layer of associations with the name of her father, a fairytale-like sense of enchantment attached to village life in Cyprus. She realises this sense of nostalgia is a product of her own Western mindset, but she can't help but see her parents' lives in Cyprus as a 'kind of romantic time', an almost-perfect life where everything was done by hand.

Sometimes Maria wonders why her parents ever left, when all they yearned for, once they came here, was to return home to Cyprus. They eventually did, after nearly forty years working night and day in the chip shop, saving up enough money to build themselves the house they'd always been dreaming of. But by that time, it was too late. Polycarpos Timotheou, the young man who left in 1961, would only live for another two years, in his beloved Cyprus. Maria feels a sense of regret that their lives in Cyprus hadn't been enough for them. She says, 'When I ask them, they talk about it as such a hardship, but to my Western mind, it seems idyllic. They didn't have a lot of cash, but they had lives close to nature, where they spent all their time outside, in beautiful countryside by the sea.'

Growing up in Catford in the seventies and eighties, in the cold, in the rain, seeing her parents' grinding struggle in the chippy, working all day by the hot, greasy fryers, the stories of Cyprus in the olden days turned it into an island paradise. And so, there is a sense that the name 'Polycarpos' carried for Maria not just the essence of her father as a person but also the spirit of the place that he once came from, and a mythological past that she'd never known herself.

•

As soon as her parents left Cyprus, carrying their suitcases onto a ship, heading for a new life in London, that world would only now exist as an illusion. But there was of course a reality, one that Maria can never really know. I only met Maria's father a couple of times, and by then he was in his fifties. I was in my twenties and he just seemed like an ordinary middle-aged man. But who was he in his younger days? What was the reality of his life, away from the idealised vision in my friend's mind. He passed away when Maria was twenty-four, so she will never really know. She wishes she could understand his motivation for coming to Britain: what dreams did he have as he was making his decision to emigrate, what was the wanderlust that propelled him over here?

I imagine Polycarpos Timotheou as a young man, working in the family fields in Maroni. It's been several hours in the dry hot sun, digging into the hard sun-baked soil, sweat pouring down back and face. He's getting ready to plant the last of the potato crop and will start harvesting the olives later this afternoon. He knows this is what his life will be if he stays here, planting, digging, harvesting, every day, every week, every month and the same the following year and the year after that. His future is mapped out by centuries of tradition and the rituals of village life. He's been helping his father tend this field throughout his schooldays and knows every inch of it. In the picture Maria has shown me, he faces the camera with big brown eyes, dark hair, and is wearing a baggy white shirt with brown twill trousers.

He doesn't look up to see the sun glinting and sparkling on the sea, across the hillside. All he can think about is how his back aches. Maybe, for a moment, he wishes he could go back to his books again, the ones he used to love reading in school. I imagine him enjoying the certainty and the satisfaction of maths, as well as the stories of ancient Greece, its gods and its heroes. He had dreamt of becoming a teacher, maybe even a doctor – but his father needs him to help run the farm. All that is over now.

But there's a new sense of possibility, of excitement when he thinks about his brother-in-law who is in England, making a new life for himself, running a business. Polycarpos wonders if he could join him, he has vague, abstract images of Britain, things he learnt in the history books at school: another great civilisation, like the Greek one, a land of opportunity, a place where he could do something other than this. Maybe he could make some money and come back to the village, build a house for his parents, one with electricity, running water. He worries they don't have enough money for when they're older, for doctor's fees if they get sick. He could make something of his life.

Maria's father came over here in 1967, but his grandfather had already been abroad, looking for opportunities to make money. He was part of a wave of migration from Cyprus to the West, spurred on by Britain's colonial influence. And once the British left in 1959, over 25,000 Cypriots made their way to this country. Quite a few of the men in Maria's family had already travelled to the UK and to America: industrious, optimistic young men, trying to find new opportunities to make their fortunes, encouraging others to do the same. Polycarpos's grandfather had, in his younger days, travelled to a few countries and returned to the village, acquiring an air of wealth and prestige. Once he was home, he bought a couple of plots of land. He had also brought back a bag of gold coins, which his wife had turned into a necklace of coins. She wore it about the village. This cemented the stories of family wealth surrounding Maria's great grandfather and he became known as 'The Richest Man in the Village'. In actual fact, despite the appearance of wealth, he had gone abroad and failed to make it. But it didn't matter, like the others who emigrated, the village story was that Polycarpos's grandfather was a successful and rich man.

By the time Polycarpos was growing up, his grandfather's plots of land had all been divided up among his children and there was very little money to go around. There weren't many opportunities for Polycarpos in a small Cypriot village like Maroni, and possibly, for a bright young man, there was an overwhelming feeling that life was happening somewhere else, somewhere very far away. It reminds me of a short story by Chekhov, called 'The Schoolmistress'. The tale depicts the monotony of life for a young teacher in a small Russian village, and describes her thoughts as she's riding on a cart through the countryside on a beautiful spring day. Chekhov sees the world through the teacher's eyes describing the beauty of the countryside: the 'languid transparent woods', the warm 'breath of spring', the 'marvellous fathomless sky'. The seductive descriptions of the landscape are, however, soon undercut by the schoolteacher's hatred of her life, its relentless tedium and its absolute lack of choices. Chekhov writes:

She felt as though she had been living in that part of the country for ages and ages, for a hundred years, and it seemed to her that she knew every stone, every tree on the road from the town to her school. Her past was here, her present was here, and she could imagine no other future than the school, the road to the town and back again, and again the school and again the road . . .[1]

Reading this description of village life in nineteenth-century Russia, it's easy to imagine that Maria's father had similar feelings of constraint as he made his decision to emigrate to Britain. And as Polycarpos Timotheou made a new life in London, spurred on by his own fantasies, hopes and dream, the reality he left behind was slowly transformed. It became, in his daughter's mind, an Edenic vision of a homeland that doesn't exist, and perhaps never did. And the name she contemplated for her son carried elements and flavours of those enchanted stories that she had heard about the place that he came from.

A Suburban Ethnic Girl Grows Up
Britain, 1980s

When I dig deeper into why the question of what to call her son was such a pressure for Maria, what slowly emerges is something much more emotional, more painful than I quite realised: a set of psychological tensions that for Maria reached back into the past, to her teenage years, that focused on her relationship with her parents, and with her father in particular. The question of tradition wasn't solely about her nostalgia for a lost heritage – although that was undoubtedly important. Or even about honouring the struggles that her father had been through in life. It was more complicated than that, it went to the very heart of who she is, and how hard she had to fight to be that person. I didn't quite understand at the time, but she was in the middle of this existential struggle when I started getting to know her, when she was eighteen.

The first few times I hung out with Maria in Brighton I assumed she was working class, English, a cockney. I didn't know what her surname was, and I had no idea that she was actually another suburban ethnic girl like me. For a start, she was white. She was striking, with a perfect, artsy black bob, porcelain pale skin and a slash of pink lipstick. She used to get her hair cut for free at Toni & Guy in the town centre because the hairdressers loved using her as a model – she had that eighties art college cool. She had a sort of doll-like but edgy vibe and dropped funny scathing lines into the conversation and laughed all the time. I just thought she was a *proper* Londoner. I used to love it when she spoke – I had my suburban west London twang – lots of 'innits' and dropped *T*s – but hers was the widest accent I'd come across at college, which for all its lefty hippiedom was a middle-class enclave. She was like no one else I met in Brighton. Funny, clever, artsy, but also *really* cockney.

But of course, it turned out Maria wasn't a proper cockney, or even English. She seemed confident, creative and the same as the rest of us, getting educated and beginning her own path in life. But despite the fact that she was white, I soon realised that her family were much more like a traditional Indian family than mine, and that meant that her life at the time was incredibly hard and much more complicated than it was for the rest of us.

A Greek Cypriot Teenager and Her Father
Catford, London, 1984

By 1984, Maria's father, Polycarpos Timotheou, is no longer a young man. He has been working in The Tasteful Fish Bar for seventeen years now. He and his wife Barbara have three children: two nearly grown-up sons and their daughter, Maria. She is no longer a little girl, no longer wearing puffy princess dresses, but a teenager, who goes to Catford Girls High School on the Bellingham Road and speaks with a broad south London accent like everyone around her.

Polycarpos and Barbara still work until midnight in the chippy, saving every penny they have, dreaming of the house they are going to build when they eventually return to their village in Cyprus. Polycarpos disciplines his children in the way he knows, remembering how he was brought up in the 1940s, back in Maroni. For Maria, life as a teenager became one long conflict with her family. The feeling of 'Them and Us' had intensified, but it no longer felt happy and cocoon-like, enveloped in the love of her Greek grandmother, who had now returned to Cyprus.

Maria wanted to do what her friends at school were doing, hang out, go shopping, but was always told no, she couldn't go out. At all. Home now felt more like a prison. It was, she tells me, 'they've got their ways, and we've got ours'. But *our* ways, she says, seemed very isolated. 'We couldn't do what the English do, you can't dress a certain way, you can't have boyfriends, you can't wear too much makeup, that's what the English do.'

As she grew up, Maria and her father grew further apart. Though they lived in the same house, they inhabited completely different worlds. They had a different belief system and values – he, as I said, was a deeply religious man, who lived by the old rules and traditions. He insisted everyone pray every night, made sure they all went to church regularly. When he was dying, says Maria, his Greek Orthodox faith gave him a lot of comfort. He felt there was something waiting for him and believed in the idea of heaven and hell. And he wasn't unusual in this – it was the same for the whole community that Maria had grown up in.

All three Timotheou children had been baptised and named after important saints – a reflection of how religion was embedded in ordinary family life. Her brother Chris, after St Christopher (the patron saint of travellers), and Timothy, the first-born son, after Polycarpos's father, Timothakis. (Timotheos, another version of the name, was the first Christian bishop of Ephesus.) Maria remembers how her father had very high expectations about his children's behaviour and the sort of people they should become. For Polycarpos, this was intrinsically connected to the idea of morality and virtue, and, in particular, he had set ways of thinking how a young girl should behave that could be traced back to traditional life in his village. It's not surprising – it was how everyone was brought up, with girls being treated very differently from boys. Maria recalls how her father thought women should 'always be tidy and neat, how they should carry about a handkerchief in their handbag, not just a tissue'. They should, he thought, always have some money on them, because 'you never know, they might get stranded somewhere'. He believed in good behaviour as a route to becoming a good person. And this was a huge thing when it came to Maria, as it was all down to the daughter to maintain the family's good name.

But Maria was living in a different world, she was a teenage schoolgirl in 1980s Britain. She dyed her hair, started smoking. Her Greek Cypriot home life started clashing constantly with the life that she led at secondary school. She loved it there, loved hanging out with the local English girls from the nearby council estates and African-Caribbean girls from Deptford, who came from strict, hard-working immigrant families like hers. School was freedom from an increasingly strict home life.

Catford Girls High School was a typical inner-city secondary school in the eighties. It was, Maria told me, 'pretty low aspiration', very few of the girls were encouraged to go to university; some got pregnant and left before they did their O-levels. Most were expected to become housewives, or at best learn to type and become secretaries. Maria herself wasn't interested in anything academic and spent a lot of her time in lessons mucking around, hanging around with the disruptive kids. But she had spent all those endless holidays in her parents' chip shop, bored, drawing on scraps of chip paper, and she had eventually become *really* good at drawing. And her brother, Chris, who was much older than her, had himself become interested in art and photography – he talked to Maria about artists that he liked, gave her art books to look at and told her about galleries she might want to visit. She started looking outwards, saw that there was a world out there, outside of Catford, outside of her family, whose controlling behaviour felt more and more insufferable and stifling.

She had always done well in her art exams, so she decided on her own initiative to apply to art college. Her parents didn't know anything about it. No one from school had encouraged her, and none of her friends was going on to college, but she did it anyway. She surprised herself and everyone around her when she was accepted.

She got her A-levels and then told her parents that she wanted to go to college. That's when things got really bad. She suddenly faced the biggest challenge of her life.

Her parents were determined to stop her – there were huge arguments, shouting. Her father forbade her from going. Her mother had left school at eleven, and her father, despite his own love of learning at school, didn't think college was appropriate for girls. She was eighteen, it was time, her parents believed, for her to get married – to someone Greek Cypriot of their choosing. Polycarpos Timotheou was in many ways a loving father, but he couldn't tolerate the fact that his daughter was disobeying him. Who did she think she was? He felt she was dishonouring the family by deciding to go off on her own, by not agreeing to get married to a Greek boy from the community. Her mother agreed, they were going to find her a husband and force her to have an arranged marriage.

It was a confusing, upsetting time for Maria – she couldn't understand why it was so wrong to want to go to college, something most parents would be proud of. Her family's controlling behaviour, her father's disciplining, caused her lasting anger and pain. She craved her freedom, and it was a huge amount of pressure on her shoulders as a young girl – she knew if she went to college, she would cause her parents incredible suffering and she even risked losing them forever.

She left anyway and started her degree in art at Brighton Art College in 1987, an enormous step for an eighteen-year-old girl from her background. (She says without a student grant she would never have been able to do it – if it was now, she would have remained trapped at home.) She was desperate for her family to accept her as she was, wanted to keep their love, but wasn't prepared to give up the power to decide for herself what she wanted to do with her life.

•

Over the next few years, the pressure from her parents continued. While she was at college, they were still trying to force her to abandon her degree, come back to Catford and have an arranged marriage. She often laughed it off, but I can now see what a struggle it must have been at the time for a young girl living away from home for the first time, going against her family and her upbringing, to stay at college and get her degree.

Her life afterwards as a working twenty-something – unremarkable to most of us – was shocking to her parents. Her mother, Barbara (pronounced Var-vaah-rah), had had an arranged marriage at the age of seventeen to Polycarpos. They'd both come from a deeply conservative society, where the idea of a young unmarried woman living on her own, working and having relationships with men, was more than unthinkable: it was shameful. And when Maria did eventually get married, in her thirties, it wasn't to someone Greek but to Xavier, who was half-Nigerian and half-French, who she'd met at a party in Brixton.

There was a gulf of understanding between herself and her parents. And it's still painful, that feeling of emotional distance she had from them, especially from her father who died over thirty years ago. While he was alive, Polycarpos Timotheou, like many immigrant fathers, never really understood his daughter, and was often a disapproving figure. And when we really dig into why the question of what to call her son was so hard, she goes back to all of this. It's right there in her head again. The feeling of always being the bad daughter, who brings shame on the family.

She's always felt the pressure, it's always there. The fact that she's a disappointment has never gone away, really.

It's a feeling that she's lived with all her life. It lies deep within her consciousness, its origins in the trauma of her teenage years and in her turbulent relationship with her father. 'The things I did as a teenager,' she explains, 'the independence I craved, the way I wanted to be like my friends, wanting to go out and do the things that they were doing, and then, going to art college – something that should have made my parents proud – that caused irreparable damage in my family.'

These were the conflicted feelings that lay behind the decision about what to call her son.

·

It's all way back in the past now, but she says that for many years she was obsessed by it all, always struggling against feeling like a disappointment in her parents' eyes. She doesn't make a big deal of it, but I find it incredible that she made it to college at all, that she then went on to have a successful career in television – despite her working-class, immigrant background, despite having to continuously struggle against her own family.

That's the story behind the tension that's always been there. That's the *pressure* that never goes away. And here it was once more as she became a parent herself. Here she was again, not doing her duty, and not naming her son after his grandfather Polycarpos.

·

After thirty-eight years of standing behind the counter, serving fish and chips and working until midnight, Maria's parents moved back to Cyprus. They built the house they'd always dreamt of in Maroni, overlooking the Mediterranean. But after just a year there, Polycarpos Timotheou became ill with cancer, and passed away another year later.

Maria remembers sitting at his bedside while he was dying. She remembers thinking to herself, 'I completely forgive you for everything. I forgive you for the bad things. I forgive you for the control you had over me, all the shouting, everything, I just forgive you. And I'm really sorry I couldn't live up to what you wanted.'

There was something that emerged, after all the fights, the years of arguments, the years of hiding her true life. It was the fragments of chatter, memories of afternoons spent in their battered Wolseley, her dad driving them to Green Lanes, or deciding they should all have a day out to Buckingham Palace; it was her father's voice, talking to customers in the chip shop; it was him telling them all to be quiet because *Mastermind* was on TV. It might have been obscured, left carelessly lying somewhere, but she picked it up eventually when she had her son. She looked at it. Something was there at the core, that had lain uncorrupted by the fights, the arguments. It was love. She knew her father had loved her. This had remained.

•

She realised her parents were just people who'd had a difficult life. She says they grew up with a mentality that was, 'let's face it, a bit backwards'. She now sees them as people that were brought up in a rough way themselves, without a lot of love, often beaten, and they came to a country they didn't understand. They'd never seen anyone stray from the path: everyone grew up in the same village, got married, and there was a whole extended family around: aunts, uncles, grandparents, cousins. Instead, she says, her mother and father found themselves 'alone in this little house in south London, having to raise children, and didn't really know how to do it'.

In the end, when Maria thinks of her father, she says, 'I knew that he was trying to do his best in his own terrible way.' He was just trying to protect her. So, the anger faded – even though she's aware of everything it took from her over the years. But the ambivalence was still there, and she would make her own way once again when it came to choosing a name for her son.

•

Maria had to accommodate all the conflicting feelings she'd felt throughout her life: her love for her *yiayia,* for her family as a little girl, combined with the distance she'd felt as an adult, her regret about her lack of closeness to her father. So when the time came to name her son, she decided on a compromise.

Polycarpos would be his middle name. But it would work differently from an English middle name. It wouldn't be, as it often is in Britain, an afterthought, never to be mentioned apart from as a joke, or filled out on a passport application. In her son's case, if her mother or the rest of her family back in Maroni wanted to carry on using it as a first name, they could. (And in fact, when Maria did take her son to Cyprus when he was little, that was the name they used.)

A compromise to try to honour her father's memory, to follow tradition in a way that she felt she was able to.

And to stay true to her Greek Cypriot childhood, she decided she had to give her son a 'good Greek first name'.

The search was now on.

•

'Hello ev-ary-baady peeps.'

A Greek man in dirty overalls and white t-shirt

He runs a doner kebab shop

A big rolling kebab on a skewer

A thick moustache, and a few days' growth on his face

It's the eighties, and *Saturday Night Live* is on TV, the come-dian Harry Enfield, blacked up (or rather browned up), play-ing one of the most popular comedy characters of the era: Stavros, the Greek Cypriot owner of a kebab shop.

Millions of people sat in their living rooms across Britain when we were teenagers and laughed along to this version of blackface. Of course, it wasn't actually blackface, because that wouldn't be acceptable, the Black and White Minstrels having been banished to the TV hall of shame. But in this case, brownface seemed to be fine, with the joke being that these people were simpletons, as shown by their imperfect grammar and their Greek accents. Unfortunately, this was one of the very few Greek Cypriots we all saw on TV.

The reality was that the kebab shop owners that Stavros represented, as well as the much-mocked Indian corner shop owners – the Patels, the Sharmas – were all immigrants trying to make their way; starting small businesses, as the English often wouldn't employ them; working until they were bone tired, for years on end; dreaming of a better future for their children. But their names have become associated with ridi-cule. For Maria, the daughter of a chip shop owner, this was always demeaning.

Maria wanted a name for her son that would make him proud of being Greek, not one that had become something of a joke. 'I didn't want a name like Stavros or Costa,' she says. 'I didn't want something that was ever part of something that was mocked.' 'Look at Stavros,' she says. 'It comes from Stavrakis,' and when she says it in Greek it sounds like a completely different name, elegant and with that characteristic forceful roll of the 'r'. 'When people think of a name like Costa,' she adds, 'people also think "Oh yeah, that's your typical Greek guy who runs a kebab shop".' Costa, she tells me, is short for Constandinos, which is actually, she says, such a beautiful name, but it doesn't work once transplanted to Britain.

Neither did Maria want a name where her son's Greekness just disappeared and melted into a sea of Englishness. She wanted a marker of her family's Greek identity, something that reminded her of where she belonged. She tells me flatly, 'I didn't want something that could be turned into a boring English name.' She goes through a list of Greek names that are commonly used by Greek Cypriot parents living over here.

'So Yanis,' she says, 'becomes your common old John.'

'Or Georgios' (pronounced Yor-yee-oss, with a majestic guttural rasp at the start) 'becomes George, as in George Michael.' She also adds that everyone she knew seemed to be called George at one point.

On the other end of the scale, Maria loves names like Achilles (which she pronounces Aa-Kheel-ays, again with a rasp on the 'Kh'). The trouble is, in Britain, naming your child Achilles would seem too pretentious, too pompous, too upper class. Greek mythology – so ordinary and accessible to Maria – is associated with a certain type of elite British culture: Oxbridge, public school, and posh. The opposite of what

Maria is like and reminds her of the kind of people she has no desire to be associated with.

•

As Maria was going through her huge dilemma of what to name her son, I had just given birth to my daughter. I also remember how choosing a name for her was very much connected to the whole question of who I was – culturally – and what I wanted to pass on of myself. Naming a child is an emotional act. For both Maria and me, everything around us is British: we no longer hear the language that we grew up with, the language of home; most of our friends haven't had the same upbringing as us, and we both married outside our own communities. Maybe we were searching for some kind of redemption, for not sticking to the paths we were meant to follow. In the fight against the patriarchal values of her father, Maria gained her freedom, but she also lost a part of who she was. As she was choosing her son's name, what part of her Greek heritage was my friend trying to hold on to?

Alexandros Polycarpos
Bounds Green, January 2008

Eventually, the process of naming her son reflected Maria's own form of accommodation with her Greek identity. It was a rediscovering of a looser, more expansive idea of Greekness than the one she had grown up with, one not so obsessed with rigid rules, strict codes of behaviour and a morality rooted in patriarchy and religion. And it was one that involved a pride in the culture that her parents hadn't quite felt.

She eventually decided on the name Alexandros, a classical Greek name. The most famous bearer of the name was Alexander the Great – a god-like Greek hero. He was so successful, his empire so vast, that he mutated into a quasi-supernatural figure. He was, according to some legends, descended from the semi-divine Achilles; according to others he was the son of the all-powerful Zeus. It's a name that embodies the timeless power of story and legend: Alexander was king of Macedon at the age of twenty and by the time he was thirty, he ruled over one of the largest empires in the ancient world, stretching from Greece to Turkey and reaching all the way over to northwest India. His story has endured for over 2000 years, part of Greek mythic tradition, celebrated in fabulous tales, through statues and in the names of cities found all over the world, most famously Alexandria in Egypt. This is the man who spread the glories of Greek civilisation across the globe and throughout time.

My friend Maria, choosing a name as she sat in a house in Bounds Green in 2008, with her now ex-husband, hoped that one day her baby son would be seduced by the magical power of his story. She imagined it weaving its way into her baby boy's consciousness when he was older, entrancing him, luring him towards the glory of the ancient Greeks and helping him discover a pride in her own Greek culture that had somehow evaded her when she was a child. Her parents, too busy working, probably didn't have time for all that, she thinks now; it had been all about survival.

There's a strength in the name.

What Maria wanted to do, she says, was to tell her son a story when he was little. 'You were named after this *big important* figure' – she does a funny impression of a parent telling a child a story. I start laughing when she adds that Alexander was probably 'a bit crazy, this bloodthirsty character', but it's the excitement of the tale she's interested in, the distillation of myth and legend, as a child might understand it.

I don't think for Maria it was about the factual details of Alexander's life, his great military campaigns. It was that opening out of the imagination she was after, crossing that border between supernatural and human existence, between reality and the otherworldly. Not because she literally believes in it – but because it's powerful, optimistic.

Maria's choice of name was an obvious marker of her own heritage, but she was wary of it being shortened to Alex – too English sounding as a diminutive. It would immediately wipe out any sense of Greekness. So, she decided, from the very start, to shorten it herself – to Alexi. That's what we all call him. She added that characteristic Mediterranean 'i' at the end to make sure her son's name remained rooted to its Greek Cypriot origins. Alexi – unusual enough, but not unpronounceable in Britain, and different enough, importantly, for her baby to know of his Greek heritage.

•

Alexandros is a name that symbolises strength, courage, and it's interesting that Maria chose the iconic name of a Greek conqueror for her son. Myths, legends, they seem so unconnected with our everyday lives, but as we go through time they reveal themselves as intertwined; they function as sources of identity. Alexandros. Not someone who could ever be mocked, and who himself was always the invader. Maybe Maria's choice of name says something about immigrant life in the seventies and eighties, about the struggles her parents went through, about their vulnerable status in this country. Through naming, perhaps she wished to bring into existence a reversal of that dynamic.

There's another, wider historical dimension, too, that plays a part. Maria's family were from an island that's been repeatedly invaded over hundreds of years – by the Greeks, Egyptians, Persians, Ottomans, the British and the Turkish, among others. During those family car drives in the seventies, alongside the usual chatter, Maria would overhear mutterings of something darker, of the horror her family and many Greek Cypriots felt when their island was invaded by the Turkish army in 1974. It's all long ago, but the island remains divided today. Perhaps at the back of Maria's mind, when she talks about a 'good strong name', it's not just the childhood memories of mockery, at her parents' accents, their funny food, her funny surname. Perhaps there's another aspect to her choice of name, one of national pride.

•

The story of Alexi's two names – Alexandros and Polycarpos – is full of layers upon layers of myths, of stories of different kinds. Not just the fabulous legends, but those of her parents' lives, that have themselves vanished into the unreality of the past. Their Greek syllables allude to the fairytale-like existence of olden Cyprus villages, lost in time, the fragmented memories of the funny aunties who dipped in and out of Maria's childhood weekends. Alexi's names embody the stories that Maria tells about herself, they hold the emotional power of those stories, and symbolise the parts of her Greek identity she wants to keep.

•

Alexandros Polycarpos or Alexi for short.

Alexandros, Αλέξανδρος, Alexander.

The man who spread Greek civilisation across the world.

Man

God

Warrior

A story that Maria tells her son.

Polycarpos. Her father's name, carrying all the emotional complexity of their relationship.

Polycarpos, a young man who loved learning, came to Britain in the sixties, who felt bewildered by his British children.

A man who did his best, who tried to be good, had his own dreams, aspirations.

Two Greek names carrying the world of Maria's childhood, her grandmother, the funny aunties, smoke-filled Sundays, her widowed mother. Tales of her parents' lives, which have themselves faded into the unreality of the past. Their syllables catching the magical threads of olden Cyprus villages, lost in time. The story of a family, fragments of Greekness, ambivalence, arguments, fighting, love, all flowing through Maria's baby's name.

Vicki Denise Marie Seneviratne:
A Collision of Civilisations

BBC, Pebble Mill
Birmingham, 1992

There was a big group of us, sitting in the smokers' corner, in the canteen at BBC Pebble Mill, in Birmingham. That's when I met Denise. It was my first job in television, working in the Asian Programmes Unit, which was stuck all the way up on the seventh floor at the back of the building. BBC Pebble Mill. It's one of those grey concrete sixties buildings on the edge of Birmingham, which itself was full of other grey concrete structures: the old Bull Ring shopping centre, spaghetti junction, the M5, M6, M60. *Pebble Mill at One* was recorded from here, a popular daytime programme in the nineties: two white presenters sat cosily on their sofas, beaming slightly soporific lunchtime chats into nation's living rooms. Shows like *The Archers* and *Countryfile* – those other cultural bastions of middle England – came out of here as well.

Apart from us and Afro-Caribbean Programmes Unit next door, it was a sea of white here in the canteen. But you couldn't ignore us, the young Black and Asian women – we sat there smoking, laughing, chatting loudly:

Amra
Rosemary
Nav
Ninder
Marie
Miriam
And Denise.

I'd never worked with so many young people of colour, all in one place. Everyone seemed very sure of themselves, politically aware. Maybe that's what it had taken in that era to get into the BBC, into a job in TV. Most of the young Bengali women I'd grown up with either didn't go to college or if they did, tended to become solicitors, pharmacists, dentists – stable professions that were acceptable to our anxious immigrant parents. In the Asian Programmes Unit, everyone was clever, had their point of view. Denise was really sharp: someone introduced me to her, she was sitting there with a cigarette in her hand, with her black bob, bright red lipstick, quick and funny, with a Midlands accent.

'This is Sheela, she's one of the new researchers.'
'Oh hi, I'm Denise, let's have a gab later,' she said, taking
a drag of her cigarette.

It would be months before she'd stop to have that chat. She was always rushing around, filming, going out. She was making a programme then about young Asian girls who'd run away from abusive homes and been forced into prostitution. It turned out to be a revelatory film – I had never seen anything like that at that time. The Asian Programmes Unit and the Afro-Caribbean Unit were the first of their kind – they felt like part of a wider moment when Black and Asian people seemed politically aligned – we'd all experienced the racism of the era, our parents were all born into colonial rule. And Denise was brought in to represent a new generation of people in Britain, the children from mixed-race relationships, who were now grown up and ready to make their mark.

•

That day we met was nearly thirty years ago. Soon after that, we both moved back to London and became close friends. We lived in the same block of flats in Islington, and we were in and out of each other's pockets, both working in TV, spending our Saturday nights out down the Medicine Bar on Upper Street, dancing around late at night. When we were out of work during our freelance careers, we'd often spend hours sitting in one of our flats, chatting, drinking tea, coming up with ideas for films.

We'd spend weeks, sometimes months, doing unpaid work, writing up proposals, meeting people. I remember an idea for a series we put together, pitching it to various TV companies, called *Guerrilla Girls*, about Asian female freedom fighters. One day we went off to East Ham – Denise had managed to arrange a meeting with the leaders of the Tamil Tigers, the formidable Sri Lankan rebel army. That was the first time I remember the question of our names ever coming up.

We turned up that day to a dingy, beige-carpeted terraced house, a bit like our parents' houses, with the same smell of spices and recently cooked curry. This was the Tigers' headquarters in Britain. I think they gave us tea and some bhajis, and we spoke to the women. Sitting there in their saris and cardigans, with their phials of cyanide around their necks, they talked about their lives as armed fighters, ready to die for their cause in the Sri Lankan jungle.

It was a strange day; we both still remember it decades later – it was an insight into a brutal struggle. We ended up getting a taxi back from East Ham. For some reason, a fragment of the inconsequential conversation Denise and I had with the cab driver on the way home stayed with both of us. It always made us laugh whenever we thought about it over the years. The driver was having a bit of a flirt and asked us our names. 'Sheela and Denise,' I said with my London twang. He checked us out again in his mirror as we sat there: two young Asian women, brown skin. The taxi driver refused to believe us. He thought we were making fun of him, having him on, how could we both be called such ridiculously English names, looking as we did?

•

Denise and Sheela may sound like similar anglicised names, given by immigrant parents during a certain era. Her parents, like mine, had also settled in England in the early sixties, but, actually, behind Denise's name is a very different and extraordinary story.

And unlike my name, Denise's has been adapted and changed – twice.

The first time was way back in the past, when she was a nine-year-old girl. She used to be called Vicki then. But her mum didn't like the way her Sri Lankan dad pronounced it. He always called her 'Wicky', which she hated. So the name Vicki was cast off, like a coat that never quite fitted. She became Denise to the world. But her original name remains to this day on her passport, a faint nominative imprint of the little girl she once was, a mixed-race child, growing up in Leamington Spa in the 1970s with her Sri Lankan father and her Middle Eastern mother and her three brothers, with the vicious race politics of the Midlands swirling around them.

The second time she changed her name was twenty-five years later, when she was a presenter on a popular prime-time TV series, called *Beam & DaSilva*. I remember it as I was one of the researchers on the show. It was on ITV at 7.30pm – just as viewers sat down to have their dinner. She was co-presenting, along with a man called Roger Beam. They were an investigative duo, uncovering all kinds of dodgy dealings – rogue landlords, illegal immigrants, scandals at Westminster Council.

The conceit was that Beam and DaSilva were running a sort of detective agency, a couple of private investigators – kind of like Bruce Willis and Cybill Shepherd in *Moonlighting*, I guess, or maybe *Starsky & Hutch*. There were noir-ish shots: dark streets with rain-slicked pavements, grainy undercover footage, and an opening image of Denise and her co-presenter appearing out of the shadows. People loved its entertaining tabloid style and at its peak, it was watched by around 8 million viewers.

There weren't that many Asian women on-screen in current affairs television at the time – and there she was, a young smart, streetwise brown woman, alongside a non-descript older white man, Roger Beam. The show's title, *Beam & DaSilva*, tripped off the tongue nicely. It was, of course, unthinkable that Denise should use her actual (Sri Lankan, Sinhalese) surname: Seneviratne. The executives all agreed it was far too much of a mouthful; everyone laughed at the thought of it. It's pronounced SENI-VI-RAT-NEE. Not actually that hard. But it was out of the question.

And so, Denise changed it to DaSilva. Her first name, Denise, at least sounded English, and now she had a surname with a European ring to it. It was actually a Portuguese name, her Sri Lankan grandmother's maiden name, a legacy of the island's Portuguese colonisers who'd ruled over it in the eighteenth century. Looking back, the overall effect of the name change was to make Denise seem unplaceable: exotic, but not too exotic, brown-skinned but with a name that obscured her Sri Lankan heritage and wouldn't turn off the show's mainly white viewers.

Even Denise assumed her surname would be unacceptable for ordinary British people. She'd grown up with it being ridiculed, pronounced wrongly, had to spell it out all the time. And this was the early nineties – there was no Romesh Ranganathan, no breakfast news host called Naga Munchetty, no BBC 5 Live presenter called Nihal Arthanayake saying his 'difficult' name out loud every afternoon on national radio. It was thirty years ago and seems like another world: John Major was prime minister; the IRA were still bombing mainland Britain.

Denise's two changes of name are actually part of a more complex story. One that starts somewhere in Spain or Portugal, in the late 1500s, with the expulsion of the Sephardi Jews by King Ferdinand II of Aragon and Queen Isabella of Castille; that moves on to France, then to Sri Lanka and Egypt during the most turbulent events of the twentieth century before reaching Leamington Spa, a mid-sized Regency town in the Midlands, in the 1960s.

The French-Sounding Version of Denise
Leamington, 1970s

When we met that day in the Asian Programmes Unit, all those years ago, I'm sure Denise would have introduced herself at the time with the French version of her name, pronounced more like 'Dur-neez', with a soft, low, humming 'D' at the start. She really hated the English pronunciation, a slightly high-pitched 'D'N-EECE'. A caricatured version of the name, which brings to mind someone from *EastEnders* shouting loudly. She's always hated it being pronounced the English way. And now, twenty-six years later, it's the first thing she mentions when she talks about what it was like growing up with her name.

'I LOVED the name Denise,' she says, pronouncing it with that full-on, dramatic French accent, giving it that sultriness associated with the language. As a child, she wanted to identify with her French side. It was much more desirable. She emphasises to me how she got a *much* nicer reaction from people (who would initially think she was Indian) when she told them that her name was French and that her mum was French.

People would say, 'Ooh how interesting! France, how lovely. You're European!' With this French version of the name, Denise felt she would have access to all the seventies associations that came with Frenchness: it was stylish and sexy, had good food, good wine. She loved having to explain that her mum was French and spoke French as her first language. She didn't tell anyone that her mum was actually Jewish.

•

Although Denise is mixed race, she is quite dark-skinned, and when I met her, in her twenties, she had thick black hair. She looked Asian, but that European name, and her explanation of it, immediately distanced her from the Leamington Spa Punjabi community of her 1970s childhood. She was Denise and not, for example, Gurpreet, or Kiranjit. As a child, she didn't want to identify with the Indian women she saw wearing saris and slip-on sandals, a coat over the top, walking alongside the Sikh men wearing turbans.

It was a question of survival. She watched as the Sikh children got called 'Paki', got abused for having long hair, tied in a top knot, with a handkerchief. She remembers the mockery, 'look at him, he's got a bun in the oven'. She internalised the grim everyday racism of the era and didn't want anything to do with the Asian part of herself. She loved the fact that she had an escape, that she could always let people know she was half French through the name Denise. It was a portal to an alternative identity, a symbol that she could use to transport herself to an imagined, much more glamorous existence.

When she recalls the racism, she does a perfect impression of the sneering voices of the (white) children around her. She overheard people saying they 'couldn't stand those women with their saris and those cardigans over the top'. When she repeats this back to me now, I almost feel the shame and fear, as if I'm there again, a child out with my mum. Denise's mimicry is perfect because we also became – in our heads – our own abusers. We all saw ourselves and other Asians through the eyes of the racist world around us. We also couldn't stand the women in the saris. I remember despising people who had Indian accents, my own resolutely London twang is a relic of that sense of self-hatred that I also possessed. Similarly, Denise remembers how she always hated it when Indians she met in Leamington tried to talk to her in Punjabi or Hindi. She didn't want anything to do with them. She wanted to be French, wanted to be as white as possible, and her name was a convenient route to this alternative identity.

Clementine Yohai
Alexandria, Egypt, 1920s

The real story of Denise's name starts with her mother, whose own name was Clementine, a French name that became popular in the late nineteenth century, and was common among the aristocracy, including Princess Cleméntine of Belgium, the wife of Napoleon V, and Princess Clémentine of Orléans, the youngest daughter of King Louis-Philippe I of France. It's the female version of the male name Clement – originally from the Latin 'clemens', meaning 'merciful, gentle, mild'. It appears that Clementine's name suited her – Denise has always described her mother as a gentle and sweet-natured person. However, Clementine's classically French name with its European pedigree didn't fully reflect her complex cultural heritage. Her family were, in fact, Sephardi Jews originally from the Middle East, and her surname, Yohai, is a Hebrew Jewish surname, which dates all the way back to the eighth century. The Yohais were part of a Jewish community living in the south of France up until the First World War, when they left, together with both of Clementine's grandmothers, to settle in Egypt.

•

Clementine was born in the port city of Alexandria and grew up there in the twenties and thirties. It was by all accounts a beautiful, cosmopolitan place, and Clementine spoke mainly French and some Italian at home, and lived among a mix of Greek, Spanish and Italian neighbours. Alexandria's heyday had begun in the late nineteenth century as British and French colonialism reached its height, and it became a major centre of business and transport from all over the world. It was a gateway to the East, via the Suez Canal and a medley of Europeans – Italians, Greeks, French – were attracted there by its shimmering Mediterranean coastline, its vibrant culture, and its architecture, where neo classical colonnades sat alongside villas with intricate Arab facades. It was by all accounts a beautiful cosmopolitan city, and Clementine spoke both French and Italian, and mingled with her Greek, Spanish and Italian neighbours. Although it was in Egypt, its large European population created a liberal, open atmosphere where Jewish families such as the Yohais lived side by side with Muslims, Christians and other religious communities, and people from all nationalities would often stroll along the famous beachfront, maybe stopping for tea in one of the high-ceilinged cafes along the way.

The Yohais were an educated, affluent family. Clementine's father worked for Barclays, the British-owned bank. Her two brothers, Joseph and Albert, both had a university education, while Clementine and her two sisters were sent to one of the best Catholic convents in the city, run by the Sisters of Vincent de Paul. In later life she would recount to Denise how her classmates included French, Spaniards, Italians, Greeks, Syrians as well as the children of rich Egyptians. Clementine loved school and studied there until she was twenty; she adored the Catholic nuns who taught her. The Sisters of Vincent de Paul were missionaries, and Clementine cherished their message of love and kindness: it suited her personality, and, despite her strict Jewish upbringing, she converted to Catholicism herself. Denise still remembers the huge oil painting of Jesus hanging on the wall in their house in Leamington, a gift from the nuns to their favourite pupil.

On the face of it, Clementine's conversion to Catholicism was an unusual, even strange, decision. Denise doesn't know much about her mother's precise ancestry, but the Sephardi

Jewish community were mainly descendants of Iberian Jews expelled from Spain and Portugal in the late fifteenth century, hounded out by the Catholic Church – the same institution Clementine had decided to join. They were expelled during the months and years leading up to the Spanish Inquisition in 1492 by the Catholic monarchs Ferdinand and Isabella, a brutally repressive period of European history when tens of thousands of Jews fled the region, and those who stayed were forced to convert, tortured or even burned alive at the stake.

Clementine's family escaped to France – so this is where the origins of Denise's name lie. The family lived there for centuries, but were eventually prompted to move again: leaving Europe at the beginning of the twentieth century, travelling across the Mediterranean and into North Africa; finding a home where they could live in peace, in the welcoming atmosphere of Alexandria. And so this was the context for Clementine's conversion. Perhaps Clementine wanted to throw off the shadow of persecution, escape the narrative of suffering and embrace the welcoming love of Jesus.

Clementine Yohai
Egypt, 1940

Clementine went to visit a psychic when she was a young woman. It was just for fun, but she would remember what the woman said to her for the rest of her life, and she in turn would tell her daughter, Denise. The psychic told Clementine she would be separated by water from her two beloved sisters, Adrienne (named after her grandmother) and Bertha. Clementine didn't think anything of it, but the woman's words turned out to be a precise prediction.

Clementine left school having completed her Baccalaureate – she had enjoyed studying and Denise remembers how she always loved reading French novels. But her life as a young woman from a cocooned, well-off Jewish family, living in cosmopolitan and cultured Alexandria, was about to come to an end. The Second World War broke out when she was nineteen years old and within just two years, the British would be fighting Nazi forces in North Africa. Intense fighting was going on just sixty miles east of Alexandria and, at that point in the war, Britain seemed close to defeat. There were suddenly hundreds of soldiers stationed in Egypt, defending British-controlled territory including the Suez Canal, a vital transport link to British India and the valuable oil reserves of the Middle East. Clementine who by then was looking for a job, decided to train as a typist, and started working for the British Army.

It was in those tumultuous times, as hundreds of thousands of soldiers moved around the world, that a serendipitous encounter led to this young woman, Clementine Yohai, a French-speaking, Egyptian-born, Sephardi Jew, turned Catholic, meeting Warrant Officer Seneviratne – a young Sri Lankan soldier in the British army, serving in Egypt. Clementine was already dating another soldier, but she was attracted by Henry's strength, his confidence and charisma. He wooed her for months but she kept saying no – she was worried about what her family would think of him. He was, after all, a 'black man' – a derogatory term for all dark-skinned Egyptians. Not only that, but he wasn't Jewish – he was a Sinhalese Buddhist. But Henry wasn't going to give up. That's what Clementine loved about him, says Denise, that he was hard; he would 'fight with anyone, he wouldn't let anyone trample him down.' Clementine eventually gave in and started going out with him. Her family were horrified by the relationship, but she was in love. She wrote a letter to them saying she was old enough to make her own decisions in life, and in 1949 Clementine and Henry eloped and got married.

So it's here, in the Middle East, that the biggest and deadliest war in human history brought together two young people. And it's here, in this moment, that we can trace the multiple threads, the civilisational forces, that weave their way through Denise's name.

Vijayatungage Henry Seneviratne, Denise's Father
Western Sahara Desert and Egypt, 1942

It is 1942 and Denise's father is twenty-two years old, an officer in the British Army. His first name is Vijayatungage, after his Sri Lankan father, but Henry is the name everyone knows him by. He is a 'Desert Rat' – a soldier in the British Eighth Army, the formidable force that will defeat the Nazis in the Sahara Desert, including their most famous victory, the Battle of El Alamein. Alexandria, on the verge of being taken, will be saved by the Eighth Army, and El Alamein will be a turning point in the war against Rommel. This will become one of the most mythologised events in British wartime history. The Eighth Army will be lauded by Churchill in his speeches, make newspaper headlines across the world, and celebrated on Remembrance Day for decades to come.

Churchill will even travel to the Western Desert to congratulate the Desert Rats after their heroic victory. 'In days to come,' he will tell the soldiers, 'when people ask you what you did in the Second World War, it will be enough to say: "I marched with the Eighth Army."'[1] Denise will always remember how proud her father was to have fought as a Desert Rat.

When Henry Seneviratne and his comrades arrived in North Africa, Britain's position was desperate. Egypt and the Suez Canal were under threat from Rommel's German forces. America was yet to join the war and the Nazis were overrunning continental Europe. France had fallen, and 43,000 people had been killed in Britain by air bombing offensives. The situation seemed hopeless.

In the terrible heat of the Sahara, this was a new type of war. The Eighth Army faced a vast, unfathomable wilderness: hundreds of miles of desert, wind-whipping sandstorms, cholera and dysentery rampaging through the ranks. In this brutal terrain there were very few roads, so everything depended on tanks and the men who crewed them and looked after them – men such as Denise's father, Henry, who was an expert in tank engineering: he and the 200 soldiers who served under him would be a crucial part of the victory to come. 220,000 British Commonwealth soldiers would die in the North Africa campaign – most belonged to the Eighth Army, but Henry was lucky. His technical expertise was his salvation, and he was spared from direct fighting. He would survive the war, go on to marry Clementine, have a family and live until the age of seventy-two.

•

Seneviratne is a Sinhalese Buddhist name made up of two parts: 'senevi' means 'leader in the army' and 'ratne' means 'precious stone, or gem'. Combined, it means 'precious leader of the army', a prophetic name, given the man Denise's father would eventually become, and how his years in the British Army would shape the rest of his life. But Buddhist naming traditions in Ceylon (as Sri Lanka was called until 1972) were diluted by the influence of the British, who ruled there for 133 years. The name Henry, of course, could not be more British – a potent symbol of how deep the imperial rulers penetrated the Sinhalese psyche at the time of his birth, in 1920.

Henry's brothers and sisters also had British personal names: Cyril, Benedict, Evelyn and Lanceline, another symbol of how life for families like the Seneviratnes was inextricably intertwined with British colonial rule in Ceylon. Henry's father was head butler at a magnificent colonial-era hotel called The Galle Face Hotel, in the capital, Colombo, known as the 'best hotel east of Suez'. Every day, he would have served members of the ruling British imperial elite in its luxurious surroundings, including the Governor of Ceylon, who was a regular visitor. He had a prestigious but subservient role, working within the very heart of colonial power, servicing its every need, as he and his staff changed bedsheets, polished shoes and served gin and tonics to the British rulers.

And so, having grown up hearing stories of the British elite from his father, it's not surprising that Henry ended up joining the British Army at the age of sixteen. His decision also offered an escape route out of poverty – although Henry's father worked in the privileged world of an elite British-owned hotel, his own family lived in extremely basic accommodation on the edge of Colombo. His wages were meagre, and he had to provide for his entire extended family. For his son Henry, the army was an exciting opportunity, and he would get to travel the world, representing the military might of the British Empire. During his years in the army, he was stationed all over the world, serving in Kenya, Tripoli, Beirut, Britain and Aden, his identity as British solidifying, the Seneviratne heritage drilled out of him with every salute, every march past, every call to serve King and Empire.

Denise's father was still a teenager when he joined the army, and it was during these formative years that he worked his way up through the ranks, absorbing the ideology surrounding him, following orders, risking his life and devoting himself to the institution that enforced colonial rule in his own country. It was through discipline and immense determination that he eventually became a warrant officer, one of the most senior ranks in the army. A dark-skinned Sri Lankan man, in charge of an all-white platoon, during Britain's pivotal campaign in North Africa. As he often told his children in later years, this wasn't easy. He had to fight every step of the way to assert his authority over his white subordinates. But he was strong, he didn't care what people thought of him. That's what Clementine had loved about him, that he was a fighter, and that's what Denise remembers about her father.

Henry and Clementine Seneviratne
British Army Base, Tell El Kebir
Egypt, 1955

It is a decade since the war ended and Clementine and Henry are a mixed-race couple, living in the married quarters of the British Army barracks in Tell El Kebir, just thirty miles from the Suez Canal. Henry Seneviratne is still a soldier, but also a young man worrying about how to make a living, with his elderly parents and impoverished relatives back in Ceylon constantly asking for money. Life is difficult – Clementine's Jewish family still disapproves of her marriage and she only sees her sisters occasionally. Denise's mother fills in official documents with her married name, 'Mrs Clementine Seneviratne'. The traces of her Jewish heritage are wiped from her signature. Her wedding was a Catholic ceremony, and Henry (who thinks all religions are the same) was happy to convert to Catholicism to keep his bride happy.

Clementine had gone the war blissfully ignorant of how close the Nazis had come to destroying everything she knew. Though she was working in an office at a British Army base, she didn't pay much attention to the military talk around her, and she remained largely unaware of what was really happening on the battlefields of the Sahara, just a few miles from the city where she grew up. But after the war, of course, it would have been impossible to ignore the scale of the Nazi genocide. Like millions of others, she would have seen the black-and-white Pathé newsreels, showing the torture and mass killings that had taken place in the camps of Auschwitz, Belsen, Dachau. She would have seen the newspapers' images of the massed heaps of bones that were discovered after the war, the rows of skulls, the emaciated survivors, the unimaginable horror.

She may now have thought it was best to wipe her Jewish past from every aspect of her life. And it was easy enough with her new name. She was now a white, French-speaking, Catholic young woman married to a warrant officer in the British Army. Maybe this is where the real process of denial about her Jewish identity began.

But as the fifties went on, the couple were caught up in yet more turbulent historical forces that would alter the trajectory of their lives and would have reverberations for their children in the years to come. There were tectonic shifts in the Middle East, as Britain, France and the United States fought for power and influence in the region. The creation of the new Jewish state of Israel, after the horrors of the Nazi camps, had immediately sparked a major regional conflict – the 1948 Arab–Israeli War. Hundreds of thousands of Palestinians were displaced from their homes, fuelling the Arab nationalism that was sweeping through the Middle East.

Egypt's own Jewish community was now viewed with increasing animosity – they were regarded as loyal to the country's enemy, Israel. Many years later, as an old lady, Clementine would recount to her daughter Denise what a terrifying time it was, filled with fear and violence, with chilling echoes of pre-war Nazi Germany. Denise isn't sure of the exact details, but sometime during this period, Clementine and the rest of her Jewish family were stripped of their Egyptian citizenship. She became stateless. And so, in 1949, when Clementine married Henry, a British soldier, she too became a British citizen.

But a new nationality with a new, non-Jewish name wasn't protection enough. Many Egyptians also hated the British and were desperate to get rid of them – they were regarded as the de facto colonial rulers of the country, as well as the architects behind the creation of Israel. In 1952, King Farouk of Egypt – widely seen as a puppet of the British – was ousted in a military coup led by the popular nationalist leader General Abdel Nasser. Alexandria rapidly lost its cosmopolitan European flair, and armed revolutionary gangs roamed the Jewish neighbourhoods, beating up residents; there were several killings of Jews. As a uniformed officer in the British Army, Henry, too, was in danger. It became unsafe for the couple to leave the army barracks where they lived. By now they had two young sons. Everyone was afraid, and threat surrounded the Jewish population.

In 1955 it became clear Clementine and Henry had to get out of Egypt. Many people like them were facing injury, incarceration or even death. Henry received a military transfer to Libya – the couple's escape route out of the country. Before they left, they made one last dangerous visit to see Clementine's parents, with Henry disguised as a local Arab. Clementine didn't know it at the time, but this would be the last time she would ever see her parents.

They thus escaped Egypt – just in time to avoid the chaos of the Suez Crisis in 1956. Though Egypt had been nominally independent since 1922, in reality the British, together with the French, had control of strategically important areas in the country, most significantly the Suez Canal, the vital transport link to India and the East. In 1956, just a few months after Clementine and Henry left Egypt, General Nasser national-ised the Suez Canal. In response, the British and French swiftly invade; hundreds of their citizens were immediately expelled.

In the end, Britain and France failed to prevent the canal being blocked by Egypt, and having achieved nothing, they were forced to withdraw. Meanwhile, hostility and intimida-tion towards Egyptian Jews intensified and an estimated 25,000 of them left the country during the next few years, many stripped of all their assets and in fear of their lives.

Clementine, now hundreds of miles away, watched as her world broke apart: the rest of her family were forced to flee Egypt, just as her ancestors had fled Spain and France. Being Jewish once again meant being persecuted, facing violence, possibly death. And Clementine would be separated from her beloved sisters, her brothers and her parents for the rest of her life.

•

As Denise's parents stared from the bow of the ship that would take them away from the Middle East, across the Mediterranean, towards the cold winds of Southampton docks, they set in motion the life their daughter would eventu-ally lead.

That's why Denise would wake under grey skies, would go to school with English children, be taunted her long 'unpronounceable' surname. She would be in England – not in Alexandria, nor under the hot skies of Colombo – because an empire was falling, because shafts of red and black had scorched the earth in a war that spanned the globe. And because her parents had moved through it all, like butterflies in a dust storm.

Clementine Seneviratne Names Her Daughter Denise
Leamington Spa, 1963

And so the words of the psychic came true. It's the early sixties and Clementine is separated from her sisters. Adrienne lives in Israel, Bertha in Ohio in the United States. The three sisters are divided by three different seas: the Atlantic Ocean, the Mediterranean and the English Channel. Clementine is thousands of miles away from where she grew up – she's in Leamington Spa, a cold grey English town, living in a small box-like bungalow, on a road full of identical houses, the windows like blank, unfriendly eyes.

Having escaped the turbulence of the Middle East, Clementine and Henry are now in England, the country that Henry has always held in the highest esteem. Clementine hopes it will be a place of safety, of refuge for her family; she is making a new life with her husband and three sons. But it's not easy, being Clementine Seneviratne, a French woman married to a brown-skinned man, being a mixed-race family in 1960s Britain. Leamington is nothing like the friendly, open neighbourhood that she grew up in Alexandria. No one wants to mix with them – not the English, who are their neighbours, or the Asians that live nearby. She is a housewife; her sons are at school and she is alone all day. She hears rumours of attacks on Asians; there are taunts in the street, and her two young sons are frequently beaten up and abused at school.

She is lonely and sits at the teak dining table, writing long letters to her three sisters on thin blue airmail paper. She makes her handwriting tiny so she can fit in as much as possible. Denise remembers seeing the replies arrive, the fragile blue envelopes with the 'airmail' sign printed on the front, precious bits of news that had arrived by plane and boat from Bertha and Adrienne. Clementine would show the letters to Denise when she was older, and Denise tells me, with some emotion, that her mother absolutely loved her sisters; in her heart she remained so close to them.

In the letters, Clementine shared her memories, feelings, her longing to be with her sisters again. All of this – her nostalgia for her French-speaking childhood, the light and the air of Alexandria, the taste of the pastries they used to buy from the French bakery, the old winding streets of their neighbourhood, her love for the nuns at her old Catholic convent – swirled, collided together, until it formed another atmosphere, which Clementine escaped to in her mind. And so, when her only daughter was born, Clementine gave her a name from this imaginative space of light and magic, that contained all the happiness of her Alexandrian childhood, passing on the identity that she created for herself, an identity that was French, cosmopolitan, European and Catholic.

She chose for her daughter a name from this world: Denise, a French name of the era and a popular name in sixties Britain. And her middle name, Marie, after the Virgin Mary, a sign of Clementine's deep religious devotion.

Denise adored her mother, and often spoke about her mother's childhood in Alexandria, her mother's love of her old Catholic convent. Clementine passed that on to Denise, who was baptised and grew up going to mass every week at their local Catholic church in Leamington. But there's also some sadness, and some frustration. Denise says it was always 'denial, denial, denial' in their house: her mother denying her Jewish heritage, her father denying his Sri Lankan heritage. She feels her mother was quite naïve and always told Denise to say, if asked, that she was French. But Denise also realises it was complicated. It's hard to blame Clementine: she was a young Jewish woman who had lived through the war and watched her family being forced out of Egypt. It's not surprising she gave her daughter a name that was so obviously European, a popular French name, behind which her daughter's Jewish heritage remained hidden.

·

Whatever hopes of assimiliation she may have had, Clementine would have seen that for her daughter, out and about on the streets of Leamington, it was being half-Asian – much more than her Jewish heritage – that was the problem. She was bound to have noticed the derogatory attitudes and the abuse suffered by recent dark-skinned immigrants to the area. A French name was never going to be enough to protect her child. Leamington, in the heart of the Midlands, was affected by the same vicious strain of racism that had been part of British life since the arrival of its ex-colonial subjects in the fifties and sixties.

In 1965, when Denise was two years old, a giant burning wooden cross, six feet long, was wedged into the front door of a local Indian community leader's house, on Avenue Road, Leamington – three miles from where the Seneviratnes lived. The burning cross was the signature of the Ku Klux Klan, and the victim was Dharam Singh Rooprah, a turban-wearing Sikh. A brick was also thrown through his window. Clementine might have seen the story when it appeared in the local newspaper, the *Leamington Courier*, with a headline about the KKK appearing for the first time on the streets of Britain.

Denise was growing up in the Midlands, not far from where my father lived when he arrived in this country. The same part of the country, the same atmosphere. She thinks she was about six years old, it was 1969. She remembers children calling her 'Wog' and throwing stones at her. She came back home, crying, asking her father, 'Why are they calling me Wog? What's Wog?'

•

Her French-sounding name also didn't protect her at school, especially from the taunts about her surname. Although Denise itself was perfectly acceptable to the white children around her, Seneviratne was a long, unfamiliar name that no one could pronounce. It drew the racism towards Denise, marked her clearly out as an immigrant.

'I hated Seneviratne,' she says.

She goes through the sneering comments, and it's horrible listening to it:

Son of a Rat

Son of Acne

Ratty

Having to spell it out constantly, S-E-N-E-V-I-R-A-T-N-E.

Seneviratne was so obviously foreign. Of course, it was perfectly possible to pronounce, but in that era, no one thought they should have to bother. As soon as it was uttered, it was an invitation for mockery, abuse and shame. At one point, as an adult, Denise had considered changing her name by deed poll, she hated it so much.

The Seneviratnes
Leamington Spa, 1972

It's unsurprising that Denise really didn't like her surname, that she never identified with its Buddhist Sinhalese heritage. However, the racist environment around her wasn't the only factor in how she felt about it. There was also her father's complicated sense of his own identity, a powerful legacy of his decades spent in the British Army, which he carried into civilian life with his family.

He was a disciplinarian, a rather isolated figure in seventies Leamington Spa, going to work every day in his immaculate suit and army-style polished shoes. He liked to be smart, says Denise, he always wore a hat, a trilby with a feather in it, and drove a big Austin car, which Denise used to call the Black Beauty. He worked as an office clerk at Potterton, a local boiler company. According to Denise, he felt British before anything, having fought in the British Army, having been a 'Desert Rat' and a warrant officer in charge of hundreds of white soldiers.

He told his children to ignore the racism on the streets. Better still, they should fight back, just as he had done in the army. 'He used to tell me, "When anyone calls you a Wog, tell them it is a Western Oriental Gentleman. Put your head up high and say that's what it stands for."' The term is said to have originated in the Middle East, during the colonial era, and was an insult coined by the British for local westernised Arabs, who, despite their efforts to fit in with their rulers, were still regarded as 'wily' untrustworthy foreigners.[2] As a British officer stationed in Egypt, Denise's father would no doubt have heard the term being deployed against the indigenous Egyptians. It's easy to imagine how he would have thought it was certainly nothing to do with him. He was from Sri Lanka, not the Middle East. Above all he was a member of the British armed forces. But, says Denise, the local English kids in Leamington didn't care about all this, they didn't differentiate. 'We were all brown,' she says, 'they still called us "Paki", still made fun of my surname, to them we were all the same.'

Henry never used his Sri Lankan name, Vijayatungage. He had been in the army since he was sixteen, had been trained and educated by the institution and had given his life to it. It's no surprise that he thought of himself as British. Indeed, *all* colonial subjects were legally classed as British citizens until the introduction of the Commonwealth and Immigration Act of 1962. They were allowed to come to this country without restriction and were *encouraged* to think of themselves as British, part of one giant global entity that was the British Empire. And so, when Denise's father, and thousands of others like him, migrated to Britain in the sixties – expecting a warm welcome from the Mother Country – and were faced with the racism and even violence, it was a shock. They often tried to ignore it, or to rise above it.

•

Denise's father was just a child himself when he joined the British Army. His own consciousness shaped by a centuries-old colonial ideology that existed long before that moment. The overriding message of this ideology was that to be white was to be superior, civilised, while to be Black or brown, the subject of a colonised culture, was to be lesser, substandard. Writing in the 1960s, the philosopher and critic Frantz Fanon explored the psychological effect of this process – in *Black Skin, White Masks*, he described how 'an inferiority complex' was created within the colonised mind through the 'death and burial' of local, indigenous culture. The only way to escape their 'jungle status', to elevate themselves, was to adopt the cultural standards of the mother country.[3] In other words, success for the colonised involved assimilating and becoming as culturally close to white society as possible, to its structures of power, to its value system, its language, its social codes.

Both my father and Denise's were educated when the British were still in power in the Indian subcontinent. They were young, they believed the best way to survive, and indeed to thrive, was to adopt the cultural norms of their rulers and excel at them. Denise's father became an exemplary soldier – his polished shoes, his immaculate suit, his army demeanour in their family home in Leamington, were legacies of that pride, and of that ideology. My father arrived in Britain in 1959 and was determined to become as fluent in English as possible. It was both a sign of status and a question of survival in highly adverse conditions. His English has always been grammatically perfect. He too is immensely proud of this, sometimes irritatingly so. He didn't see it as subjugation – he saw it as an accomplishment, which of course it also was.

But that colonial mindset was also damaging; both for them and for us, their immigrant children, and it left us confused about who we were. Denise inherited her surname from her father – a traditional Buddhist Sinhalese name – but she loathed it. There was no sense of pride or history to attach it to. No one seemed to see any value in either of our cultures. The imperial ideology that underpinned British rule in Sri Lanka and India had got into our heads. It created I feel, a Fanon-type split within our psyches, where we often disliked and disavowed the Asian parts of ourselves.

The Name Vicki Vanishes
Leamington, 1976

Denise thinks her father's attitude also created a complex and difficult relationship with the Asian community that lived in Leamington and the wider area. His experience serving in British colonies all over the world meant that he saw himself as very different from, and perhaps superior to, the Punjabis who lived nearby, who had only just arrived from India in the sixties and seventies. As a family, they were isolated because her father didn't feel the same as them, nor did they have any Sinhalese friends or family around them for support. And so, the Seneviratnes lived at a distance.

If you had walked down Denise's quiet suburban road in Leamington Spa in 1976, each semi-detached house would have had inside it a white family. Except for the Seneviratnes. Nearby a local fascist, Robert Relf, advertised his house as being 'For Sale – to an English family only'. Leamington Spa gained national notoriety in the summer of 1976 when his large racist sign, displaced on his front lawn, was found to be in breach of the Race Relations Act. The tabloids took up the fascist's case and presented him as a victim of 'draconian' equalities laws. The story made the national news, with many locals supporting him, and there were demonstrations across the Midlands organised by the National Front.

And so, this is where Denise was growing up – in Leamington Spa, a town both proud of its genteel British regency heritage and often violently angry at the recent influx of Asians. Not only were the Seneviratnes a mixed-race family marooned in a sea of white faces, but some of their neighbours were also virulently racist. And Denise's parents – in their different ways – continued to live in a complex state of denial about who they were.

This precariousness over identity was reflected in the confusing approach to their names within the home. The children had all been given anglicised Sinhalese first names, after their father's first name, Vijayatungage.

Victor, Victor, Victor and Vicki were the four siblings' first names.

It was, says Denise, part of her father's own attempt to carry on a Sinhalese naming tradition, where the first name is the patronymic or an ancestral name, and often has 'ge' at the end of the name. In this tradition, the second name is usually the personal name and the final name is the surname. So Denise was called Vicki, a Westernised adaptation of her father's first name, Vijayatungage, and her three brothers were all called Victor, the male version of the same name. In Sri Lanka everyone understood the system and the second, personal name would be the one most often used in daily life. But here in England, with the patronymic at the start, people assumed these *were* the children's names.

'It was silly to all have the same name,' says Denise. She still laughs at the absurdity of it.

According to Denise, no one really knew what it was about; the tradition wasn't reinforced by any Sinhalese community around them, nor was there any attempt to impart the meaning behind it, or to place it within the context of their family history. There was, of course, no family to explain things anyway – Denise never met her Seneviratne grandparents or any of her aunts and uncles in Sri Lanka. And ultimately, when the siblings did all drop their first names, their father, Henry, showed no great interest in continuing to assert his Sinhalese heritage.

And so, my friend became Denise Seneviratne, and I never knew her as Vicki. But she still thinks about that original name, the name given to her by her father, the name he used to call her when she was a little girl. It's the first thing she mentions when we start talking about her name, all these years later.

•

The shedding of Vicki, her dislike of Seneviratne, were part of growing up where she did, at a particular point in Britain's history. And Denise's feelings and experiences were, in many ways, connected to what Liz and I were experiencing at the same time, as young children. In Leamington, when Denise was thirteen, in September 1976, an elderly Asian woman died after young men poured petrol over her and set fire to her sari. (The *Coventry Journal* reported that there was no racial motive to this.)

And this was part of a much wider pattern of horrific attacks. During the five years between 1976 and 1981, across Britain, thirty-one Asian and Black people were murdered.

They included:

Gurdip Singh Chaggar, aged eighteen, a student, stabbed to death in Southall.

Altab Ali, a Bangladeshi garment worker, murdered in a park in Whitechapel while walking home.

Michael Ferreira, murdered in Hackney.

Ishaque Ali, another Bangladeshi textile worker, killed walking in the street in Clapton, Hackney, with his nephew.

Akhtar Ali Baig, killed in Newham.

Mohammad Arif and Malcolm Chambers, murdered in Swindon.

Sewa Singh Sunder, murdered in Windsor.

Famous Mgutshini, stabbed to death outside Liverpool Street Station.

Fenton Ogbogbo, murdered in south London.

A disabled Sikh woman burnt to death in Leeds after an arson attack on her home.

A young boy stabbed to death after casually flicking an apple core at a passing driver.

Parveen Khan and her three children burnt to death after petrol was poured through their letterbox and set alight, in Walthamstow.

Temples, gurdwaras, community centres, shops were all targets for attack and vandalism: fascist graffiti was every-where, bricks were thrown through windows, petrol-soaked rags pushed through letterboxes, violence, arson and murder were commonplace, and police often denied that there was a racial motive for these attacks.[4]

It all explains why, as children, we grew up with a sense of an unnameable threat. It was a part of everyday life. Denise remembers being chased down the road by some youths, being called a 'black bitch', being called a 'Paki' and having things thrown at her. She heard about an Asian boy being stabbed for going out with a white girl and remembers the National Front handing out leaflets outside her secondary school. We didn't know then how much we were traumatised by all this hatred, weakened by it, in our responses to the world and to aspects of ourselves.

We all felt it, in different ways, me, Denise, Liz.

A Fightback
Leamington Spa, 1980

But Denise's story has a different trajectory to mine and Liz's, maybe because she was a bit older, maybe because she had to be tougher than us. Maybe because, like her father, she was a fighter. She says she ended up going round with hard girls for protection, skinhead girls, who no one would mess with. Denise remembers how the teenagers she knew at that time, in the late seventies, in Leamington and Coventry, had all grown up together, Blacks, whites and Asians, all listening to the same music: reggae, ska, Motown. She was going out all the time, and knew everyone. She remembers how everyone used to go to a little place called the Buttery Bar on a Friday night, a disco adjoining a local hotel, how they all hung round in a huge, racially mixed group. 'Tipsy, Trevor, me and a girl called Parveen,' she tells me. Denise was a Mod – in her tiny tartan mini skirt, her sixties-style bob and a green parka – and there were skinheads there too, but not the vicious ones that wanted to beat her up. She looked great, loved the music and the

fashion, and people liked being around her; she was confident, she was fun, she liked a dance.

.

The Midlands, Leamington, Warwick, Coventry. Little edge-
of-town places like Cubbington and Black Down. Places that
were being destroyed by Thatcherism, factories closing down
and high unemployment, fuelling the far right. But among
teenagers like Denise and her friends, Black and white music
had started to fuse, with an underlying political, anti-racist
message. It was cool to be mixed race and there was suddenly
a strength through the music and the fashion of the time.
Without being particularly aware of it, Denise was suddenly
in the epicentre of one of this country's most significant
cultural moments: the birth of two-tone – where Black and
white musicians, who'd grown up in this country, took
Jamaican ska, punk and soul and turned it into a new musical
form and a movement of its own.

Just a few miles up the road in Coventry, a multiracial group
of teenagers started a band and called it The Specials. Over
the next two years or so, 'Gangsters', 'A Message to You,
Rudy', 'Too Much Too Young', 'Rat Race', 'Stereotype', 'Do
Nothing', 'Ghost Town' would all hit the Top 10. Terry Hall,
the lead singer, was out and about in Leamington; Pauline
Black, the mixed-race lead singer of the band The Selecter,
often played gigs in the town. Racially mixed groups of musicians, Black guys wearing pork pie hats, and skinheads got up
on stage and stuck two fingers up to Margaret Thatcher and
to the far right, a defiant show of racial unity.

It was around this time Denise started going out with Mark,
an anti-racist, white skinhead. She and Mark were often
abused on the streets; there was violence, fights with other,

far-right skinheads, known locally as the Anti Paki League. She remembers going off on a Saturday morning to Nottingham one time, to demonstrate with the Anti-Nazi League against the National Front: she remembers arriving there and bricks being thrown at their coach, seeing hundreds of young men goosestepping, carrying flags with swastikas. It was terrifying.

•

Names, their meaning and how they were received by the world were important at this time. Pauline Black, the lead singer of The Selecter, had in fact changed her surname from Vickers to Black, in response to the racism of her own adoptive English family. For Denise, her own surname, signifying her mixed-race background, was no longer a shameful burden. The people she hung round with were often of colour and there was no question of being mocked and abused for for being called Seneviratne. They were all part of the same struggle. And anyway, it was all about going out, dancing, clothes, Ben Sherman shirts, suede heads, Black kids with pork pie hats, going to blues parties where they'd dance to reggae, soul and ska.

•

Denise was part of a fightback. It wasn't always overtly political, but something was happening at the level of the ordinary. Young people, Black, white, sometimes Asian, sometimes mixed race, people like Denise, were suddenly finding a tribe they could identify with. It wasn't always like this with two-tone – once the music spread to other parts of the country, its audience was different. As I said, in west London, where I lived, it was the music of the racist skinheads I'd grown up with, with their Harrington jackets, their DM boots, beating up the Asians in Southall. But its origins in the Midlands were undeniably idealistic, and for Denise, being in the middle of it was life-changing. Before her teenage years she feels she had no idea who she identified with, she just didn't want to be associated in her mind with 'those Pakis'. Now she started to feel a sense of strength. People were interested in where she was from, it was good to be different, it was fine to say her father was from Sri Lanka, to explain that her surname was Seneviratne.

Manchester Polytechnic, 1985

Identity is a funny thing, a slippery, mutating entity, that we're constantly searching for. Music, alternative culture, went on offering more ways to create a new one. By the mid eighties, as she reached adulthood, it was mainly Black culture that Denise was identifying with. She discovered hip hop, loved dancing to Public Enemy, A Tribe Called Quest, went to blues parties. And it was through music, clubs and going out that, as a young adult, she found people of colour to hang out with. It was in the political message underlying hip hop and reggae, in the music of soul singers like Aretha Franklin, Nina Simone and Stevie Wonder – forged during the civil rights era – that a lot of Asians, like Denise, like me, found a place where we could *be*, something we could partly identify with.

She reels off names of some of the clubs she went to in Manchester:

PSV, the Reno, the Gallery, the Hacienda

Outside the white spaces of Manchester college life. Music, dancing, drugs, getting dressed, a bottle of wine before going out. Cigarette in hand, a long dress, with the back cut down to her waist. Dancing until five in the morning.

I ask her to describe PSV, and she says it was a working men's club in Hume, a rough part of the city, three storeys high, where you couldn't see for all the dope smoke. She remembers lots of rastas, hard boys, students and the music – reggae, soul. She went there for the music, had brilliant nights out.

In these spaces was a freedom. I remember it too. Dancing – music – was an identity. We could be ourselves, Sheela Banerjee, Denise Seneviratne, it was absolutely fine. It was better than fine: as young Asian women, we were confident, walking around with a strong sense of who we were.

BBC Asian and Afro Caribbean Programmes Unit Pebble Mill, Birmingham, 1991

Denise describes being in the Asian Programmes Unit, all those years ago at BBC Pebble Mill, as a time of real change, an epiphany, almost. Talking to Sri Lankan political activists, working alongside Oxford-educated Urdu speakers, working-class Punjabis from Southall, meeting other mixed-race people – of Caribbean, Asian, Sri Lankan heritage – day in, day out. She says, 'being there helped me to develop my understanding of racism – I could politicise it in a way that wasn't just about fighting skinheads, dancing and music.' And she realised that 'we were all isolated; it didn't matter whether you were mixed race, Black, or in a very white environment, like Oxford. We all had our crosses to bear. It transpired we *all* felt we didn't fit in anywhere.'

And for the first time in her life, Denise visited Sri Lanka. She was sent there to make a TV series about the civil war between the Tamils and the Sinhalese, a brutal conflict rooted in the old colonial policies of divide and rule. That's where she first met the leaders of the Tamil Tigers, who agreed to talk to her, despite her surname, Seneviratne, a name which immediately signalled her Sinhalese heritage, a name from the enemy side. And as she started travelling around the capital, Colombo, Seneviratne was, for the first time in her life, a common name, unremarkable; just as Banerjee was for me when I arrived in India. And Vicki, her first name, hovered like a ghost from the past, making its presence felt, speaking of relatives long gone, of a naming system long abandoned. She tried to find her father's family, her aunts and uncles: Cyril, Benedict, Evelyn and Lanceline. But they had all died. She visited the Galle Face Hotel, sat at its long, glamorous bar, saw where her Seneviratne grandfather had once worked, serving drinks to all those colonial gentlemen. And she saw, as she carried out her research, the deadly legacy of their rule, a brutal war splitting Sri Lanka in two: the Sinhalese and the Tamil populations, fractured forever. 'It was massive,' she says, 'to go there for that long, to find my roots. It was kind of seminal, you know.'

Denise Seneviratne
London, 2023

I've known Denise for so long now – we've been through our twenties, thirties, forties and now our fifties together. She can always make a party out of any situation, get chatting to absolutely anyone. We still laugh about those days when we were unemployed TV producers sitting around in our flats. We didn't always feel like coming up with ideas or looking for jobs – sometimes we'd just end up drinking sherry in the afternoon, like a couple of old ladies.

She's also one of the brightest people I know, but at one point she nearly gave up trying to make films, tired of the elitism and racism of the industry we were in. She's now a senior figure at a major channel, a commissioning editor, one of very few working-class brown women who've made it in British TV. It's taken a huge amount to get there, incredible tenacity. That's part of the fight that she's always had.

•

We were on the phone the other day, as I was walking to the local swimming pool, and we were chatting a bit more about her childhood, about her father. She surprised me by saying he was actually quite sweet once he was older, he'd stopped being such a disciplinarian, shouting at his children. He eventually abandoned the Catholicism he had adopted as a young man to marry her mother – towards the end of his life, she says, he went back to being a Buddhist. Her parents, she says, loved spending time together; they lived in their little two-bedroom flat in Leamington and used to go out for day trips together to places like Stratford-upon-Avon. 'He really loved her,' Denise says. After all the stories she told me about her name, about race, colonialism, her parents' flight from Egypt, it turns out her mixed-race name was, ultimately, like many such stories, about love.

Hugh St Paul Whyte: Three Different Names at Three Different Times

It's cold, really blowy, it's summer by the seaside in Britain. It's 2021 and I'm in Whitby. It's great – the sea is ice cold, with huge waves, but we've been in for a swim and there's an incredible sandy beach overlooked by dramatic cliffs. There are hordes of (British) tourists – it's just a few months after lockdown and the English coast is rammed. Whitby has the ruins of a magnificent abbey perched on one of those clifftops, and it's here that Bram Stoker's Dracula ended up after escaping from Transylvania – as an Eastern European, he's possibly the most famous foreigner ever to have visited the town. This weekend, as well as the hordes of families strolling around, clutching their ice-creams, hundreds of pale-faced goths have descended on Whitby for an annual music festival. There's a jolly atmosphere, there's a kind of fizz and crackle of a British bank holiday: the beeps and buzzes of the fruit machines, the colours of the fairground rides; I keep smelling the sharp smell of warm vinegar coming off fish and chips, cooked in one of the many chippys that I go past on the seafront. We're all here for a week's holiday – I'm with one of my best friends, Sharon, and her family, including her brother-in-law, Hugo. There aren't many people of colour among the crowds, apart from me and Hugo. I notice a few Asian Muslim families perched on their blankets, spreading out their home-made food, their children playing on the sand.

Hugo joins us when he can – he's really busy, with Zoom meetings during the day; he's a program manager with a big software company in Germany. We pop round to where he and his family are staying and have a cream tea, in the middle of the Yorkshire countryside. It's a soft yellow brick cottage overlooking the hills of North Yorkshire. We've traipsed through beautiful little glens and woods to get there. It makes me think of what he's told me about his childhood, growing up in the Jamaican countryside as a little boy. It was a different time then, and it was the start of the story of Hugo's name. In fact, it's the story of his *three* different names, each with its own complex personal resonances.

Junior
Potois, Jamaica, 1969

'Junior!'

'Come over here and give me a hand with the floor,' shouts Hugo's great grandmother, Betsy. She's 107 years old. She does everything. Despite her immense age she was 'country strong', remembers Hugo. But her knees were painful so she couldn't bend down and needed help sweeping the floor.

That was in the 1960s, when Hugo was a child. When everyone called him Junior. He's sixty-two, and now it's just his brothers and sisters who refer to him by that name. And when they do, Hugo is taken straight back to the person he was as a little boy. Its effect as immediate as a Proustian madeleine, summoning the sights, the sounds, the people, the feelings from over fifty years ago. It's almost as if he can touch the red soil of his great grandmother's land in Jamaica, in the hills outside Montego Bay. He remembers his childhood as a magical time, filled with a sense of joy and abundance. His grandmother grew custard apples, mango, sugar cane, pineapples, yams. The family kept pigs, goats and chickens. Everything they ate – apart from fish – came from their own land.

Every day, he walked several miles to school. He knew everyone, and everyone knew him, the little boy called Junior. It was pure fun and bliss, Hugo tells me. 'We'd go from one house to the next, picking up friends along the way, and suddenly there would be thirty kids, joining from all over the place.' They'd all walk to school together, going past rivers, seeing cows, sheep, walking past huge mango trees. They had a game of throwing stones to make the fruit fall from the trees. Towards the end of the mango season, Hugo recalls, there were always a few mangoes left so high up that they became trophies for anyone who could bring one down with a good throw.

•

Junior was his pet name, part of a naming tradition followed by most Jamaicans. A name filled with fun, love, affection. In Jamaica, pet names are also known as 'home' or 'yard', or 'duppy' names. 'Duppy' is a word of African origin, meaning 'spirit' or 'ghost', part of a folklore tradition dating back to a time of pre-slavery. Its origins lie in the Ga language, spoken by the Ashanti in Ghana, and gestures towards the African cultural heritage of most Jamaicans. Usually, those close to you will call you by your pet name and its use symbolises, like a Bengali *dak naam*, the emotional bonds that you share. But it can also take on a wider currency in Jamaica – nearly everyone in your village or town might know you solely by this name, not just close friends and relatives. A pet name can be based on physical appearance ('biggie', 'fatty', 'sprat'); on personal traits ('sly'); on preferences ('coke', 'sugar'); or, as in Hugo's case, on family relationships. The name Junior arose out of his status as the youngest boy in his family, so it carries for him a deep emotional charge.

Within this Edenic world, skin colour wasn't an issue for Hugo – everyone around him was Black. But race, colonialism, slavery lay like a snake in the background of all their lives. His great grandmother, Betsy, a pale-skinned woman, unusually for most people on the island, had inherited a large plot of land from her father. Hugo doesn't know how his family came by this land in the first place, but often there was a dark side to gifts such as these. They were sometimes the result of sexual relationships – possibly coercive or violent – between white plantation owners or overseers and the enslaved women who worked for them. Jamaica was a country formed by the dark history of slavery and by three hundred years of British coloional rule. It only gained its independence in 1962, one year after Hugo was born. Unknown to ten-year-old Junior, questions of whiteness surrounded his name, the power and politics of race suffusing its past and present, woven deeply into its syllables, and propelling the transformations it would undergo in the future.

•

Junior's registered name was Hugh St Paul Whyte. As a little boy, barely anyone used it, but it was there, on all his documentation. His aunts all commented on what a beautiful name it was. It lay ready and waiting for when Junior would become an adult and make his way in life, enter the realm of the official world, which was a much more serious affair, requiring a name with weight.

Hugh: an archaic name, popular in Britain around the late nineteenth century, with echoes of a previous generation of middle- and upper-class Englishmen. Patrician, lordly. Statesmanlike. A gilt-framed picture on a wall of a grand personage comes to mind. An Englishman with big sideburns. A name from another world, another time. It is a name with a lineage that is Western, that is white. It was originally popular among the medieval French aristocracy, who introduced it to Britain during the Norman conquest of 1066. The English version comes from the Old French personal name *Hu(gh)e*, and this in turn can be traced to German roots: it's the short form of various Germanic compound names beginning with the first element *hug* meaning 'heart', 'mind', or 'spirit'.

It was a name chosen in 1961, the year Hugo was born, by his mother, Winifred Whyte, a young Jamaican woman living in a country that was still ruled by the British. Sir Hugh Mackintosh Foot (Baron Caradon) had until recently been the hugely popular colonial governor – he was the brother of Michael (the former leader of the British Labour Party) and father of Paul (the prominent British socialist). Naming baby boys after colonial governors and political and military leaders was a common practice in that era among parents throughout the Caribbean. Winifred had already named one of her sons Winston. That these kinds of names, Hugh, Winston, Lloyd (after the former Prime Minister David Lloyd George) – upper class, English – were so popular among Jamaicans indicates how deep the connections – both emotional and cultural – between Britain and Jamaica were.

Hugo's middle name, St Paul, reflected Hugo's parents' religiosity. Hugo's mother, Winifred, was a devout Christian – a Baptist – and a regular churchgoer, like most of the people around her. Paul was a popular name for baby boys at the time, and use of the prefix 'St' was still a common practice on the island in the sixties. In Britain, however, it was rarely used. The presence of those two letters, 'St', in Hugo's name hinted, once more, at a bygone era, and was another aspect of his official name that pointed to the legacy and influence of British aristocratic classes.

•

Whiteness – and its power and privilege – was not just embedded in the history of his first and middles names; it was there most strikingly in Hugo's surname.

Hugo tells me he thinks Whyte was originally a Scottish surname, and a quick search online reveals he's right. The Whytes were among a group of distinguished noble families from Scotland, with their own family crest. The name Whyte is derived from the Old English word *hwit*, meaning 'white', and would have been attributed to a pale or fair-haired person first used as a nickname and then a surname. (Similarly, the Scottish surname Campbell is from a Gaelic nickname *cam beul*, meaning 'wry or crooked mouth'.) The aristocratic lineage of the name Whyte means there are records, archives, family crests. It has a history. It dates back to the medieval era when a Scottish nobleman called *Uuiatett Hwite* first appears in archival documents. He was recorded as being present when his village, in the modern region of Berwickshire, was granted a Royal Charter during a visit by King Eadgar of Scotland sometime around the twelfth century.[1]

But the fact that Hugo – someone of African Caribbean

heritage, born in 1961, on the island of Jamaica – bears the Scottish surname Whyte tells a very different naming story to this one of noblemen, crests and archives. It speaks of the global slave trade – with Britain at the very heart of it. Hugo's ancestors would have been African: kidnapped, tortured and trafficked to the Caribbean by British slave traders sometime in the eighteenth century. The Whytes were part of a cohort of slave owners, overseers and slave bookkeepers – a generation who travelled from Scotland and extracted wealth from Jamaica and its enslaved population.

Hugo's forebears in turn were the captured people who had this surname forced upon them, or may have adopted it themselves, after emancipation. Ultimately, it was a surname that arose out of a brutal system of economic, sexual and physical exploitation. Contained in the surname Whyte is the origin story of slavery and the foundations it laid for the subsequent power and wealth of the British Empire.

The presence of this surname among Jamaica's Black population is about the relationship between two countries: Britain and Jamaica, darkly intertwined in a grotesquely uneven dance of racial and economic power. Britain was the biggest slave trading nation in the Atlantic world during the eighteenth century and its traders sent nearly a million captive Africans to Jamaica between 1655 and 1805. The population of enslaved people in Jamaica was much lower – just over three hundred thousand – as thousands of Africans died due to the particularly horrific conditions, much worse even than those endured by enslaved captives taken to the United States.[2] Those who survived, having been trafficked and traded, were used to grow sugar and coffee – the main crops of the British slave-owning class.

The Scottish origins of the surname Whyte point to the special colonial role of Scots. Scotland and its merchants were huge beneficiaries of this trade in trafficked human beings. So much so that in just a few decades at the turn of the eighteenth century, the Scottish economy grew from one of the weakest in Europe to one of the most powerful. The vast warehouses where Jamaican sugar was once stored are still standing in the Scottish town of Greenock, once a major port and shipbuilding centre. Sugar production began in Greenock in 1765 and at its peak there were fourteen huge refineries exporting sugar from plantations in Jamaica to the rest of the world, the most successful of which eventually became Tate & Lyle. And to this day, across Glasgow are numerous statues and street names that honour the merchants who participated in the slave economy.

Hugo's Whyte forefathers did not, however, benefit from any of this wealth and are not memorialised in the same way. There are no monuments with their names engraved beneath them, and their original African names are unrecorded. Most captive people brought to Jamaica were from West Africa, a region where names and naming ceremonies were a hugely important part of the culture. Though the enslaved community often continued to use these names among themselves, none of them appear in Jamaican slave lists. Instead, white plantation owners set about systematically renaming their slaves, part of the process whereby Africans became their property, along with their livestock and land.[3] That missing African name *is* in many senses the story – its absence symbolic of all that was stolen from the Africans who eventually became the Whytes: their family, tribe, culture, history, political life and, most importantly, their freedom.

•

And so those enslaved Jamaicans who bore the name Whyte have left little historical trace. When I search for the Jamaican name Whyte, the most frequent names that come up are James Whyte and Andrew Whyte – two of the most celebrated Whytes in Jamaica and among the island's wealthiest slave owners. James Whyte was born in Scotland and acquired a small sugar plantation in Jamaica in 1811. He started off with just twelve enslaved people, but after the Napoleonic Wars demand for Jamaican sugar and coffee increased and Whyte began to get very rich. He acquired more slaves, and soon became an important figure in Jamaican slave-owning society and part of the island's ruling elite, so much so that he has an entry in *The Dictionary of Canadian Biography*. This is the historical legacy of the surname Whyte in Jamaica; these are the names we still get to see.

After running a highly successful sugar plantation, James Whyte's fortunes dipped and he emigrated to Canada. His biographical entry notes: 'The plantation economy was suffering from low prices, an overpopulation of slaves and a growing sense of insecurity, heightened by the abolition movement in Great Britain and the slave rebellion of 1831.' The entry presents itself as an impartial, neutral account; James Whyte is described in approving tones as a successful and notable figure, first in Jamaica and then in Canada. The mention of the 'slave rebellion' seems almost incidental – its main purpose in this account is to provide context for Whyte's life story and explain his eventual departure from Jamaica. But this 'slave rebellion of 1831' was the hugely significant Baptist war, an eleven-day uprising during which 60,000 of Jamaica's 300,000 enslaved people revolted against their white masters, the largest slave uprising in the British Caribbean. It was, in fact, part of a wave of major slave uprisings across the Caribbean, including the Haitian defeat of the French government by an 80,000-strong slave revolt.

None of these tumultuous events is found in the entry for James Whyte, and *The Dictionary of Canadian Biography*, which is still online today, goes on to note that 'the outlawing of slavery in 1834 by the British parliament, with compensation to the owners, afforded Whyte an opportunity to liquidate his assets and leave the colony.' Again, he is viewed as an upright and enterprising figure, taking advantage of his 'opportunities'. There is no hint of criticism of a man who became rich from the captive labour of other human beings, and of a system that 'compensated' his loss of income after the abolition of slavery in Jamaica. Whyte may also have been the surname of Black Jamaicans who were part of the slave rebellions on the island, but their histories are once more unrecorded, their stories lost.

Hugh St Paul Whyte
Walsall, England, 1971

It is now over three hundred years since the first British slave ships, carrying their cargo of trafficked human beings, arrived in Jamaica. It is 1971 and one of the millions of their descendants, Hugo, has just arrived at Heathrow Airport. The first time he has set foot in the United Kingdom. He still thinks of himself as Junior as he stands in front of the British immigration officer who looks at his passport. A ten-year-old boy, dressed in a new green suit, specially made for this momentous journey by a local tailor.

As the immigration officer waved him through, Hugo's life was about to change.

And so was his name.

Junior landed in Britain on an overcast autumnal day and joined his parents, Basil and Winifred, and the rest of his brothers and sisters, whom he'd not seen for six years. His family didn't have much money and they lived in a small house in Glebe Street, opposite the General Hospital in Walsall. Junior had never seen a hospital before, and he remembers waking up on his first morning in this country and seeing this huge, bustling building, right outside his window. It was a sight that, even now, he remembers with fondness.

•

Walsall General Hospital, like hundreds of others in this country, would have been filled with other recent arrivals from the Caribbean: nurses, porters and orderlies. In 1962, just two years before he began his virulent agitation against immigrants, Enoch Powell, then a Conservative minister for health, had toured the Caribbean, begging people to come and work in Britain. They would, he pleaded, be helping the Mother Country, help build it out of the ruins of war, help create the newly formed British National Health Service. Jamaicans were also encouraged by the British to come and fill vacancies in other sectors, such as manu-facturing, transport and hospitality.

And so, Hugo's parents arrived on a great tide of migration that had begun in the forties and early fifties. They were part of the Windrush Generation: tens of thousands of hopeful people who came from Jamaica to work in this country. The first arriv-als were 492 Jamaicans on board the Empire Windrush, which landed at Tilbury Docks in June 1948. The young men, who are photographed smartly dressed, with suits and trilby hats, were welcomed with open arms, with a national newspaper headline proclaiming: 'Five Hundred Pairs of Willing Hands'.[4]

Hugo's Uncle Martel was the first in the family to be lured over with promises of good jobs and a warm welcome. Jamaica had become independent in 1962, but it was an impoverished country after hundreds of years of slavery and colonial rule. More recently, in 1951, a hurricane had ripped through the island destroying houses and infrastructure, which meant by the early sixties, the newly independent Jamaica and its population were on their knees. And so the Whyte family joined the tens of thousands of young Jamaicans who headed to Britain in search of a better life. Many of them settled in the Midlands, along with other communities from former colonies, in places like Birmingham, Walsall and Coventry, working in the steel and ironworks and other heavy industries.

•

But by the time Hugo arrived here, in the early seventies, Enoch Powell had changed his tune. As I've discussed in previous chapters, he now wanted foreigners out of Britain. His campaigning had been having an effect. Hugo's arrival also coincided with the 1971 Immigration Act, created, it seemed, with the ultimate purpose of keeping people of colour out of Britain. It was the culmination of several pieces of government legislation; only those with a parent or grandparent born in this country were now allowed in, meaning that, in the majority of cases, only those immigrants with white skin were permitted to settle in Britain.[5]

•

Junior, a little Jamaican boy, just arrived from the ex-colonies, was precisely the type of person that newly passed immigration legislation was designed to exclude. Junior was also the type of person that Enoch Powell had been warning the British population about in recent years. Powell had been doing the rounds in the very place that Hugo came to live. He had given a speech at Walsall Town Hall in February 1968, in which minority children were singled out for attack. He painted the picture of a lone white girl, swamped by their threatening presence:

> *Only this week a colleague of mine in the House of Commons was dumbfounded when I told him of a constituent whose little daughter was now the only white child in her class at school.*[6]

And later that year, in his 'Rivers of Blood' speech, Powell reserved his most toxic language to specifically describe children of West Indian immigrants. Children like Hugo. They were, according to Powell, 'wide-grinning piccaninnies', a highly charged racial slur, commonly used in the United States to refer to the children of enslaved African Americans. It was, writes the historian and broadcaster Olusoga, a 'precisely calibrated attack on the younger generation', the children of immigrants – who Powell argued could never become 'Englishmen', even if they were born and raised in this country. They would, he warned, 'gain the whip hand' and eventually overpower the native-born, white population.[7]

•

The moment he arrived from Jamaica, Hugo stepped into this particular current of Britain's race history. He arrived in this country as viciously racist language – categorising Black people as savage, brutish, and intrinsically inferior – was being used daily in political and media discourse. The infamous Smethwick general election campaign was just eight miles away from Walsall. It was, as I've said earlier, won by a Conservative candidate whose central slogan was 'If you want a n****r for a neighbour, vote Labour'. These ideas, the toxic language, were not just flowing around nationally – in the newspapers, on TV – but right next to where Hugo lived.

•

The Whytes had settled in Goscote, a deprived area on the outskirts of Walsall. Despite its poverty, Hugo has good memories of the place: there was a river running through it, lots of nearby fields to play in with his brothers and sisters and the neighbours were in fact very friendly. His father had a job as a bricklayer in the Wednesbury Steelworks – a large factory employing hundreds of people. Basil Whyte was laying bricks for the tunnels into which the molten steel was poured, a backbreaking and low-paid job. But Hugo's mother, Winifred, was partially deaf – seventy per cent – and found it very difficult to get work. She was, Hugo remembers, quite well educated, but her hearing meant her options were limited. She tried working in the hospitality industry, and was a chambermaid for a while, but was forced out by the cruel behaviour of people around her. She didn't say much about this to her children, including Hugo, apart from the fact that she came into contact with the 'worst kinds of people'.

•

Within the Whyte household, to his brothers and sisters, Hugo was still known by his pet name, Junior. But he had to grow up quickly and exist within a new reality: 'Junior' had to go, and for the outside world he had to use, for the first time, his official name. Whenever his mother introduced him to anyone, filled in any forms, his name was now Hugh Whyte.

Hugh Whyte
Forest Comprehensive, Walsall, 1971

At the age of eleven Hugo started secondary school, just a short walk from where he lived. It was called Forest Comprehensive. The school had acquired a new name at the same time as Hugo did, having formerly been W.R. Wheway School for many years. But the school's new name didn't cover up its reputation as one of the roughest, most underachieving schools in the area. It had been built in the 1950s to serve the new council housing estates that surrounded it: Blakenhall Heath, Goscote (where Hugo lived), Harden and Coalpool, some of the poorest areas in Walsall. An ITV documentary in which the school featured depicted violent bullying, money extraction and extreme levels of poverty. 'It was,' says Hugo, '*very very* deprived.'

•

As he started at Forest Comprehensive, Junior was now Hugh to his classmates. There were no other Hughs in his year. It was an old-fashioned name, even among the English. But Hugo didn't think anything of it – this was just his more formal name that was now being used, as he had always expected it would be.

•

'What's your name?'

The new boy was asked and he replied, with his Jamaican accent:

'Hugh Whyte.'

It was immediately a problem. As is often common with Jamaican English, Hugo didn't pronounce the 'H' strongly at the beginning of his name. So 'Hugh' was easily turned by the other children into 'You'. 'When the two names were put together,' explains Hugo, '"Hugh Whyte" suddenly became "You White". And you know, people say it quickly and it's like "Are You White?"'

That was the joke. '"Are you white?" And clearly,' he says, 'I'm not.'

Hugo starts laughing when he tells me this. He can see the funny side of it. But at the same time, he didn't particularly like it. Partly, he thinks it was just one of those things, kids having fun. 'But,' he says, 'I never liked saying that word, "Hugh", and I still don't.'

'I never use that word.'

•

Hugo remembers National Front signs scrawled on the walls outside his school, and a general air of 'nastiness and menace' that was common to a lot of schools in that era. Cut lips, bruises and beatings were normal. The problems in the school, he thinks, were also very much connected to class. Poverty, unemployment, poor housing all fed into it. 'It wasn't even racism,' Hugo says, 'it was violence.'

I can still hear the traces of Hugo's Jamaican accent in his voice today when we talk about the story of his name. In Jamaica this was how everyone spoke, it wasn't an issue. But once he came to this country, his name became, overnight, he says, 'a thing of fun' – and much worse too. What can a bunch of teenagers, brought up in a society saturated with deprivation and violence, do to a name like that? They can do a lot.

Hugo's name became a lightning rod, drawing towards it the racism in the classrooms, absorbed in turn from the world outside the school gates. Every time Hugo spoke his name – with a cadence and musicality that were obviously foreign – he was stepping unknowingly into poisoned territory. This was a society built on a linguistic code that had its roots in imperialism and slavery; it fused into a strict hierarchy of language that persists in Britain, even today. At the top of this hierarchy was British Received Pronunciation – RP – the speaking style of the English upper classes, those who went to public schools and to elite universities such as Oxford and Cambridge. Pronounced with this accent, the name Hugh began with a whispery, over-enunciated 'H', its breathy syllables a marker of prestige and status. On the other hand, the English of the colonies – such as Jamaican English – was openly derided, especially in the seventies, and treated with general contempt. A noted educational campaigner of the time, Viv Edwards, described in her research how Jamaican patois was regarded as 'sloppy' or as 'jungle talk' and the children who spoke it were judged to be intellectually inferior.[8]

I know and recognise this attitude, having grown up seeing my parents and my community ridiculed for their Indian accents. At the same time, I noticed that other foreign accents – American, Australian, French and Italian – were admired, even emulated. These were, as it happens, white speakers of the English language.

There was, of course, nothing of note, nothing funny, about the name Hugh Whyte in Jamaica – as I said, relatives often commented on how beautiful the name sounded. Now, at the age of sixty-two, Hugo reflects that his parents gave him the name in innocence, but it ended up in a 'quagmire of race and immigration'. Language, race and class came together in a toxic combination, weaving their way through the school, affecting how Hugo was treated and creating a discomfort within him every time he uttered his own name.

•

However, the story of Hugo's name is not just about the racism of the time, it's about *his* reaction to it, how he positioned himself in relation to it, to survive, and how he moved through life afterwards. As I said, Hugo doesn't tell the story of his name with any bitterness; in fact when I start speaking to him, he tells it with a storyteller's gift for humour, making fun of both himself and the world in which he suddenly found himself. Of course, it was funny, he was an innocent abroad, a Black boy in a viciously racist society, with a name that embodied white-ness. Plenty of times when he's telling me about it, he starts laughing himself. He says there's no point in dwelling on it.

So sometimes the story of his name is funny, but some-times there is, of course, a serious point to it: he doesn't want to be consumed by 'this thing called race'. He's seen too many of his friends dragged down by the bitterness. As an adult he also thinks that it's important to put racism into its context, to be aware that his own experiences as a child, the things his family and forebears suffered, didn't happen to them in isolation. He says when it comes to questions like 'Why am I living in Goscote?', 'Why did my parents come over?', 'Why were they looking for work?', a lot of the answers go back to slavery, to colonialism. He says, 'You have to be aware of history, of the economic context of racism, the power structure of racism. You have to be able to navigate it all.'

But Hugo also thinks things were different for him because he had already spent a large part of his childhood in Jamaica. The racism couldn't touch him in the same way that it did those of us who were born here and had our consciousnesses shaped by a culture and a country that were often hostile to us. He tells me, 'I never experienced racism in Jamaica, I just didn't know what it was. So over here, I never really saw racism and it didn't have the same impact on me as others.' He tells me, 'I never got in a funk or a rage about racism. I didn't let it get on top of me, I didn't let it cloud my view of the world or of white society in general.' Ultimately though, he's clear eyed – he says there was a lot of racism about in the seventies, 'but to me it was just about surviving'.

Hugo Whyte and 'The Magnificent Seven'
Forest Comprehensive, Walsall, 1972

'The Magnificent Seven. Once you've met them you'll never forget them. Yul Brynner, Chris . . . the leader. The Magnificent Seven who fought like 700.'

(Trailer from *The Magnificent Seven*, 1960)

Yul Brynner: handsome, tough, wearing a black shirt, on horseback, rides into town and defeats a gang of evil bandits. *The Magnificent Seven* – they're smarter, stronger, funnier than the gang who are tormenting the villagers. It's the Wild West, but Yul Brynner and his gang of men save the day.

•

Most of us who grew up in the seventies know that film – it was regularly shown on TV. And as soon as we hear that rousing Hollywood orchestral score, so typical of the western, we're transported into the heroic landscape of the cowboy world. Yul Brynner and his crew outwitting the violent gang with their ingenuity, gun skills and physical strength. They're super-smart, tough. And they always have the last laugh.

•

After a few months, Hugo settled in at school, making friends, including with another Black boy called Lennox. They all used to have a laugh together in class. As he does now, Hugo reacted with a lightness to the jokes about his name; he didn't like it, but he was quick-witted and laughed off the teasing and the derision.

The real problems were outside the school, and the threat of violence he faced as soon as he came out of the school gates. The lower years – including his – were housed in an annexe two miles away from the main building, adjoining another Walsall secondary school. It meant the younger children were isolated, prey to violence from the older boys in the neighbouring school, which also suffered from a similarly brutal and rough atmosphere.

After school, Hugo would walk home on his own, making his way through Blakenhall Heath, one of the roughest council estates in Walsall, going past a grim-looking pub, The Oak, with 'Blacks Out' scrawled on its red brick wall. He'd be nervous: there were often groups of older, vicious-looking teenagers from the school next door, hanging around. They would lie in wait, sometimes brutally assaulting some of the younger children. One time, they cornered Hugo, following him as he walked home, surrounding him and kicking him to the ground, hurling racist abuse. They only stopped when a woman shouted at them from her window.

The threat of physical violence was, as Hugo puts it, 'ever-present, a constant companion'; but it was how schools were in those days, 'nasty and rough'. He stresses that life at school wasn't all bad, that there was a 'lot of light with the darkness'; he made lots of good friends, some of whom he still knows today. But, he says, Walsall was a typical seventies town, 'it had that air of threat that was around in a lot of places then.'

There were seven Black boys in his year when Hugo started secondary school. All eleven years old, making their way home in ones and twos. Terrified. The colour of their skin made them more visible in this environment, much more susceptible to being a target. So they made a plan. They'd make sure they were never alone, always sticking together while in school and when walking home. And for a laugh they called themselves 'The Magnificent Seven'.

It worked – they fought back, together, and they stopped getting beaten up. Hugo never found himself cornered on his own after school again. When it came to violence, to the racism, first, says Hugo, he 'laughed it off', and then adds that he 'punched it off', eventually getting a reputation in school as someone not to be messed with. 'The Magnificent Seven' became lifelong friends, especially Hugo and Lennox, who showed the newly arrived Hugo the way. Such as what the 'Blacks Out' graffiti on the wall of the pub really meant. Hugo had thought it referred to the blackouts – the power cuts – that had been going on in Britain at that time. Lennox told him that 'no, it wasn't that kind of blackout'. It was, Lennox explained, 'telling us Blacks to get out.'

•

Hugo laughs now at his own innocence but thinks in the end it protected him. He's thankful that he wasn't attuned to racism, that he didn't always see it for what it was, and feels that, in a way, he was blessed. It was as if he could take his imagination and his feelings to a place of playfulness, despite the hate. It was almost as if he danced above it; he lifted himself to a different plane. He wasn't going to bother engaging with it but took himself to what Du Bois described as a 'region of blue sky and great wandering shadows'.[9] For Hugo it was a lightness that has stayed with him for life, combined with an instinct for pure survival.

.

As he went through school, Hugo had 'The Magnificent Seven' by his side, but his name was still a problem.

Hugh Whyte . . .

You White?

Are you White?

Day in day out.

The name had become a millstone around his neck. As a child, if you're unlucky enough to bear a name that is a daily burden, you just have to put up with it. Your name stays the same and racism doesn't just go away. Hugo was also up against insidious forces that were – unlike the jokes about his name – largely invisible. This was an era of deep-rooted discrimination against working-class Black children. The Black filmmaker Steve McQueen, who has made a semi-autobiographical BBC film about the issue, describes his own experience of secondary school in London as 'hell', with 'shitty classes' where working-class Black pupils were disregarded and set up for failure.[10] Many Black children during the era when Hugo was at school were routinely assumed to be educationally subnormal and often sent to 'special schools' with shockingly low teaching standards.

Hugo looks back on his time at school with mixed feelings. He got on really well with some of the teachers, and is still in touch with some of them. But, on the whole, he thinks this was an era of negativity towards Black pupils. Forest Comprehensive was also carrying its legacy as a secondary modern; a place for pupils who had failed their 11 plus, a place where no-one was interested in academic qualifications. Barely anyone went to university; many of the teachers, despite their best intentions, were ground down by its rough, brutal atmosphere and had given up on the idea of academic success for pupils such as Hugo, who was not only working class but also Black.

Hugh Whyte
Walsall Public Library, 1973

Hugo doesn't want to paint a picture of the 'bad white society' without acknowledging the part that his own parents were playing. He doesn't blame them – they were just trying to survive – but he also reflects that a lack of academic expectation was part of the Jamaican working-class culture he came from. At home there wasn't much money – Hugo's father's income as a bricklayer at the steelworks had to support all six of them. He doesn't remember his mother or father ever coming to parents' evening. Like most Jamaicans he knew, they weren't that interested in what went on at school. 'These were people from the countryside, working-class people who came here to do menial jobs,' he explains, and 'the expectation was that you left school and went to work.' He says, 'Again, you have to understand the reason they had to leave Jamaica – it's about class and if you look further back, it comes back again to history, to colonialism, to slavery'. They had tough lives, their ancestors were enslaved, tortured, their families brutalised. Hugo reflects, 'The way that slave societies were structured and the coping mechanism when slavery goes, those characteristics remain in place, including that lack of focus on education.' Some people, he adds, like his mother, saw the benefits of the education system and were grateful. 'But,' he laughs, 'she wanted me to become a chef. "People always need to eat," she would say.'

The lack of money at home meant there also wasn't a lot to do, especially in winter. The television was a rental model and had a meter in the back. Hugo remembers that 'you had to put 50p in it every time you wanted to watch something'. So he says, 'we had to be very selective in what we all watched'. The only alternative was to read, he tells me. Hugo ended up spending a lot of his time in the local library – he used to go two or three times a week, especially in the first few years of being in Britain. He remembers how he *loved* spending time in that quiet 1970s building, loved getting books out. He particularly liked ones that explained things, science books that he could understand, physics, chemistry, biology, that kind of thing. He developed a passion for reading that would stay with him for the rest of his life. He didn't realise it at the time, but he was, in effect, giving himself an education.

Hugh Becomes Hugo
Wolverhampton and Bilston Athletics Club, 1973

What really saved Hugo at school was sport – he was a gifted athlete. Wolverhampton and Bilston Athletics Club – coincidentally in Enoch Powell's constituency – was the top athletics club in the country at the time, regularly producing Olympic champions. One day a coach from the club, Bob Roberts, and one of its directors, Charles Taylor, came along to a sports evening at Forest Comprehensive when Hugo was competing. Both men were working with athletes who ran for Great Britain and were scouting for new talent. They saw Hugo and immediately knew they had spotted a champion; they invited Hugo to join the club and start training. But, once more, there was no-one at home to help or encourage him: no money for kit or trainers, no-one with enough time to take him to the training ground eight miles away, in Wolverhampton, after school.

The coach and the manager decided they had to help the young teenager. They took Hugo under their wing; they understood that life was difficult for him. 'They knew my family was poor,' says Hugo, 'so there were countless things like "We need to get you some spikes, don't worry, we'll sort it out." Little things like that.' Bob Roberts and Charles Taylor made a great team. Coach Bob was, says Hugo, 'a kind and gentle soul, who did so much for everyone but wanted nothing for himself'. He was 'more than kind' adds Hugo, 'to his *very very* bones he was a great human being'. While Charles was a retired headmaster, disciplined, full of confidence, with 'an incredible posh accent'. He and Coach Bob took it in turns to drive Hugo from Walsall to Wolverhampton three times a week, as they realised Hugo's parents wouldn't be able to manage it. They did this for many years. When Hugo talks to me now, it's obvious that he won't ever forget what these two men did for him.

And one evening, when it was Charles' turn to drive Hugo to athletics, he turned to him and said, 'You know something, Hugh's a little bit old fashioned, it'd be so much more interesting if you were called Hugo.' What did Hugo think? Charles didn't like the whole 'You White' thing, he could see what a burden it'd become. Hugo jumped at the chance, he liked it. And in an instant the problem with his name was removed. From then on 'Hugh White' became Hugo to everyone, to his family, friends and everyone at school.

Hugo. It brought with it a little bit of European chutzpah, some Iberian glamour. He probably didn't realise it at the time, but Hugo was, and still is, one of the most popular boys' names in France and Spain, with a name day dedicated to it, on 1 April, across many European countries.

Coach Bob and Charles Taylor were like a pair of guardian angels, changing a name that had oppressed Hugo, and looking after him in so many other ways too. He was halfway through secondary school, had a new name and he loved it. Other things also started to change for Hugo. He was picked to compete for Great Britain, he travelled all over Europe, to Paris, Amsterdam, and appeared on TV. It was exciting. Hugo says, 'The teachers were happy for me, it made them and the whole school proud. It was a rough school, so there was not a lot to be proud of.'

And all those hours in the library paid off. Hugo bucked the trend of low achievement among young Black working-class boys and did exceptionally well in his exams at the end of his third year. He says, 'When it came to exams I wasn't afraid. I loved exams actually!' His teachers moved him into the top set – he was the only Black boy there. Just before he left school, one of them sat him down and gave him some advice, telling him to work hard, to maybe try for university even though his friends were leaving school, all going off to earn money and have a good time. 'I was really grateful to him – he really explained to me what "deferred gratification" meant,' he remembers.

And so, unlike most people at his school, Hugo made it to university, got a degree, did a Masters in computer science. All this time he kept reading, he still loved books. He became educated about Black history, he read writers like James Baldwin, his favourite was *Go Tell It on the Mountain*; the semi-autobiographical story of another intelligent Black teenager, another outsider. And he became a software consultant, a really successful one, and has worked for some of the largest businesses in Europe – Unilever, Oracle, Electrolux and the big pharmaceutical companies.

Hugo Whyte
Walsall, 2023

Hugo is not bitter about what he experienced. He says too many of his friends were destroyed by feelings of anger and rage about the racism of that era, including, he says, one of the 'Magnificent Seven' , who died recently of cancer, having faced a challenge with alcohol for much of his life. He doesn't care that his name caused him such discomfort that it had to be changed. Instead, he mainly laughs about it – it's a funny story he sometimes tells about the past. Race is not something he particularly wants to think about a lot. His partner is white, also from Walsall, and they have three mixed-race, grown-up children.

He's quite philosophical about it – Martin Luther King, Gandhi fought these things, he tells me, but not everyone wants to fight. He says: 'The way I look at it, I have three score years and ten on this planet – that's seventy years give or take a few. As far as I know I've never lived before and I won't be living again. In the history of the world this is my only time. I am not going to waste it on things outside of my control.' When it comes to racism, he says, 'I can rationalise it. I know it's part of a bigger historical picture. Individually I don't have the power to change it. But I do have the power to decide what I do in response to it.' He compares it to being a canoeist in a river: 'You have to understand the currents that you're moving in. My choices may be limited, but I do *have* choices.'

•

Two years ago, he went to the funeral of his friend Lennox from those olden days, the days of 'The Magnificent Seven'. He tells me he wishes he'd spoken at the service; he regrets not speaking up that day. He wishes he'd told everyone in the church about Lennox and about 'The Magnificent Seven'. He would have told everyone about what Lennox meant to him as a young child growing up. He tells me now what he had really wanted to say:

When I got to England I was quite green about racism. I didn't fully understand it. And it was Lennox who explained the lay of the land and how racism works. He was a savvy young boy, and he really looked after me. I would have told the story of how 'The Magnificent Seven' came about and I would have told them that it wasn't just a case of us twelve-year-olds wanting to be like Yul Brynner and his posse. I would have told them it was because we shared a school building with kids that were three or four years older than us. And who wanted to beat the shit out of us. In that first year of secondary school, I would have said there were seven Black children who had to bear the brunt of this racist violence. So we stuck together and we called ourselves 'The Magnificent Seven'.

•

It's all a long time ago now, the 'You White' thing, 'The Magnificent Seven'. In all that roughness there are, for Hugo, also a lot of good memories. 'I'm not too sure I'd change any of it,' he tells me.

Mainly now, when he's not working, Hugo loves being in his garden. He has a passion for growing plants. And he keeps bees too, he makes honey – when we began our conversation this was the first thing he told me about. It brings to mind that abundant, self-sufficient world he grew up in, as a child on his grandmother's land in Jamaica. He's always loved bees, he says and explained how homemade honey is so much nicer than the stuff in the shops which is pasteurised.

It goes back to the time when he was a little boy called Junior.

He was a country boy then, he tells me. 'When we walked those four or five miles every day, on our way back from school, there was a guy who used to keep bees. We always used to look out for him.' Hugo can still feel the heat of the day. He says, 'We went up a steep incline and there he would be. It was a bit of fun and when we'd see him he'd sometimes give us each a bit of honeycomb.'

That's one of the starting points, when he looks back on life, Hugo tells me. 'And when someone calls me Junior I can remember exactly who I was then.'

'These are the moments,' he says, 'that stay with you.'

He must have been seven or eight years old. His name was Junior. He was living with his incredible great grandmother Betsy, who grew her own food, looked after her great grandson at the age of 107, while his parents tried to build a new life. And somehow Hugo has carried that world with him, the sense of who he was when he was on Betsy's farm, still a little boy called Junior. Every time he hears the name, he remembers that mixture of innocence and strength that he had as a child, from growing up in a culture that didn't hate him, with a great grandmother that loved him, with friends of the same colour that wouldn't have thought to make fun of his name or his skin colour. His brothers and sisters still call him by that name, and when they do a part of him is right there again, in that place of love and affection where the question of race had never touched him.

Sheela Banerjee:
The Journey of a Second-Generation Indian Name

My name has never changed.

It was unaltered by marriage. I was never going to take on my (white) husband's surname. It felt too patriarchal. More importantly for me, it would have completely changed how I appeared to the world. I would have become Sheela Cannell, a woman who sounds like she's white, a British Celt, with a first name that's spelt slightly wrong.

Unlike most Bengali children, I was also never given a *dak naam*. So there was no *Tinku*, *Tumpa* or *Mithu* for me. And so here I am, a British-born Indian, in my fifties, still carrying the name I was given at birth – Sheela Banerjee. A sign, a transparent envelope that has surrounded me all my life.

But a person's name is not a static entity. How I feel about these five syllables and what they represent is constantly changing, under the influence of my own psychological and social journey. How others perceive the name also evolves. The name evokes different feelings in different spaces, and in different times. Its texture alters according to the race and class of the person hearing or reading it, like a reflection in a pool that shifts as the ripples pass through it, by the clouds forming their shadows.

Here is the story of my name, as it passed into the world of my adulthood, as I left Hayes, left the Bengali cocoon that I had grown up in, and fully inhabited a British life. No more living in a liminal immigrant world, no more going backwards and forwards to India, to my parents' homeland. I was going to live here forever. I was to become British.

Here is the story of my name as I went with it through my journey in life, a vertiginous up-and-down trajectory, which at times felt like it would destroy me. Here is the story of my name, reflected in the story of Britain itself, as the country changed. As it was forced to accept us, the children of immigrants, who grew up here, spent our adult lives here and felt a right to belong here, in a way that our parents never could.

Harrow, West London, 1984

I'm sixteen, at sixth form college, in Harrow. Sheela is acceptable, perhaps a bit old fashioned. People sometimes mistakenly call me Shirley or Sandra, other similarly unfashionable names. Luckily however, Sheela is unexceptional – my parents have achieved what they set out to – it's a name that's never caused me any problems. But my surname is a different matter. Right now, I am focused on shedding everything my Banerjee name signifies.

•

I was metamorphosing during my college years. My Indian surname – the clear badge of my cultural heritage and my family – was at odds with who I was trying to be, my outward appearance a visible sign of the change in my identity. I couldn't help it, I was becoming more and more a part of the British world around me as I got older, more and more influenced by it. The shell of my Bengali upbringing was receding.

Sheela Banerjee is now a name I want to outgrow, the daughter of immigrants, a studious Asian girl, doing maths every evening with my mother. I want to escape the stain of being brown, of being afraid, of being suffocated by my Banerjee family. The Friday and Saturday nights with my aunts and uncles and cousins, singing Bengali songs, with my mum sitting on the carpet, with her harmonium, in our front room. Eating fish curry with my hands, picking the bones out with my fingers, the pressure to do impossibly well at school, to look pretty. Everything had to go.

•

Every morning my routine is a sort of ritual banishing of my Indian surname and everything it stands for. I wake early to get ready for college, stand in my parents' bedroom, in front of the round mirror that's built into their teak dressing table. Torn jeans, a tangle of jewellery. My mum's Revlon lipstick and rose powder-compact on a lace doily, alongside my dad's Old Spice aftershave and his oblong wooden hairbrush. In the mirror, my freshly washed silky Indian hair needs to be trans- formed. Holding the hot crimpers by my head, I hear my hair fizz as I clamp the tongs shut, the scorching singe of the ridged metal turns my hair into a mass of wiry frizz. I spray gusts of Harmony Extra Firm Hold hairspray and backcomb until there isn't a single girly shiny strand of hair left. It all has to be rough and punky. One side is completely shaved. I put on my red lipstick and eyeliner and I'm a different person – the lipstick turns me into a woman, and my hair takes me into an imagined realm of possibility, of nights in dingy pubs, concerts, a world of dirt, grunge. My ideas are all in my head: from glamorous tales my friend Erica told me at school on Monday mornings about her Saturday nights out in a goth pub in Ealing, and from religiously watching *The Tube* on Channel 4, on our portable black-and-white TV in the dining room. In reality, I hardly went anywhere, my parents had barely allowed me out up until this point.

I was in the middle of doing my A-Levels. I'd started bunking off maths lessons, going to the pub in the middle of the day, to smoke and talk politics. I realised I belonged on the British streets around me, I was someone who was no longer nervous or timid, I was no longer that immigrant Sheela Banerjee, a little girl just back from India, with a name to match.

I was now British. But it was an idea of Britishness that still felt overwhelmingly white. I hardly ever saw anyone like me on TV. No one Indian ever seemed to do anything particularly admirable, nothing I looked up to. No film stars, directors, pop stars. No writers that reflected my life. Until 1985, when Hanif Kureishi's film *My Beautiful Laundrette* came out. It was the first time I saw an Asian woman on screen who was a bit like me – young, angry, and she wasn't in a sari. It was a blast of energy. There was some kind of energy in all of us too. Things were moving and shifting politically. Marches, strikes, Ken Livingstone's GLC, and later the Poll Tax riots.

•

It is the miners' strike for many months. I get involved: I sell papers, I march, I organise meetings. I start to read; I join the Labour Party Young Socialists. It's January 1986 and I've just turned eighteen. Every Saturday night for weeks I make my way to the cobbled pavements of a street in east London. I spend two hours travelling from Hayes, taking the overground, two tubes, until I'm outside Rupert Murdoch's printworks in Wapping, in the freezing cold, with huge shiny brown horses charging at us. I'm with hundreds of strikers. Perhaps I don't really care about the printworkers, but we're here to defend the idea of unions.

It all somehow connects back to the extreme and hellish poverty I saw in India as a child, the mountains of stinking rubbish all over Kolkata, where people lived and scavenged for scraps to sell, the limbless beggars everywhere. Empire, racism, capitalism, all of that was coming together in my mind, all part of the same long fight. I met other like-minded young people in Southall and Hayes, a complete mixture, second-generation Punjabis like Nina, as well as Paul, Derek, working-class English young men from west London, who I was not afraid of, who had no issue with what the name Sheela Banerjee represented. I started to understand that we have to work together with the white working classes, they don't always have to be my enemy.

•

My feelings about the old Sheela Banerjee, the one I'm gradually leaving behind, are in state of flux. I'm ambivalent about who I really am. Sheela Banerjee: on the simplest level it means that I am female and Bengali. It symbolises everything that a Bengali person carries in their head about what it means to be female. The centuries of arranged marriages, the selfless mothers, aunties, doing all the cooking, putting themselves last, the absolute focus on 'good' behaviour, on looking right, being subservient and studious. Our names are a code that tells this whole story, the generations of females behind me, whose surnames have been erased, a sign of their powerlessness in the society I am from. Although my mother and my aunts were educated and got jobs (the first in their families ever to do so), the legacy they carry is one of a deep-rooted patriarchy. At seventeen, there is so much about being Sheela Banerjee – an Indian *girl* – that I want to escape.

As a teenage girl in the Bengali community, I've grown up always being looked at, appraised. Many Bengalis – especially in India – aren't polite, they don't self-censor: opinions and prejudices are stated without consideration of their impact on the listener. 'She's too thin, not very good looking . . .' I've overheard other young girls being talked about in the same way. I've internalised the idea that, to be of worth, I must be pretty. My looks are always to be a subject of discussion and I will be judged on them.

There's a photo of me aged thirteen, in an ill-fitting pencil skirt, with long skinny legs, standing between my mother and a Bengali aunty in our garden in Hayes. I look gawky, self-conscious. We have been back from India for a year, I am just starting to grow. I have overheard comments at Bengali gatherings about my figure and looks. I don't fit into this society's idea of beauty. In India where I've just been living for a year, the girls considered good looking are light-skinned (known as *forsha*), curvy like the Bollywood film stars, not flat-chested like I still am. By the time we left India I had started to tower over all the other girls and my legs were like sticks. I had watched the older girls turn into young women, and those who were thought of as attractive started to glide around exquisitely in expertly folded saris, tightly wound around their curves.

It's this Indian ideal of beauty I carry around with me. There is a Bengali word that's often used to describe a young woman who is good looking: *shunduri*. In this case, it is a noun, unlike adjectives such as 'pretty', or 'beautiful'. If you are a *shunduri* that is your identity, that's the first thing you are to the world and you embody it within the whole of your being. There is no similar word for a boy, and my male cousins I grew up with never have to endure the same dissection of their looks and the endless fixation on their appearance.

These ideas of female beauty were still being played out as I grew up in the eighties in Britain, but now, as a young woman, I was fed up with it. I latched onto the tail end of a generation of punks, my appearance designed to say 'F you' to the whole thing.

•

But setting aside this version of myself isn't that simple. I was trying to escape the constrictions of being a Banerjee, a particular cohort of middle-class educated immigrants. A group that was still floundering in many ways with their children, anxious for them to succeed in a way that they hadn't been able to. As a child of Indian parents, I was also under intense pressure to succeed academically. My mum had spent every evening after a day's work making sure I did extra maths and English; my exam grades, like all my cousins', were a subject of intense scrutiny by our wider family. But rejection also wasn't something I actually wanted. Contained in my name was an attachment, something I cherished, something deep within me that was drawing me in.

•

It's Saturday night. We are at the Gangulis' house, yet another Bengali gathering in someone's living room, full of suburban families. The Roys, the Chatterjees, the Nandis and a host of other Bengalis are here. I'd wanted to go out with my friends but I've been dragged along to this dull event instead. Someone has brought out a harmonium and it's my mum's turn to sing. I sit on the carpet, bored, as she starts pushing the bellows and pressing the small ivory keys. She sings a classical Bengali song that I've heard her sing countless times, as she cooked or did the washing up.

That evening, as I listened to the song, for the first time I started to pay attention to its labyrinthine melody and the emotive beauty of the words.

Shey din dujonay
(That day, two people)

Duley chinoo boney, phulodorey badha jhulo naa
(Were in the forest, on a swing intertwined with flowers)

It's a song of pain and memory, speaking of an intense moment in the forest between two people, and like a lot of classical Bengali songs, fuses a sense of romance with the beauty of nature. It's by Rabindranath Tagore, the artist, songwriter and freedom fighter, whose songs, poems and stories are known by everybody in West Bengal. Tagore's songs, known as *Rabindrasangeet*, are sung at countless gatherings, as people are doing their housework, on the radio covered endlessly by famous singers.

I asked my mum to teach me the song, and over the next few months I learnt a few more of them. I started singing the odd song myself at different gatherings. Sometimes it was in a rented hall, a community centre, more often it was just an impromptu session in people's front rooms. Sometimes I'd sing along with my friend Swapna (*Shop-naa* – a name which has seldom been correctly pronounced by a British person). She was the daughter of the Gangulis and had also learnt a few of the songs from her parents, who, looking back, were really talented singers themselves.

It didn't seem like a big deal, singing was very common at Bengali gatherings. It took me back to those days in India with my cousin Tuktuki, singing Hindi songs on the veranda after the electricity had gone out, fireflies in the air. Swapna and I sang together quite a few times, once at a concert my parents and their Bengali friends organised, in a hall at University College London. We were nervous as we went on stage and arranged our saris, sitting by the side of the harmonium. My hair, I remember, was still resolutely spiky. My singing wasn't particularly good, but I remember people clapping along, I think they were surprised and pleased that a teenager, especially one who looked as stroppy as me, had decided to take an interest in the songs of their childhood.

Sussex University, Brighton, 1987

As I finished my A-Levels, I had begun to shed the layers of internalised stigma. As well as Swapna, I had started hanging out with other Bengali friends in West London pubs. Millie, Lily, Dip and Tip – not one of us, coincidentally, had a full-on Bengali name. I went off to college, to study politics at the School of African and Asian Studies in the radical environment of Sussex University. And it was here that everything about my name, Sheela Banerjee, underwent a further transformation.

•

I'd never lived anywhere like Brighton before – full of hippie shops and food stores selling loose chickpeas and lentils, with people often wearing batik print clothes, jewellery from India. The threat I'd felt in outer West London had suddenly vanished. The town would be buzzing at night, with clubs on the seafront, in converted churches, in tiny basements playing jazz all night. All of this was sandwiched between the expanse of the sea and the hills of the South Downs.

I'd only ever been to Brighton for day trips to the beach with my family. We'd been the original 'Bhaji on the Beach' crowd, long before Gurinder Chadha's film of that name came out – with all my relatives eating *luchi aar aloor dom* (puris and potato curry) on the beach and drinking delicious hot, sweet tea out of thermos flasks. We'd eat our food, swim in the sea, go to the pier and go on the fairground rides. But we were very separate from the English people around us, and I'd had no idea that there was this hippie, arty, cool hinterland that existed behind that typically British seafront.

Although Sussex was still, in 1987, a largely white campus, the exciting intellectual atmosphere, the political activism, awakened my consciousness of my Indian heritage. Throughout school I was never taught anything by Asian or Black writers. All my teachers had been white except for my maths teacher Mr Sharma, who, as I said earlier, was derided and made fun of because of his Indian accent. Here, the first seminar I ever attended was led by an Indian lecturer with an Indian name: Homi Bhabha. He was brown-skinned; he too spoke with an accent – but here at Sussex he was hugely respected, a leading cultural theorist, who taught us about the critical links between colonialism and literature. Through him, I quickly discovered writers like Chinua Achebe and Edward Said, and became aware of how racist stereotypes were part of a broader ideology. The casual racism of my everyday life in Hayes, the perpetual sense of threat on the streets, the years of name calling, were put into the context of centuries of British imperial power. I started looking back at the world I had grown up in through a different lens.

•

In my second year I'm taught by a professor who's Bengali, like me: Partha Mitter. Although in tutorials we rarely refer to our shared heritage, we both know from our surnames that we share a common Indian ancestry. There are only four of us doing his course on Indian art, and I immediately feel at home with him – he looks like an intellectual version of one of my uncles, and there are only four of us doing his course on Indian art. Back home, one of my parents' closest family friends were the Mitras, and my professor's surname, Mitter, is an anglicised version of the same name.

Each week we meet in his little study and discuss pictures painted by Western travellers visiting India for the first time, the magnificence of Hindu temple art in Orissa and how culture and society are wholly intertwined. I start taking more photographs. I remember going shopping with my aunt to Southall and taking my camera with me, an SLR that I'd got for my twenty-first birthday. Quite soon after that I decide I want to make films – documentaries. I don't know much about it, but I'm really excited, I love the idea of using a visual language to say something political about the world I see around me.

And for the first time in my life, in the late eighties, on this left-wing campus, Sheela Banerjee becomes a surprisingly good, even moderately cool name to have. During my tutorials, during student protests, at Labour Club meetings,

chatting in someone's room late at night, it's positively ok –
it's good to be brown, to be Indian. For me this is a total
novelty, and I like it. Yes, there's an element of being exoti-
cised, but I don't really care, it's better than being attacked,
feeling inferior, and in Brighton I can relax for the first time.
And politically, around me things are changing too – in the
1987 election four MPs of colour are elected to parliament –
Bernie Grant, Paul Boateng, Diane Abbott, and for the first
time in 118 years, an Asian, Keith Vaz.

I suddenly start noticing a few voices that sound like mine.
I see a young woman called Meera Syal on TV; she's doing a
monologue about being a teenage Asian girl. Gurinder
Chadha, an Asian woman my age, from just down the road
in Southall – who went on to make *Bend It Like Beckham* –
has made an amazing short film called *I'm British But . . ..* I
love it. Just the title and the opening image of a fluttering
sari hanging on a washing line seemed to sum up my existence: kind of British, kind of Indian, with the sari, an
emblem of my mother, my family, always in the
background.

Banerjee: It's Not My Actual Name
Kolkata, 1990

After university, I decided to go back to India for a visit – for
the first time as an adult. I was going to stay in our hometown
of Chandannagar, as well as visit Kolkata.

I'm more comfortable being a Banerjee now than I've ever
been before. But I'm only beginning to understand the history
of the name and how it is intertwined with India's colonial
past.

Banerjee was very much a reminder that the British had, until very recently, ruled over us. For Banerjee is not in fact my original surname. Even though my surname had always, in Britain, marked me out as very definitely Indian, Banerjee, as I've been told by many Bengalis, was actually a creation of the British Empire. It was probably introduced at some point in the eighteenth century as the British consolidated their power – an anglicised version of the Sanskrit name Bandyopadhyay, as our colonial masters couldn't be bothered to pronounce the original.

It was the same for a slew of upper-caste Bengali Brahmin names: Mukhopadhyay became Mukherjee, Chattopadhyay became Chatterjee, Gangopadhyay became Ganguli.

Bandyopadhyay by no means disappeared, and it's still used among Bengalis, but it seems that Banerjee gradually took administrative precedence over it. This at least is the account I'm given by family members, some of whom have never accepted the change in name and still go by Bandyopadhyay.

Banerjee, then, I discover, is a bastardisation of my real name. Every day as I wrote 'Banerjee', said it out loud, it summoned a tiny but tangible reminder of the presence of the British in the country of my forebears, a memory of subjugation. As I've got older, I've increasingly come to feel a distance, even a distaste for Banerjee as a name. As I've mentioned previously, its predecessor, Bandyopadhyay, is an ancient Hindu surname. Yes, it contains the dark stain of caste, but it also carries my Indian Bengali heritage – good and bad – and tells the world where my family are actually from, going back thousands of years.

•

I became much more clearly aware of all this colonial history on that trip back to India in 1990. Wandering round the streets of Kolkata as a twenty-two-year-old, I was seeing India with different eyes – looking back on the place I'd lived as a child from a new perspective. It felt like the city was saturated with its legacy as the capital of British India, not sure whether it loved or loathed its former colonial master. The British Empire began in Bengal and was powered by exploiting its wealth. Everywhere I went was a reminder of the British presence: the architecture of the grand, decaying Kolkata houses, like my cousin Tuktuki's house in north Kolkata; the major government buildings in Dalhousie Square; the enormous, filthy Howrah Station and, next to it, the majestic steel architecture of Howrah Bridge, dominating the skyline over the River Hooghly. Then there were the elite English-medium public schools – like the one I'd been sent to as a child – with their gated walls and their neat British-style school uniforms. On the one hand I was told endlessly about all these major British-built landmarks, taken off to admire the Victoria Memorial or to the Eden Gardens cricket ground. On the other hand, there was also a huge nationalistic pride: everywhere around me were paintings of Gandhi and Nehru, India's first prime minister, accompanied by inspirational quotes. The Bengali freedom fighter Netaji Subhas Chandra Bose was also widely celebrated. (Bose was violently opposed to the British and even joined forces with the Nazis to try to get rid of them.) There were images of him stencilled onto walls, with his trademark glasses and military uniform, statues on street corners, and people would string garlands of flowers around pictures of him and offer up their prayers.

•

As I travelled around Kolkata that summer, got on buses, went to the passport office, I noticed that the old British street names persisted, despite the fact that officially they had been changed. It was slightly confusing, but I realise now, this was a place where names were power, and the struggle was ongoing. They were incredibly important to the pride and defiance of a country that had only become independent less than fifty years before. It would still be a few more years before the city's official name would be changed from the colonial-era Calcutta back to its original Bengali title, Kolkata, but for now, place names had become the focus of the communist West Bengal government.

I often found myself near the centre of the city, with road names such as Clive Street and Amherst Street. The most famous of these was Dalhousie Square, an oasis of grand colonial-style buildings, the former heart of the British Empire in India and now home to major government offices. It had been named after the Marquess of Dalhousie, the Governor-General of India from 1847 to 1856, but had been renamed, with a different street sign proclaiming it to be *Binoy Badal Dinesh Baag*.

Binoy, Badal and Dinesh were the first names of three beloved young Bengali revolutionaries, aged twenty-two, twenty and nineteen. One summer's day in 1905, they got dressed in formal European clothes, walked through Dalhousie Square into the Writers' Building – the epicentre of the colonial rule – and shot dead the British Inspector General of Prisons, a man notorious for torturing Indian nationalist prisoners.

There is still an official plaque on the entrance to the Writers' Building commemorating the heroic acts of the freedom fighters – a sign of continuing reverence for what was considered at the time to be an act of terrorism by the British authorities. Moments away is Clive Street, named after Robert Clive, the first Governor of Bengal, a man reviled for his violent and rapacious rule over Bengal. It was renamed Netaji Subhas Chandra Road – after the Bengali nationalist I discussed earlier. But, despite the deep affection for these figures, in day-to-day life people still used the British names – for example, everyone still called *Badal Binoy Dinesh Baag* by its old name, Dalhousie Square – and the shadow of the empire was still very much present in the popular consciousness.

Chandannagar, 1990

During that trip, I went back to where my family was from, Chandannagar, for the first time in many years and stayed with my aunt – my *Choto Mashi* (youngest aunt, on my mother's side). Her house overlooked the greyish brown waters of the Hooghly River, a distributary of the Ganges, and each morning I'd go and stand on her flat roof, watching the small boats go past and people bathing on the steps leading down to the water. The places I knew as a child had started to acquire a different significance. This quiet, unprepossessing spot – muddy and full of scraps of rubbish – was, in effect, where the story of my bastardised surname began. This was the site of one of the most important victories in the history of British imperialism in India.

In the mid-eighteenth century this small stretch of river, dotted with primitive settlements and villages, became the site of the major European powers battling it out for global trade domination via the control of Bengal's riches. The French created a trading post at Chandannagar with their own fort and standing army, trading in indigo, spices, cotton and silk, under a licence from the Mughal-controlled ruler of Bengal, Siraj-ud-Daulah. It became a thriving city, with thousands of French-built houses and a population of one hundred thousand. Once just three sleepy villages, Chandannagar now became the main centre for European commerce in Bengal, with British-controlled Kolkata at this time its poor cousin.[1]

However, in 1756 the British East India Company, led by Robert Clive and his private army, fought their way into Chandannagar and defeated the French. Although it was a fairly scrappy affair, it turned out to be one of the most significant military victories in Indian history. A few weeks later the British moved further upstream and vanquished the Muslim ruler Siraj and his army in the Battle of Plassey (or *Polashi*, as it's known in Bengali). This was, in effect, the end of the Mughal empire in India. In a celebratory procession afterwards, they paraded Siraj's dead body on the back of an elephant, marking the beginning of British control of India for the next 200 years.

•

I find it hard to think that my parents' hometown was the site of such a momentous historical event, one that would affect all our destinies. The place didn't feel like the stuff of history books. When I lived in Chandannagar as a child in the seventies this was all long forgotten. It was just a small suburban commuter town, messy and chaotic, and as a six-year-old, I used to go by rickshaw to my school, St Joseph's Convent, situated on the banks of the river, with no sign of the epic battle that was once fought here.

When the East India Company arrived in India and took over Bengal, this was the wealthiest region of India, 'a glittering jewel in the medieval world' according to the Indian politician and writer Shashi Tharoor. At this point in history, 1756, when the British took de facto control of India, it was the largest economic power in the world, its share of the global economy was twenty-three per cent, equivalent to the whole of Europe put together.[2] (It had declined, according to Tharoor, to a mere three per cent of the world economy by the time the British left. Not everyone agrees about the figures and conservative historians, such as Niall Ferguson, continue to view the British Empire in a positive light.)[3] A million weavers spun and wove the finest cotton in the world. The silk produced was some of the most exquisite ever seen, and Bengali exports were in demand across the globe, particularly in the fashionable drawing rooms of Europe. As the East India Company established its stranglehold, India's wealth was ruthlessly and systematically extracted, and the British turned Kolkata into the new capital of its global trading empire.

This is the context for how my surname came to be changed to Banerjee: a system of racialised supremacy, based on brute military force and economic coercion. Over the coming decades the East India Company imposed crippling taxes and destroyed centuries-old industries in order to support industrial production in Britain. The Indian textiles industry was almost destroyed – the British vandalised cotton looms, carried out widespread violence against weavers and brought in extortionate tariffs to prevent the export of woven cotton. Millions of skilled workers were left destitute. Bengal experienced some of the worst famines in human history and Britain undertook perhaps the largest transfer of wealth from one country to another that the world has ever seen.

This was the context for changing my name, from one that had evolved in the region over the millennia to one that eighteenth-century Englishmen could pronounce with ease.

•

But the alteration from Bandyopadhyay to Banerjee is not just about the exercise of brute force. Less comfortably, for an anti-imperialist like me, my Bengali Brahmin forebears were often complicit in the management of empire. There was sustained and close supportive contact between upper-middle-class Bengalis and their British masters. We worked with the British – advising them, doing business with them, and acting as intermediaries in the exploitation of our homeland and the lower castes beneath us.

It was in Kolkata that my ancestors, the Bandyopadhyays, would have mingled and done deals with the British, part of a mutually beneficial and ambiguous relationship between rich upper-class Bengalis and the huge influx of rapacious and predatory British traders. From the mid-eighteenth century onwards, as wealth was systematically extracted from the Bengal heartlands, a class of high-caste Bengali businessmen arose – with surnames like Tagore (originally Thakur), Banerjee and Mukherjee – they were essentially go-betweens who did business with the East India Company and made enormous fortunes. The writer and poet Rabindranath Tagore's grandfather, Dwarkanath Tagore, traded in indigo, sugar and Bengal coal; he became so rich that he was known as 'The Prince' by contemporary Englishmen.

An elite group of Brahmin scholars also helped the British to draw up laws to administer the country and consolidate their power. These were known as the 'Gentoo Laws' – a bastardised version of ancient Indian texts that created an inflexible hierarchical system. Flexible local traditions and values, decided within each caste, were replaced by a system of rigid Brahmin domination.

The 'Code of Gentoo Laws' became a powerful and influential document over the next two centuries. It appears that Brahmin scholars used their prominent role in this process to enshrine their own privileged position in colonial society. Brahmins went on to dominate a whole raft of professions – in the civil service, the law courts, the railways and academia, and their surnames still predominate in the upper echelons of these professions today.

•

My name is about the subtleties of the relationship between ruler and subject. As the Banerjees – upper-middle-class Bengalis – became quite close to the British, there was a psychological and cultural transmission of values. They were educated in the British schooling system, taught to speak English, and taught a British version of history. At the same time, this was still an unequal and uncomfortable relationship. As Indians, we were still under their yoke, still a subjugated race, which is why I imagine my centuries-old name was changed with such casual disregard.

This ambiguous dynamic meant that as a child, I had looked at India with a dual vision. On the one hand I was Sheela Banerjee, an Indian girl, but on the other I saw the country with superior eyes, the British part of my consciousness. It was patronising and wrong, but I couldn't help it. I was steeped in two hundred years of colonial history, I saw everything with my coloniser's eyes, seeing everything Indian as slightly inferior.

It's hardly surprising – the influence of the British had saturated my own family. My grandfather, Ram Chandra Banerjee, was born in 1907, under British rule. He spoke English, and after he'd left the priesthood, became the general manager of a company which supplied porters and teashops to the British-owned railways. He eventually ran his own teashop in a large commuter station in a Kolkata suburb. When I went back to visit India, I was reminded again of how my family were proud of this British connection. I also remember how I used to love visiting the teashop as a child: the crowds, the dusty jars full of biscuits and the chai walas scurrying about with their giant silver tea urns. For my grandfather, it was a way of earning a living, but of course, in the process, people like him couldn't help but absorb some of the values and cultural norms promoted by the British. He remained intensely religious and fought, like my maternal grandfather, to get the British out of India. But the influence of the British filtered down to his son, my father, who always dreamt of coming to England. Like all successful imperialists, the British perpetuated powerful myths about the superiority of their culture and way of life, favoured certain sections of the population – in this case the Bengalis – and used them to communicate their ideology. My altered name contains within it this complex story, of the close, sometimes uncomfortable contact between the two sides.

•

It was around this time, after getting back from India, that I became more curious about the origins of *Sheela*. I asked my mum about the meaning, hoping, for the first time, that it was a 'proper' Indian name, not just a marriage of convenience between India and 1960s Britain. She told me the name comes from the Hindu god Shiva, and the Sanksrit word 'sheel' – the long black stone that's used to pray to him. I remember seeing these black stones everywhere in India when I was a child – in temples, in my grandparents' prayer room, smeared with sandalwood and garlanded with flowers.

It meant I could, to some extent, put aside the British associations of Sheela and embrace its Indian-ness. The memories and associations were important to me. I began to see what a rich cultural heritage I'd grown up with in London: having all my cousins, aunts and uncles around me; the hundreds of Bengalis that gathered at religious festivals; my parents' huge network of friends; how all that was a source of strength and support. I grew up within a huge London Bengali community: the Gangulis, the Roys, the Bhattacharyas, Dr Chatterjee (who my dad and uncle played cards with during the summer holidays), the Mitras, the Ghoshes, the Biswases in Harrow, the Chandras in Southall, the Sarkars, the Bagchis.

There was still of course a lot that was problematic in my community – the patriarchal values, the damaging conservativism, hadn't gone away. But something had shifted in me, in quite a fundamental way, during my few years after leaving home. Maybe I'd grown up a bit, maybe it was studying so many things that illuminated our history. I had a confidence and a new interest in the Bengali world I'd come from. I was getting used to the idea that being Sheela Banerjee had its plusses, it was an identity that I could finally feel comfortable with, and maybe even explore in the wider world, beyond university.

Brighton, 1990

It's 1990, I've finished university and am living in Brighton. I'm twenty-two. Young, confident, determined. I'm going to try to start making documentaries. I'm convinced that if I try hard enough I can do this thing: make films that have meaning, about the lives of ordinary people, make work that is political too, maybe show aspects of the world I know that I've never seen depicted on TV. The place I'd come from,

India, the Bengali culture of my family, my childhood as a Bengali growing up here – I saw that there was so much to say about these places and our experiences living here.

I have so much I want to say, but I have no idea what to do – how to get into this world. I need connections to get anywhere near the world of film or TV. (This is years before the internet, smartphones, or even small cameras, so I can't just start making my own films.) Even getting some work experience seems completely impossible and out of my reach. There's no one to ask for advice. My parents cannot be of any help – my mum is a lab technician at Brunel University and my dad is an insurance salesman. Their Bengali friends mainly work in low-level admin jobs – in local authorities, libraries, small businesses – or they are doctors – GPs in obscure parts of the country, like Merthyr Tydfil or Lowestoft. I have no friends with mums or dads in the media.

I have a degree, but that is all. I watch as a few people at university mysteriously get media work, seemingly with no previous experience: at the BBC, one on a daytime talk show. I am baffled and wonder how on earth it happened. But I don't care, I persevere. I get together with a friend, another Greek Cypriot called Maria, and we manage to get arts council funding for a low-budget film, about a group of local Bangladeshi women, an invisible community suffering from domestic violence and lack of support in this mainly white seaside town. We even get the actor Rita Wolf – another Bengali with a hybrid name – who played the character I so admired in *My Beautiful Laundrette*, to come and do our voiceover.

Sunrise Radio, West Hounslow, London, 1992

'I'm Sheela Banerjee, and this is the news at nine o'clock on Sunrise Radio.'

I say my own name about ten times a day.

I read news bulletins every hour, after the jingle plays and a voice sings, 'Sunrise Radio – Britain's largest Asian radio station'. And it actually is – around three hundred thousand Asians, in London and across the country, tune in to listen to its mix of latest Bollywood songs, old Hindi hits, news from India and Pakistan, and news about the Asian community here in Britain.

With a name like Sheela Banerjee, I fit right in. I am among a whole host of Indian and Pakistani presenters: Tony Patti, the turbaned morning breakfast presenter; Ravi Sharma, who comes on mid-morning, popular with female listeners who love the old Hindi movie songs; then there's the glamorous, smiling Pakistani DJ who presents a show every evening, playing ghazals and chatting in Urdu.

I often complain about working there – three of us working in the pokey newsroom, putting together thirteen bulletins a day. It's really hard work and the pay is abysmal (no minimum wage back then). But I am happy there. Maybe because it is like working with my aunties and uncles: the women often come to work wearing salwar kameez or saris, and the men wear those baggy blazers that I'd seen my father's generation wear and speak with thick Indian accents. As I sit in the studio ready to read the news, I hear the old Hindi film songs I grew up with, the high-pitched voices of Lata Mangeshkar and Asha Bhosle, coming through my headphones.

The studio sits in a drab office block, down a side street in West Hounslow. But the station is a phenomenon, it has an incredible reach: until now thousands of Asian immigrants living in this country have never had a station like this – something that connects them daily to the continent they left behind decades ago, that tells their stories. It's wildly popular with my parents and their friends. Everyone Asian from the older generation listens to it. Every Asian corner shop I walk into, as I buy a bar of chocolate or a loaf of bread, I hear Sunrise Radio coming out of a tinny radio, with presenters often speaking Hindi, Urdu or Punjabi. Major Bollywood stars like Amitabh Bachchan frequently pop in to do interviews; thousands of Asians living in west London gather in our tiny car park at the front to catch a glimpse of them. Sometimes I'm embarrassed about working there – it feels a bit cheesy and is aimed mainly at my parents' generation – but it's fun, and in the tiny newsroom we're mostly allowed to pursue stories that we think matter.

I don't realise it at the time, but I am also up close to the politics of race in this country.

Every day I interview and report on the activists that are pushing for change in British society: from the feminist group the Southall Black Sisters, who fight against forced marriages and inhuman immigration laws, to the Newham Monitoring Project, who are instrumental in helping to kick out the far right in east London. I often speak to Suresh Grover of the Southall Monitoring Group – he was a teenager during the Southall riots in 1981 and now is a leading anti-racist activist. He will go on to help the family of Zahid Mubarek try to get justice for the racist murder of their son in prison. These are a whole generation of people my age, or a bit older, who've experienced racism in this country, who are fighting against the far right, against laws that discriminate against Asians and Black people in this country. It's inspiring, and these people will help to bring about change. I often speak to the campaigning solicitor Imran Khan, who will be instrumental in campaigning with the family of Stephen Lawrence to get justice for their son, and will help fundamentally change the way British society thinks about race. The station is small but surprisingly influential: I talk to the Labour leader John Smith in a gym hall in Hounslow; Conservative ministers often turn up to our studios during the 1992 election, knowing that hundreds of thousands of voters listen to this station all day.

Sometimes I look back and think maybe I should have stayed in that safe Asian world, but I assumed that all this experience, this early progress, would mean that I'd eventually get to do what I really wanted to do – make documentaries with a social purpose, like the ones I watched on TV, projects that could speak to a national audience and perhaps make a difference in the world. I put my heart into that and thought if I worked hard enough it would eventually happen.

The BBC, Various Production Companies
London, Early 1990s

I sit on the floor of my flat in Islington and look through my CV quickly, as I get ready to phone some of the TV production companies I've sent it to. I'm a researcher. Sometimes I'm an assistant producer, the next level up.

I'm out of work – yet again.

Sheela Banerjee

My name is at the top of my CV.

It's the first thing that people see of me when I try to get a job. I follow it up with a phone call to the relevant executive: 'Hi my name's Sheela Banerjee, I sent my CV in last week. I was wondering if David/Nick/Simon/Charlotte has had time to have a look at it?'

I feel like a slightly desperate salesperson. I have about thirty seconds on the phone to impress these powerful characters (white, middle class). I say my name. Sheela Banerjee. They immediately know I'm not a Lucy or a Charlotte. I know I have to sound super-confident, perky, to get over being called Sheela Banerjee. I have to convince them I'm nearly the same as the Lucys and the Charlottes, like someone who probably went to Oxbridge, who is almost definitely English.

Someone like them.

That's the act I'm involved in. I tell myself I'm playing a part, to summon up my confidence. I'm trying to get beyond my name, to eradicate the coded messages that are contained within it. The whiff of working class from the 'Sheela'. And the Banerjee surname, so prestigious in India, containing so much (undeserved) cultural capital, is worse than useless in this world, a badge of Asian-ness. It just doesn't feel like a name to be respected. Maybe it's the anglicised form – Banerjee – rather than the more authentic and impressive Bandyopadhyay – even if it is a mouthful. That 'jee' at the end, like the Chatterjees and Mukherjees, now feels like it has a slightly infantile, faintly comical air about it.

It's only my perception of course. But it feels to me like there is a fairly small family of names that confer power. Names that say: a) I'm white; b) I'm (upper) middle-class (ideally from Oxford or Cambridge). Names like: Lucy. Emma. Ed. Tom. Simon. Elizabeth. Charlotte. Sophie. Kate. Sarah. David. Nick. Christopher. Charles. Richard. Claire. James. Jeremy. Etc. The individual owners of these names will usually be lovely, unprejudiced people – many become my friends – but collectively they appear to me to form a phalanx of privilege. A phalanx whose ranks I cannot enter.

It seems impossible to get a permanent job. I'm on endless short freelance contracts, and am trying to fit in, make myself acceptable at every workplace, in the hope of being kept on, given the next job. I've got plenty of experience but many people with much less are doing better. When I go to work, I introduce myself, over and over again, at every new company I work for. I never meet anyone called Sheela or Sheila at these places. It's not a name chosen by English middle-class families from my parents' generation. (I do meet one Sharon – she's working class – we become close, lifelong friends.)

•

Back then, I don't know for sure whether the foreign-sounding name at the top of the page makes it more likely that my CV will be thrown in the bin. But other aspiring TV people I know, also from minority backgrounds, often have the same suspicion. It's well documented now, decades later, that a foreign-sounding name is a significant barrier to getting an interview. (A study from Nuffield College, Oxford, for example, found that British applicants with ethnic minority names have to send, on average, sixty per cent more applications to get a positive response from employers than their white counterparts.[4])

.

And then there appeared to be an even deeper layer of prejudice operating in the particular area of TV I was trying to progress in – serious documentaries and political programmes. It seemed to me there was an even more pernicious ecology of often Oxbridge-educated commissioning editors who would commission programmes from Oxbridge-dominated prestige independent production companies with names like Oxford Films (of course!), Brook and Blakeway. Similar people also colonised particular swathes of the BBC – the documentaries department, BBC Westminster, Newsnight. Here, a certain type of person seemed destined to progress. A person with a certain background, a certain skin colour and a certain accent. The Jeremys, the Sophies, the Lauras, the Lucys. Britain's liberal oligarchy, as someone once called them.

Pretty much everyone, including me, signed up to the belief that only *very clever* people could prosper in this arena. That it was all terribly meritocratic. If you were not succeeding it was because you just weren't smart enough. This or that person, you'd hear, was supposed to be razor sharp and going places. It just happened to be that the people who got to work at these companies, who passed the entry test and then acquired the vital experience they needed to make further progress, tended to be very similar socially to the people who were employing them. A (very nice) white TV friend of mine (upper middle class, loves *The Archers*, grew up in a literary household) who was given a permanent job at the first company she ever worked for, handed documentaries to direct with barely any experience, wondered out loud, around this time, why I wasn't getting on as fast as she was. 'It's such a mystery,' she intoned over a glass of wine.

•

I did finally manage to land a job at the BBC in London – after taking a demotion. It was only a short-term contract but it was a break. The BBC was such a large institution, one of the few places that had lots of permanent jobs – hundreds of them – so I thought I'd be able to prove myself on merit. It had been a struggle, but I thought that now I was going to be ok.

But it was here, at BBC White City, the heart of where documentaries and serious political programmes were made, that I really sensed that something was wrong. Until then I was still full of hope, it was just a question of really hard work. In the grey carpeted expanse of a huge open-plan office, I seemed to be the only one like me: brown, from outer West London suburbia, state school educated (non-selective), with that slight hint of a London twang. Here with very *nice*, well-spoken, middle-class people, I suddenly feel self-conscious. That my laugh sounds too loud, that if I make a point in a meeting, it will somehow sound aggressive. Whenever I find myself in a lift with one of the executives, it always seems as if they feel awkward in my presence, as if there is a faintly bad aroma around me.

•

Though executives seem to genuinely like my work, I never quite manage to get a foothold. When I inquire about work, my CV is always 'at the top of the pile'. 'You've been brilliant,' I get told repeatedly, but they never seem to like *me* enough to give me another contract. Regardless, I persevere. I manage – again – to get a short-term job at BBC White City. (The clue to this place, I later realised, was always in the name.) While I'm back there, the BBC Director General Greg Dyke delivers his famous comment about the corporation being 'hideously white'. I look around my particular office to double check on the day I hear his comment, at all the other executive producers, directors and researchers: not a single person of colour apart from me. I feel sure I've only managed to get work here as the executives needed someone at short notice. I do my job and direct the film they want me to make – my immediate boss says he loves it. But no matter. By now, I know exactly what is about to happen. I'm out again.

·

Of course, it's not all just about *names* exactly, but when I do manage to land an interview, I am now feeling more and more that 'Sheela Banerjee', that familiar string of syllables, places me in a particular box in the eyes of the executives who were in charge.

Conversations – something like the following – took place over time:

It was one of my first media interviews, at the BBC. I'd walked through a huge marble-pillared foyer, my first time in such a building. I walked into the interview room. Two middle-aged white men in suits were sitting behind a desk, looking powerful, antagonistic. I'm nervous. I'm twenty-three, wearing the Next jacket my mum's bought me to wear for interviews.

We exchange our verbal calling cards: their names, my name, all sending a signal in that airless room about who we are, what world we come from.

'Hi, Sheela isn't it? Have a seat. I'm Alistair, this is Charles.'

(Of course, I don't remember what they were actually called – it was years ago, but I've chosen some random names that were common in the early nineties among the – mainly male – media elite. This was the Charles/William/Christopher/David/John/Michael generation.)

What I do remember is that the men were the stuffiest-looking people I'd ever come across. (Someone later told me that BBC panels back then were modelled on Oxbridge entrance interviews.) I attempt a linguistic performance, mimicking the assured white middle-class tones of my interviewers – the right mix of extremely polite but authoritative; a supremely confident, white young person, whom they will both like and value. However, my name alone is enough to turn the odds against me.

•

At one BBC interview panel, a senior TV executive falls asleep while I try to talk about the ideas that I've come prepared with (I often spend days getting prepared for these interviews, researching ideas, sometimes sending in up to six beforehand, preparing for questions that I will be asked). At another, at BBC Westminster, my interviewer (extremely posh, white, middle-aged, male) is apparently so uninterested in what I've got to say that he turns to the wall behind him and starts lightly drumming on it.

After years of plugging away, I was asked to come in for a meeting with a Channel 4 commissioning editor. It felt like a big deal, and I was hopeful. I assumed, going in, we'd be talking about the possibility of directing for the channel, which after all began its life as a progressive force. I'd once again come armed with ideas for new documentaries. Instead of inquiring about those, the commissioning editor asked me if there was anyone in my family or one of my friends who might be interested in working for her – as an au pair.

•

When I did manage to get a contract, I heard hundreds of these sorts of little exchanges:

'Meet Emma, she's lovely, she's one of the assistant producers.'

'Oh, Nick's got a brilliant strand at the BBC, I was in there having a chat with him.'

'Lucy's in charge, she's great, she's the series producer.'

'Elizabeth/Lucy/Charlotte/Sophie – she's frighteningly clever, I'd love to keep her on. We must find something for her.'

'Sheela, oh yes.' (A slightly weary sigh, denoting that it's a drag to have to consider this person again.) 'What's she done lately? Well, I don't think any of us think she'd be top of the tree for this, do we?'

This last conversation was, of course, imagined – the one I never heard. But over the years I felt strongly that something like this was definitely taking place in reality. I imagined them looking at my CV when I was out of work, dismissing me as soon as they saw my name.

It wasn't all bad. I met people that I'm still friends with, and there were people that occasionally helped me. I usually got lucky on the peripheries.

I get a job at BBC Elstree, regional TV, on the edges of London. I love it and I don't have the feeling of dread when I approach work. I travel out to Borehamwood and walk down a suburban street full of thirties semis, until I'm on the huge lot of Elstree studios, where they make *EastEnders*. We often bump into the cast of the soap – Dot Cotton queues up in the canteen next to me as we both get our chips and beans, or I bump into Grant Mitchell – the big bald one – in the BBC bar. My show is only broadcast in London and the South East, so very few of the people I met at White City are interested in this bit of the BBC. Because we are forgotten about and the budgets are so small, I can make films I actually care about. I make a documentary about two teenagers with autism, another about the agony aunt Claire Rayner after her breast cancer surgery, and I spend weeks filming on the Aylesbury council estate in south London. Over three years I make multiple documentaries and this time they keep asking me back. I feel valued and as if, finally, to some extent I was doing what I had set out to do all those years ago.

And, oh yes –

The person who employs me and keeps re-employing me at BBC Elstree is not called Charlotte or Simon or Lucy but is one of a vanishingly small number of ethnic minority non-Oxbridge execs, someone I feel entirely comfortable around.

•

But one supportive individual, however helpful, wasn't enough.

I found myself back in my flat sat on my floor, with my CVs around me, a list of letters I had to write, phone calls to companies, remembering to sign on at the Job Centre. As I filled in those income support booklets my self-esteem plummeted a little lower.

Name: Sheela Banerjee

This time it wasn't a CV, with a list of my media experience; it was endless benefit booklets, to get scraps of money to pay my rent, to buy food. I was there every few months with the unemployed at the Job Centre in Islington, trying to feel like I had a career, trying to get over the shame of being in and out of work. Filling in my name, again, my address, my last job. Attaching my last P45.

London, 2004

I'd had enough. Nearly fifteen years of never getting a firm foothold. By now I was too anxious, angry, I couldn't take the insecurity. Though no one ever aimed a racial slur at me, I felt I'd experienced a severe, yet extremely subtle, form of classism and racism. So subtle that I could never quite call it out, or even be sure. But it had curdled my consciousness, it had sapped my energy and my sense of self-worth. I'd watched as middle-class colleagues had their careers nurtured by supportive executives who'd taken a shine to them. They would be offered permanent jobs, given a chance to show their worth, while I'd be on the move the whole time, worrying about money, jealousy eating away at me.[5]

I suffered intense anxiety and was filled with hopelessness at times. The psychological damage was made worse by the fact that I was always wondering if there was in fact something sub-standard about me, whether in truth I really wasn't good enough. Maybe the Mollys, Charlottes and Lucys making the big documentaries genuinely were much more talented.

And I felt like my many years pretending to be what I was not had also brought me back into an old psychological trap. Acting out the self-hatred of my childhood, when surrounded by the power and discrimination of people who were nothing like me. Thinking with the mind of the person who despised me, seeing myself as inferior. Trying to discern the exact nature of my own failings when the failings were beyond my control.

·

This time I couldn't prove that I'd been the victim of prejudice. But I felt like the story of my name had gone full circle.

Sheela Banerjee had taken on a taint once again.

Of course, it wasn't the same as my childhood, but it felt like there was something equally unpleasant going on. Being ignored, patronised and shut out from jobs by TV executives was a bit different from being called 'Paki' in the street. This time it had been terribly polite and always unspoken. But it felt like the well-mannered version of the same thing.

I am not a physically brave person, and I'd always found violent racists frightening. But was the polite Oxbridge variety so much better? I did at least know where I was with someone who called me a 'Paki'.

Naming My Daughter

We had been trying to have a baby for a while, an IVF failure, a miscarriage, doctors at the Homerton Hospital telling us that even with IVF, our chances were very low. I had imagined myself being a mother, and alternated this with a despair that it would never happen. It was a dark time, full of needles, blood tests, anxious hospital visits, and the overriding shame and sadness of infertility.

And then miraculously, a second round of IVF worked, and I'm pregnant. I'm going to have a girl.

She will be born in the Royal London Hospital, in Whitechapel – just down the road from Brick Lane. We used to come here when I was a child – before it became a neighbourhood of successful artists, when it was just full of Bangladeshi grocers and sari shops. We'd travel from Hayes – my parents and I, my aunt, uncle and cousin – and they'd buy some frozen *rui mach* (a fish that Bengalis all love) from a dusty grocers shop with a freezer cabinet in the back filled with grey-looking frozen fish.

And now on the way to my appointment, I'd overhear Bengali words as I walked through the street market on Whitechapel Road, as the Bangladeshi stall holders chatted to one another in Sylheti, a language that's similar to Bengali. The food was familiar too – not just the frozen fish from the ponds in Bangladesh, but okra, bitter gourds, *potol* (another sort of gourd) and thin green and red chillies by the tub, all for a pound. I'd stop off at one of the local Bengali cafés on my way to my ante-natal appointments, for a kebab roll, or sometimes for a bit of dal and a freshly made fluffy, buttery nan, at Tayyabs, a Pakistani restaurant round the back of the hospital.

And so, on an overcast winter's day in December, a young midwife from Zimbabwe called Tapiwa delivers my baby into this world. I look at her face, and can't believe this could be true, that she is here.

●

Like many couples, we have considered hundreds of names. There's something quite deep at work in one's subconscious over likes and dislikes as one's eyes run down the pages of different options. Every name has a minutely different register, which would play a subtly different part in this story I carry with me, of my own name, my parents' and their forebears'.

We agree it has to be an Indian name. Our daughter will have her father's British/Celtic surname, so her ethnicity will be represented 50:50.

And in the choice of first name, unlike my parents in 1967, I don't want to feel like I'm appeasing anyone, trying to fit in with the English world around me. So I don't want a name that could be mistaken for an English name, like mine. That summons anything English.

I feel British, but I have a right also to be as Indian as I like. I belong here, and I refuse to hide my identity. I am no longer a little girl just back from India. My daughter will have a name that is not cowed. Its origins will be on display. I want her to feel the opposite of the deep shame I felt as a child, about being Bengali. I want her to be proud.

When I was a child, the biggest compliment was being told, 'Oh I just think of you as English'; all that effort to look English, sound English, had paid off. But I certainly don't want that anymore, and choosing an Indian name is part of that. Many non-white British dread and resent the question 'Where are you from?' but part of me *wants* to be asked where I'm originally from. I want people to know that I'm Bengali. I'm not the same as someone whose parents or grandparents grew up in this country. We have a very different history. My grandparents were fighting the British, to get them out of India, while theirs were fighting the Germans. Our sense of who we are comes from very different places. I have no connection to the Second World War. Or to the First. Or to anything historical in this country – kings and queens, Vikings, Romans, none of it. The only thing I'm connected to is its deadly imperial history.

We strike out a great many options. We like the name that's written in the Western alphabet as *Sulakshana* but it's not that easy for the British to say. It should sound something like *Shu-lok-khkhona* (with a kind of strong upward thrust on the *kh,* that doesn't really exist in English). As much as I don't want to compromise, I still don't want a name that's physically impossible for most British people to say and will be mangled forever.

As we pore over lists, we come across *Durga*. In Bengali it's a beautiful-sounding name.

Dthoor-gaa. It's difficult to explain with English lettering, as the sound at the start doesn't have a precise equivalent. In Bengali the first consonant is a downward-sounding *th*, like *Dth*. There's no way of writing it, and I don't think the British can easily place their tongues in the position needed to make that sound.

So for them, the name turns into *Duh–gaar*. Rhymes with burger.

Duh – the sound people make for someone who's being a bit stupid. Childhood memories of mispronounced Indian names, a lifetime of listening to my mother's name pronounced completely wrong, eradicating any sense of linguistic beauty, of its true meaning. I don't want that.

But Indian gods are non-exclusive when it comes to names. The same god might be called a number of names. In Durga's case, we come across a name that I've never heard of before, but which is one of its most ancient forms in Sanskrit.

ঈশানা
Ishaana

Pronounced in Bengali, it's ee-shaan-aa, with even stresses on all three syllables, a parade of long luxuriant vowel sounds and soft consonants. Pronounced in English, it won't sound quite like that, but the name will survive the transliteration.

•

It feels perfect. I'm not a devout Hindu. But the name catches a memory, a fleeting feeling of a building, the old town hall at Belsize Park where every year we'd go for the annual Durga Puja festival – our equivalent of Christmas, I'd say, as I tried to explain it to English friends. In my mind, the name Ishaana contains an element of that time.

I'm walking along on a side road towards Haverstock Hill. It's October, and the rain is coming down in sheets, and it's dark already. My mum is in a bright blue-and-gold silk sari, and has a black cardigan from Marks & Spencer over it, to keep out the autumn chill. We bump into other families like ours, men in suits, or new jumpers, women in saris and the children tagging along, all walking towards Hampstead Town Hall. It's cold out here, my mum's bare feet in her sandals, her sari, are inappropriate on the cold grey paving stones of the side street. The huge dark London plane trees with their black leaves form a gloomy canopy.

I walk up the steps of Hampstead Town Hall with my parents and we enter a magnificent Victorian hallway, beautiful tiles on the floors, a grand sweeping staircase leading to an ornate gilt mirror. Various Bengali children, with black pudding bowl haircuts and new dresses, hang from the wooden bars that are there to protect the mirror. I see them every year – Debjani, Swati (pronounced 'Shaathi', but sadly often reduced in England to 'Swotty'), or Pamela and Debbi (the latter is a commonly used Bengali name, meaning 'goddess', convenient in its hybridity, like Sheela). The place is thronging, there are hundreds of people here, it's as if all the Bengalis in London, from places like Alperton, Perivale, Harrow, Wembley, Mill Hill, and from other parts of the country have congregated here.

My parents immediately fall into conversation with people they haven't seen in a while, my dad cracking jokes and settling himself down by the bottom of the staircase, with the bunch of men that are the most louche, yet were the ones who in the sixties were responsible for setting up this religious festival, when they were all newly arrived students, from West Bengal. As soon as the women have got into the warmth of the hall, they've taken off the ugly Marks & Spencer cardigans, the hooded grey anoraks, and they are dazzling, in their gold-threaded silk saris, known as *Benaroshi* (the Bengali word for Varanasi, famed for its beautiful saris), tight-sleeved blouses, dripping with dazzling gold jewellery, that they only get a chance to wear during these four days of celebrations.

•

Every Bengali child who grew up in London during the seventies and eighties remembers this puja. It's held in our collective imagination, it's the first thing we talk about if we find out someone is Bengali. 'Oh did you used to go to Belsize Park?' one of us is bound to ask. The name Ishaana for me will hold this place; Bengalis recreating for themselves a place, a tiny bit of home, which they now carry only in their imaginations. The West Bengal of their childhoods, transmuted in this municipal town hall. It's that story. It's the poignancy of the story of trying to create a better life, filled with dreams and the encounter that my parents and their friends had with British society, some of it good, some of it hateful.

And what of the meaning behind Durga herself? What was I trying to pass on to my daughter? In the name Ishaana is the image of a powerful goddess who vanquishes evil. It takes me back to the large stage at the front, meant for typically English municipal ceremonies, that would have been transformed into a makeshift Hindu temple, with lots of women milling about, helping with the puja (prayers). I would tiptoe around banana leaves, heaps of garlands, loose chrysanthemums and dahlias; the smell of incense heavy in the air; and brass plates piled with squares of cream and green squares of *sondesh* (Indian sweets), sliced banana and apple.

All of these were offerings for the magnificent goddess Durga that was at the head of everything: the stage and all the hundreds of Bengalis. It's a huge clay statue; close up on the stage, I would like being next to her, with her ten arms, her smiling, victorious painted face, the thick black wiry hair.

It's like a dream when I remember it now: the building, like something out of a Kafka novel, has become larger. For four days each year, I would be running around inside that building, in a different realm, Bengali, but also otherworldly, leaving behind Haverstock Hill, London, the slick of rain on the October paving stones. As a child, I got told a tiny little summary of that story every year in Belsize Park. About how a battle was raging throughout the universe. Humanity, the gods and the whole cosmos were being threatened by the evil Mahishasura and his army of demons. The gods were really worried, I was told, because he had now reached the gates of Heaven and they still couldn't stop him. So the three most powerful gods, Brahma, Vishnu and Shiva, combined their powers to create the ultimate force, the goddess Durga. She vanquished her enemy, decapitating him, and then used her trident to pierce the demon that arose from his severed neck. Good work.

It was pretty gruesome but thrilling for a child, and Durga Puja celebrates her victory over evil. I've always loved the way she's depicted riding in on her lion, her trident aloft, a symbol of the ultimate creative and cosmic force. And Mahishasura always seemed like the ultimate creepy guy, very male, bare chested, muscly and with his thick moustache; and whenever I looked at him, I felt a momentary satisfaction at his symbolic defeat by the lovely Durga. Beautiful, but also a ten-armed female warrior goddess fighting machine.

And now the rousing story of superhero gods operates on a different level too, as a way into to a deeper spiritual level. Their extravagant unreality is a sign of how much we don't know, it's the confounding of reason; the idea that at the heart of our existence is something mysterious and unknowable.

I hope my daughter's name might one day be a window, an opening of the curtains into the unreal – it's there if she wants to look into it. The power to defeat the demon I take as a metaphor, to defeat the lure of the worldly, the demons within, and access something bigger, something mystical, something that defies reality, that enchants. A gentle invitation to delve into the mystery of existence, into the spiritual realm.

.

Gods were ubiquitous in India when I was a child, in little frames on the dashboard of an antique lumbering Ambassador taxi, in everyone's houses, on calendars, clay statues, with garlands of flowers placed round them, the incense lit as the sun started going down, in makeshift shrines on the floor, in shops, in little temples in the middle of busy Kolkata streets, celebrated all the time in numerous weekly, monthly, yearly festivals.

Durga Puja any time between September and October; Kali Puja three weeks later, Jagatdhartri Puja in Chandannagar in November; Saraswati Puja in January; puja when you start a business; a puja when you move into a new house; a puja for getting married; a tiny puja for when you do your exams. In the midst of all this life, the gods were always there, in the most mundane and everyday situations. Their presence was a question, pointing to mystery. That's what my daughter's name is to me.

Ishaana
Hackney, 2000s

I hope and believe that bearing a foreign-sounding name will not even be an issue. Ishaana will live in twenty-first-century multicultural Hackney, a far cry from the monocultural Hayes of the 1970s. Our neighbours are the Atias – Gujarati Muslims who are always smiling, saying hello. When Ishaana is one year old, they will be her first childminders, I will pass her over the wall and they will look after her, feeding her chapatis which she loves, and bringing round the most delicious chicken curry every Eid. The streets are filled with every nationality, every ethnicity – Indian, Turkish, Hasidic Jewish, Caribbean, mixed heritage, French, Punjabi.

It's not always a nice place, there was a murder at the top of our road just after she was born, crime is a threat. But at least here, the name Ishaana is entirely comfortable. When she goes on to primary school, in the small concrete playground, she will play on the monkey bars for many years with Jahanavee and Maliha (Hindu and Muslim Indian names respectively). Jahanavee's family are from Gujarat. Maliha's family are devout Muslims who've grown up locally.

Maliha and other Muslims in the class, including Ziyad and Bilal, were often away celebrating Eid. Jahanavee's family celebrated Diwali, and at home their family spoke Gujarati. There is also Nissi (Belgian Congolese); Niyah (mixed British and Malawian); Ziyad (British Pakistani); Bilal (British Gujarati Muslim); Matilda (British Jewish, French); Safa and Sophia (Turkish twins); Mimi (British); Isaac (British).

That was part of the optimistic feeling that the name Ishaana existed within, for me, in those early years of her life. I didn't worry that her name would be taken and mangled, spat out as a mockery of its original self. That she would be constantly waiting for some child to start picking on her because of her 'funny' name. Everyone here has a 'funny' name. One of Ishaana's first teachers is called Shaila Patel – a teacher whose Gujarati Indian parents perhaps had a similar idea to my own when they named their daughter with their own variation of the English Sheila. Her next teacher is called Lucin, a young second-generation Turkish woman, who loves drama and gets the children to put on a production of *A*

Midsummer Night's Dream, with fragments of Shakespearean sentences coming out of the mouths of children of every nationality and every background. Her head teacher is a warm, friendly African Caribbean Londoner called Norma. The narrow order of British names that existed when I was growing up has exploded – in Hackney at least – into multiplicity.

London, 2007

Going back further in time, to a few months before Ishaana is born, the old racist attitude to foreign names briefly resurfaces on the national radar. Jade Goody is castigated for her behaviour towards the Indian actress Shilpa Shetty on *Celebrity Big Brother*. She calls her 'Shilpa Poppadom', tells her to 'fucking go back home', Shetty is told her name is unpronounceable, told she can't speak English properly. I'm mesmerised by this weird reality TV drama. The sniggering bullying, the snide remarks, take me right back to being at school, but now, in 2007, it's different, it's publicly unacceptable. Chancellor Gordon Brown weighs in and condemns any form of racism. Jade Goody is vilified and there's no audience when she's evicted from the house. Forty-four thousand people complain to Ofcom, and it feels like the majority have rejected racism for good.

In 2007, it's possible to believe that racism is gradually disappearing in British society. I no longer get called a 'Paki' or a 'Wog' on the street – around Hackney the idea is absurd.

•

But then, when my daughter is eight, in 2016, Brexit happens, the vote to take Britain out of the European Union; ostensibly it's about control, but it seems much darker than that. I feel the ground beneath my feet shifting. I had given Ishaana her name at a time of much greater optimism. Maybe I was naïve, but I had thought things had changed since I was a child; I thought those racists in Hayes were throwbacks from another era, but now, suddenly, it was *their* views that I kept seeing in the mainstream, from UKIP, the *Daily Mail* and leading conservative politicians. I'd also ignored the dripping of poison by the previous Labour government itself: its 'war on terror', which gave Islamophobia the nod of official acceptance; the demonising of veiled Muslim women for failing to integrate; the nasty fixation on 'bogus' asylum seekers and its xenophobic call for 'British jobs for British workers', chilling in its similarity to the National Front's fascist rhetoric in the seventies. And then, with the Tories, came Theresa May's 'Go home' vans, the Windrush scandal, Boris Johnson, with his sinister playground racism, calling Black people 'piccaninnies', Muslim women 'letterboxes'.

I think I had been partly deluded, relieved at the election of a Labour government in 1997 after growing up under what seemed like an eternity of Tory rule. I'd not really understood that there was a latent racism that had never gone away, a yearning for past imperial glory that lay buried in parts of the British psyche, which both Labour and the Tories were willing to exploit and encourage.

Hackney, 2020

All three of us are at home, locked down during Covid. I've started writing this book. Ishaana is doing her lessons on Zoom, I hear tinny sounds – the words of her teacher emanate from her laptop when I pop my head around the door.

For days and weeks we are in stasis, watching the numbers of Covid cases go up. Going out to Hackney Marshes for our exercise, taking pleasure in a tiny strip of nature by the River Lea. I cycle alongside the dark polluted water. I see a grey factory warehouse, bits of slightly grim east London light industry, through the foliage. There's nothing else to do. Just try to stop worrying about money, my parents, getting Covid. We cook food three times a day.

And then, in this end-of-world time, something happens.

A statue of a slave trader comes toppling down in Bristol and a fuse is lit. I see young Black people, masks on, marching, the anger spilling out. Black Lives Matter takes off. Alongside the handmade NHS rainbow posters in the windows on our street, there are posters with a black-and-white fist and 'Black Lives Matter' written underneath.

The biggest conversation I've heard about race in my adult life happens.

I don't want to pretend I have suffered the way that the young Black people I see around me in Hackney have. I know I'm much more privileged – I'm middle class, my ancestors weren't trafficked into slavery. But this incredible movement does trigger a whole host of thoughts in me – about empire and the brutal extraction of wealth from India; the millions killed in consecutive famines in Bengal; Enoch Powell; my childhood; the sense of threat I always felt in Hayes; the uprisings in Southall; the endless soul-destroying interviews for TV jobs; the absolute and subtle force of whiteness. And how I'd experienced the same thing, again, when I went into academia.

In some ways I had been luckier that time, a wonderful professor was incredibly supportive – she enabled me to flourish, to start writing; I'd met a couple of lovely colleagues. However, as in television, the presence of a few generous individuals wasn't enough to compensate for an even more impenetrable wall of institutional racism and classism, this time hidden behind a veneer of impeccable left-wing credentials. I spent over a decade studying and working (on casualised contracts) in my pleasant, liberal English department, in the middle of multicultural east London, yet they didn't employ a single Black lecturer during the time I was there. Apart from the odd exception, its quiet corridors remained a privileged space for a certain type of person – again, overwhelmingly white, Oxbridge, with a perfectly enunciated upper-middle-class accent.

•

My daughter lives in a different world from the one I grew up in. My head teacher at my virtually all-white comprehensive school, Mrs Babbs, was often seen gliding around in a cap and gown, in some kind of parodic private school attire (even though the pupils were overwhelmingly working class) and spoke in the most over-enunciated English I have ever heard. She had us singing Christian hymns and reading out biblical parables at assembly, as a guiding moral force. There was never any hint of politics. Ishaana's head teacher at her secondary school is very different. She's an amazing, energetic woman, with a strong estuary English accent, in charge of a multicultural school, full of young Muslim girls, from Bangladesh, Pakistan, Sudan, Afghanistan, Turkey, with names like Zara and Aisha. There are no parables or hymns. Instead during lockdown, when Black Lives Matter erupted, as well as spending her days organising the hundreds of food parcels delivered to many of her pupils, sorting out laptops, and trying to keep everyone learning, she took the knee.

My daughter's multicultural identity is not a factor when she moves through this world of hers. She's not anxiously waiting for someone to take her name, twist it and turn it into a weapon of racial mockery. Why would they? In this part of London, if anyone were racist, *they* would be the pariahs. Not the people of colour, as it was for our generation – as it was for Hugo and his friends, the Magnificent Seven; as it was for me on my first day of primary school, when I saw the word 'WOG' scrawled for the first time on the back of a toilet door.

•

When the statue of Edward Colston came down in Bristol it seemed to unleash conversation about all the erasures that we've grown up with – about slavery, empire and our heritage in this country. For the first time I heard a proper discussion about Churchill's racism, his complicity in the deaths of millions during the last Bengal famine; *Girl, Woman, Other*, a novel about the lives of Black British women, won the Booker prize; Steve McQueen's *Small Axe* films for the BBC showed an Afro-Caribbean world that I had grown up alongside, and one that was barely seen on TV.

Increasingly there was also a conversation about the erasure surrounding our names. In 2021–22, as I'm writing this, stories keep appearing of celebrities of colour who have reclaimed their original names. Suddenly there is a tiny space to own our brownness or Blackness. The actor Thandie Newton announced she was reverting to the Zulu-derived spelling of her name, Thandiwe – that missing 'w' altering how the world sees her and how she sees herself. She said in an interview with *British Vogue* afterwards, 'That's my name. It's always been my name. I'm taking back what's mine.'[1] The comedian Shappi Khorsandi also decided to go back to using her original name, Shaparak – a 'fancy poetic' Persian word for 'butterfly' – a name which speaks its difference out loud, unlike the more accommodating Shappi. She reflected on why she had shortened this beautiful Persian name, saying 'I'm only now scratching the surface of how often in my life I have internalised bigotry and tried to bend in a direction which would make my foreignness more comfortable for other people – changing my name was part of that.'[2]

But, of course, this moment isn't just about celebrities. Names, like statues, like our histories, have become important to all of us. I have a British Chinese friend called Jan – a common, if slightly old-fashioned British name, a bit like mine. She too reverted to using her original Mandarin name, Jan-Ming, at around the same time. She explained why on a Facebook post to her friends:

> *I shortened it to 'Jan' around 11 years old to sound more 'English' and to try to fit in and to not be bullied. I realised only this year that I don't need to do that anymore . . .*
> *In Chinese, 'Jan' or 'Jian' means healthy, strong, capable and 'Ming' means brilliant, clear, intelligence. Definitely my name! :-)))*

'I feel,' she told me later, 'that when you say things, you bring them into existence,' and so she wanted to be acknowledged as all aspects of her name, not just the Jan part. She also wanted to accept the gift her parents were trying to give her when they named her. 'It's part of my lineage,' she told me, 'it's about honouring my parents.'

•

The names we carry unfold in place and time; we cannot know how meanings and nuances will develop, what history will bring. I cannot know what society my daughter will live in, what place she will have within it. Britain has already changed since the eruption of Black Lives Matter, and the backlash has begun, as politicians reach once more for race hatred as a way to distract from their failures. Government ministers once more echo the rhetoric of the far right, describing migrants arriving on our shores as an 'invasion'; fascist-led protests have become a regular occurrence outside reception centres housing asylum seekers.

India will change. London will change. Perhaps my daughter will live in a world where an Indian heritage will become utterly unremarkable in the multicultural mix of fluid identities. Ishaana will always be in some way Bengali but also English, Manx (from her Dad), a Londoner, but also from Hackney, mixed race. Perhaps holding on to past identities is futile in the long run, perhaps it works only for a generation or just for a few years. But for now, I am happy we gave her the name Ishaana.

Notes

Growing up as Sheela Banerjee

1 Stuart Jeffries, 'Britain's most racist election: the story of Smethwick, 50 years on', *Guardian*, 15 October 2014.
2 See for example Ekta Singh, *Caste System in India: A Historical Perspective* (Kalpaz: Delhi, 2009); B.R. Ambedkar, *Annihilation of Caste* (Verso: London 2016); Susan Bayly, *Caste, Society and Politics in India from the Eighteenth Century to the Modern Age* (Cambridge University Press: Cambridge, 2001)

Marcella Gatsky: The Journey of a Name from Tsarist Russia to Suburban Stanmore

1 Steve Belasco, host, Sounds Jewish (podcast), *Guardian* October 4, 2013.
2 Alexander Beider, *A Dictionary of Jewish Surnames from the Russian Empire* (New Haven: Avotanyu, 1993)
3 Gerald Sorin, *A Time for Building: The Third Migration* (Baltimore: The Johns Hopkins University Press, 1992), p. 19.
4 Martin Gilbert, *The Routledge Atlas of Jewish History* (Oxford: Taylor and Francis, 1995), p. 73
5 Robert Weinberg, 'The Pogrom of 1905 in Odessa: A Case Study', in *Pogroms: Anti-Jewish Violence in Modern Russian History*, eds.

John D. Klier and Shlomo Labroza (Cambridge: Cambridge University Press, 2004), p. 263.

6 Robert Winder, *Bloody Foreigners: The Story of Immigration to Britain* (London: Abacus, 2013), p. 229.

7 Winder, pp. 229–30.

8 Beatrice Webb in Charles Booth, *Life and Labour of the People in London*, Vol. 1 (London: Macmillan, 1889), p. 583.

9 Booth, p. 583.

10 Todd M. Endelman, *The Jews in Britain: 1656 to 2000* (Los Angeles: University of California Press, 2002), p. 571.

11 Winder, p. 235. (he is quoting Myer Wilchinski, 'History of a Sweater', *Commonweal*, 26 May, 1888.

12 Endelman, pp. 135–6.

13 Booth, pp. 567–8.

14 Geoffrey Alderman, *The Jewish Community in British Politics*, (Oxford: Oxford University Press, 1983), p. 176.

15 Winder, p. 238.

Liz Husain: From Hyderabad to Harrow

1 Salahuddin Ahmed, *Dictionary of Muslim Names* (London: Hurst, 1999), p. 16.

2 Beth Notzom and Gail Nesom, The Arabic Naming System, *The Science Editor* 28, no. 1 (Jan–Feb 2005), p. 20.

3 Adam Forrest, 'Metroland, 100 years on: What's become of England's original vision of suburbia?', *Guardian*, 10 September 2015.

4 David Olusoga, *Black and British: A Forgotten History* (London: Pan Macmillan, 2021), p. xvii.

5 David Gilmour, *The British in India: Three Centuries of Ambition and Experience* (London: Penguin, 2019), p. 312.

6 W. E. B. Du Bois, 'The Strivings of the Negro People', *Atlantic*, August 1897, p. 194.

7 Rozina Visram, *Asians in Britain: 400 Years of History* (London: Pluto, 2002), p. 86.

8 Visram, *Asians in Britain, p.* 89.

9 Yasmin Khan, *The Great Partition: The Making of India and Pakistan* (London: Yale, 2017), p. 27.

10 Khan, pp. 106–7; 112–13.

Why My Friend Maria Found It So Difficult to Name Her Son

1 Anton Chekhov, *The Schoolmistress and Other Stories*, (Ecco Press: New York, 1986)

Vicki Denise Marie Seneviratne: A Collision of Civilisations

1 Winston Churchill, quoted in Matthew Holden, *The Desert Rats* (London: Wayland, 1973), p. 8.
2 Derek Brown, '1956: Suez and the end of empire', *Guardian*, 14 March 2001
3 Frantz Fanon, *Black Skin, White Masks* (London: Pluto, 1967), p. 18.
4 Peter Fryer, *Staying Power: The History of Black People in Britain* (London: Pluto, 2018), p. 403.

Hugo St Paul Whyte: Three Different Names at Three Different Times

1 Donald Whyte, *Scottish Surnames*, (Birlinn: Edinburgh, 2000), p. 239
2 Trevor Burnard, *Jamaica in the Age of Revolution*, (University of Pennsylvania Press: Philadelphia, 2020), p. 83
3 Trevor Burnard, 'Slave Naming Patterns: Onomastics and the Taxonomy of Race in Eighteenth-Century Jamaica', in *The Journal of Interdisciplinary History*, Vol.31 No.3 (Winter, 2001), pp. 325–346
4 Fryer, p. 378–9.
5 Fryer, p. 388–90
6 Enoch Powell, 9 February 1968, *Speech at Walsall*, enochpowell.net/fr-80.html.
7 David Olusoga, *Black and British: A Forgotten History* (London: MacMillan, 2021), p.513.
8 Viv Edwards, *Language in Multicultural Classrooms*, (Batsford: London, 1983), pp. 5, 55.
9 W. E. B. Du Bois, Strivings of the Negro People, *The Atlantic Monthly*, August 1897, vol. 80, p. 194
10 Steve McQueen, 'Discrimination at school: is a Black British history lesson repeating itself?' By Lola Okolosie. *Guardian* November 2020.

McQueen also made the semi autobiographical drama 'Education' as part of the *Small Axe* series, and *Subnormal – A British Scandal*, May 2022, a documentary about the same subject.

Sheela Banerjee: The Journey of a Second-Generation Indian Name

1 Nitish Sengupta, *History of the Bengali-Speaking People* (New Delhi: UBS, 2001), pp. 145–54.
2 Shashi Tharoor, *Inglorious Empire* (London: Penguin Books, 2017), p. 2. This is similar to the 22.5% figure quoted by the historian William Dalrymple. See, for example, his article: 'Robert Clive was a vicious asset-stripper. His statue has no place on Whitehall', *Guardian*, 11 June 2020
3 Niall Ferguson, *Empire: How Britain Made the Modern World* (London: Penguin Books, 2004)
4 The researchers sent fictitious applications to over 3,200 applicants, and found discrimination levels 'unchanged since the late 1960s and 1970s'. 'New CSI Report on Ethnic Minority Job Discrimination', Nuffield College, University of Oxford. 21 January 2019. For a detailed analysis of name-related bias among employers, see also Pragya Agarwal, *Sway: Unravelling Unconscious Bias*, (London: Bloomsbury, 2020), pp. 346-54.
5 The true scale of the discrimination I was up against became clear to me a few years later: research carried out by Directors UK in 2016 showed that just 2.8% of directors working in factual TV were from a Black, Asian or minority ethnic background. This was despite the fact that TV production was concentrated in London, which had a BAME population of over 40%. (And if it was this bad in 2016, I'm assuming it was even worse in the period I'm describing.)

Naming My Daughter

1 Diana Evans, '"I'm Taking Back What's Mine": The Many Lives Of Thandiwe Newton', *British Vogue*, 4 April 2021.
2 Shaparak Khorsandi, 'Why I have decided to change my name from "Shappi" back to "Shaparak"', *Independent*, 11 June 2021.

Acknowledgements

I want to say the BIGGEST ever thank you...

. . . to my incredible, amazing friends who've allowed me to tell their stories, Marcella, Liz, Maria, Denise and Hugo. It's been a privilege and an honour. What an astonishing journey; it's been so powerful and moving at times. Thank you beyond words.

. . . to Sharon, who went far too early. Thank you for the magic of our friendship. I didn't know how lucky I was. I wish I was still sitting at your kitchen table with a glass of fizzy wine in my hand, so I could tell you in person what an utterly brilliant, supportive friend you have always been, how you helped me in writing this book in so many ways.

. . . to Rhona, Tamsin and Maria for the decades of laughter mainly, but also for being so fabulous to talk to, for your smartness and for always believing in me, in whatever it was I was trying to do.

. . . to my friend Alex. I couldn't believe it – it was like I'd been sent an angel when you came along and offered to help me. I can't tell you how grateful I am, not just for all the hours you spent in the British Library, chasing down those obscure details, but also for just for being there.

. . . to Mickela, you're the best mentor ever. Thank you for having my back. I have felt the strength coming straight from you, especially in those difficult moments. (And thank you for reminding me of the importance of timetabling regular breaks into my schedule!)

. . . to the people who helped me along the way, especially my PhD supervisor, Michèle Barrett. She told me I could write, when I didn't even know I could – it was such a gift, which changed my life. And to Melissa, for the way in which you were so generous and encouraging when I began on this journey, but didn't know if I could pull it off.

. . . to Barley, for the time you came along one evening, sat on my living room floor, and said 'we're starting a writing group,' and that was it – we were off, we were now writers. Thank you for always being so inspiring.

. . . to Kate, my brilliant agent, for your judgement and your clever insight, and for having that crucial vision in the first place. And a huge thank you to the team at Sceptre, especially to my two incredible editors. Juliet, thank you for believing in and championing my idea. And Jo, I'm so grateful for your intelligence, support and wisdom, and for everything you have done to bring this book into being. And a massive thanks to Nico, for your endlessly astute suggestions and all the care you have taken in getting this book through all its various stages.

. . . to my family, to my aunts, uncles, my fabulous cousins – it's all our stories in here.

. . . to my mum and dad, who have so many stories themselves, who made their way over here, took me back to India, who gave me everything.

. . . to my daughter Ishaana. You are the most beautiful gift of all.

. . . to my utterly gorgeous, wonderful husband Dollan, what can I possibly say? That I couldn't have done it without you – of course I couldn't have. But it's so, so much more than that . . .